SOMEBODY ELSE'S KIDS

Also by Torey L. Hayden
ONE CHILD

SOMEBODY ELSE'S KIDS

TOREY L. HAYDEN

G. P. Putnam's Sons
New York

Copyright © 1981 by Torey L. Hayden
All rights reserved. This book, or portions thereof,
must not be reproduced in any form without permission.
Published simultaneously in Canada by Academic Press
Canada Limited, Toronto.

Library of Congress Cataloging in Publication Data

Hayden, Torey L
    Somebody else's kids.

    1. Resource programs (Education) 2. Handicapped
children—Education. 3. Problem children—Education.
I. Title.
LB1028.8.H39 1981   371.9   80-24398
ISBN 0-399-12602-3

PRINTED IN THE UNITED STATES OF AMERICA

This book is for Adam, Jack and Lucio, but especially for Cliffie, whom I could not help, and whom I have lost to a lifetime of walls without windows. A book is such an impotent gesture, but, Cliffie, I have not forgotten you. And perhaps someone else, some other place, some other day, will know what I do not know.

SOMEBODY ELSE'S KIDS

1

It was the class that created itself.

There is some old law of physics that speaks of Nature abhorring a vacuum. Nature must have been at work that fall. There must have been a vacuum we had not noticed because all at once there was a class where no class was ever planned. It did not happen suddenly, as the filling of some vacuums does, but rather slowly, as Nature does all her greatest things.

When the school year began in August I was working as a resource teacher. The slowest children from each of the elementary classes in the school would come to me in ones and twos and threes for half an hour or so a day. My job was to do the best I could to keep them up with the rest of their classes, primarily in reading or math, but sometimes in other areas as well. However, I was without a class of my own.

I had been with the school district for six years. Four of those years had been spent teaching in what educators

7

termed a "self-contained classroom," a class which took place entirely within one room; the children did not interact with other children in the school. I had taught severely emotionally disturbed children during this time. Then had come Public Law 94-142, known as the mainstreaming act. It was designed to normalize special education students by placing them in the least restrictive environment possible and minimizing their deficits with additional instruction, called resource help. There were to be no more closeted classrooms where the exceptional children would be left to sink or swim a safe distance from normal people. No more pigeonholes. No more garbage dumps. That beautiful, idealistic law. And my kids and me, caught in reality.

When the law passed, my self-contained room was closed. My eleven children were absorbed into the mainstream of education, as were forty other severely handicapped children in the district. Only one full-time special education class remained open, the program for the profoundly retarded, children who did not walk or talk or use the toilet. I was sent to work as a resource teacher—in a school across town from where my special education classroom had been. That had been two years before. I suppose I should have seen the vacuum forming. I suppose it should have been no surprise to see it fill.

I was unwrapping my lunch, a Big Mac from McDonald's—a real treat for me because on my half-hour lunch break I could not get into my car and speed across town in time to get one as I had been able to do at the old school. Bethany, one of the school psychologists, had brought me this one. She understood my Big Mac addiction.

I was just easing the hamburger out of the Styrofoam

container, mindful not to let the lettuce avalanche off, which it always did for me, trying for the millionth time to remember that idiotic jingle: Two-all-beef-patties-blah, blah, blah. My mind was not on teaching.

"Torey?"

I looked up. Birk Jones, the director of special education in the district, towered over me, an unlit pipe dangling from his lips. I had been so absorbed in the hamburger that I had not even heard him come into the lounge. "Oh, hi, Birk."

"Do you have a moment?"

"Yeah, sure," I said, although in truth I didn't. There were only fifteen minutes left to gobble down the hamburger and french fries, drink the Dr Pepper and still get back to a whole stack of uncorrected work I had left in the classroom. The lettuce slipped off the Big Mac onto my fingers.

Bethany moved her chair over and Birk sat down between us. "I have a little problem I was hoping you might help me out with," he said to me.

"Oh? What kind of problem?"

Birk took the pipe out of his mouth and peered into the bowl of it. "About seven years old." He grinned at me. "Over in Marcy Cowen's kindergarten. A little boy; I think he's autistic, myself. You know. Does all sorts of spinning and twirling. Talks to himself. Stuff like your kids used to do. Marcy's at the end of her rope with him. She had him part of last year too and even with a management aide in the room, he hasn't changed a bit. We have to do something different with him."

I chewed thoughtfully on my hamburger. "And what can I do to help you?"

"Well . . ." A long pause. Birk watched me eat with such intensity that I thought perhaps I ought to offer him some. "Well, I was thinking, Tor . . . well, perhaps we could bus him over here."

"What do you mean?"

"And you could have him."

"I could have him?" A french fry caught halfway down my throat. "I'm not equipped in my present situation to handle any autistic kids, Birk."

He wrinkled his nose and leaned close in a confidential manner. "You could do it. Don't you think?" A pause while he waited to see if I would reply or simply choke to death quietly on my french fry. "He only comes half days. Regular kindergarten schedule. And he's rotting in Marcy's class. I was thinking maybe you could work with him special. Like you did with those other kids you used to have."

"But Birk? . . . I don't have that kind of room anymore. I'm set up to teach academics. What about my resource children?"

Birk shrugged affably. "We'll arrange something."

The boy was to arrive every day at 12:40. I still had my other children coming in until two, but after that, he and I had only one another for the remaining hour and a half of the school day. In Birk's mind it was no worse if the child destroyed my room for that period of time when I had to work with the resource students than if he tore up Marcy Cowen's kindergarten. Because of my years in the self-contained room, I had that mysterious thing Birk called "experience." Translated, it simply meant I did not have the option to get upset, that I should know better.

I cleared the room for this boy. I put all the breakables out of reach, placed all the games with small, swallowable pieces in a closet, moved desks and tables around to leave a running space where he and I could tackle one another on more intimate terms than I ever needed to do with the resource students. As I finished and stood back to assess my job, pleasure surged up. I had not found resource teaching particularly fulfilling. I missed the contained-classroom setting. I missed not having my own group of children. But by far the most, I missed the eerie joy I always felt working with the emotionally disturbed.

On Monday, the third week in September, I met Boothe Birney Franklin. His mother called him Boothe Birney to his face. His three-year-old sister could only manage Boo. That seemed good enough to me.

Boo was seven years old. He was a magic-looking child as so many of my children seemed to be. There was an illusory realness about his expression: the sort one sees in a dream. Of mixed parentage, he had skin the color of English tea with real cream in it. His hair was not quite black, a veritable mass of huge, loose curls. His eyes were green, mystery green, not clear but cloudy—a sea green, soft and ever changing. He looked like an illustration from a Tasha Tudor picture book come to life. But not a big child, this boy. Not for seven. I would have guessed him barely five.

His mother shoved him through the open door, spoke a few words to me and left. Boo now belonged to me.

"Good afternoon, Boo," I said.

He stood motionless, just inside the door where his mother had left him.

I knelt to his level. "Boo, hello."

He averted his face.

"Boo?" I touched his arm.

"Boo?" he echoed softly, still looking away from me.

"Hello, Boo. My name is Torey. I'm your new teacher. You'll come to this room from now on. This will be your class."

"This will be your class," he repeated in my exact intonation.

"Come here, I will show you where to hang your sweater."

"I will show you where to hang your sweater." His voice

11

was very soft, hardly more than a whisper, and oddly pitched. It was high with an undulating inflection, as a mother's voice to an infant.

"Come with me." I rose and held out a hand. He remained motionless. His face was still turned far to the left. At his side his fingers began to flutter against his legs. Then he started to beat the material of his pants with open palms. The muted sound they made was all the noise there was in the room.

Two other children were there, two fourth-grade boys with their reading workbooks. They both sat paralyzed in their chairs, watching. I had told them Boo was coming. In fact I had given them special work to do for Boo's first day, so that they could work much of the thirty-minute session independently while Boo and I checked one another out. Yet the boys could not take their eyes from us. They watched with mouths slightly agape, bodies bent forward over their desks, brows furrowed in fascination.

Boo patted his hands against his trousers.

I did not want to rush him. We were in no hurry. I backed up and gave him room. "Will you take off your sweater?"

No movement, no sound other than his hands, beating frantically now. He still would not turn his face toward me; it remained averted far to the side.

"What's wrong with him?" one fourth grader asked.

"We talked about it yesterday, Tim. Remember?" I replied, not turning around.

"Can't you make him stop that?"

"He isn't hurting anyone. Nothing's wrong. Just do your work, please. All right?"

Behind me I heard Tim groan in compliance and riffle through his book. Boo stood absolutely rigid. Arms tight to sides, except, of course, for the hands. Legs stiff. Head screwed on sideways, or so it looked. Not a muscle moved beyond the fluttering.

Then with no warning Boo screamed. Not a little scream.

12

A scream heard clear to next Christmas. "AHHHHHH! AHHH-AHHHH! AWWWWRRRRRKK!" He sounded like a rabbit strangling. Hands over eyes he fell writhing to the floor. Then up before I could get nearer. Around the room. "ARRRRRRRRR!" A human siren. Arms flew out from his sides and he flapped them wildly above his head like a frenzied native dancer. He fell again to the floor. Boo turned and twisted as if in agony. Hands over his face, he beat his head against the linoleum. All the while he screamed. "AAAAAAHHHHHHHHHHH! EEEEEEEEEE-E-AHHHH-AWWWWWWWWK!"

"He's having a fit! Oh my gosh, he's having a fit! Quick, Torey, do something!" Tim was crying. He had leaped up on his chair, his own hands fluttering in panic. Brad, the other fourth grader, sat spellbound at his desk.

"He's not having a fit, Tim," I hollered over Boo's screams as I tried to lift him from the floor. "He's okay. Don't worry." But before I could say more, Boo broke my grasp. One frenetic whirl around the room. Over a chair, around a bookcase, across the wide middle area I had cleared. To the door. And out.

2

"Boo? Boo?" I was in the hallway. "Boo?" I whispered loudly into the silence and felt like a misplaced ghost.

I had made it to the classroom door in time to see him careen squawking around the far corner of the corridor, but by the time I had gotten down there Boo was gone. He had disappeared entirely and left me booing to myself.

I went into the primary wing of the building. Wherever he had gone, he had ceased to scream. The classrooms were empty; the children had gone out for recess. All was quiet. Eight rooms in all to check. I stuck my head first in one room and then in another. That miserable rushed feeling overcame me. I knew I had to capture Boo and get him back, check Tim's and Brad's work, calm them down a bit about this odd boy before they went back to their class, and finally prepare for Lori, my next resource student. And all that time I needed to be with Boo.

"Boo?" I looked in the third-grade rooms. In the second-grade rooms. "Boo, time to go back now. Are you here?" Through the first-grade rooms.

I opened the door to the kindergarten. There across the classroom under a table was Boo. He had a rug pulled over his head as he lay on the floor. Only his little green corduroy-covered rear stuck out. Had he known that this was a kindergarten room? Was he trying to get back to Marcy's? Or was it no more than coincidence that put him here, head under a rug on the floor?

Talking all the while in low tones, I approached him cautiously. The kindergarten children were returning from recess. Curiosity was vivid on their faces. What was this strange teacher doing in their room under their table? What about this boy in the green corduroy pants?

"Boo?" I was saying softly, barely more than a whisper. "Time to go to our room now. The other children need this room."

The kindergarteners watched us intently but would not come closer. I touched Boo gently, ran my hand along the outside of the rug, then inside along his body to accustom him to my touch. Carefully, carefully I pulled the rug from around his head and extracted him. Holding him in my arms, I slid from under the table. Boo was soundless now and rigid as a mannequin. His arms and legs were straight and stiff. I might as well have been carrying a cardboard figure of a boy. However, this time he did not avert his face. Rather, he stared through me as if I were not there, round eyed and unblinking, as a dead man stares.

A small freckle-faced boy ventured closer as I prepared to take Boo from the classroom. He gazed up with blue, searching eyes, his face puckered in that intense manner only young children seem to have. "What was he doing in our room?" he asked.

I smiled. "Looking at the things under your rug."

Lori stood outside the door of my room when I returned carrying a stiff Boo in my arms. Tim and Brad had already gone and had closed the door and turned off the light when they left. Lori, workbook in hand, looked uncertain about entering the darkened room.

"I didn't know where you were!" she said emphatically. Then she noticed Boo. "Is that the little kid you told me about? Is he going to be in with me?"

"Yes. This is Boo." I opened the door clumsily and turned on the light. I set Boo down. Again he remained motionless, while Lori and I went to the worktable at the far side of the room. When it became apparent Boo was not going to budge, I went back to the doorway, picked him up and transported him over to us. He stood between the table and the wall, still rigid as death. No life glimmered in those cloudy eyes.

"Hello, little boy," Lori said and sat down in a chair near him. She leaned forward, an elbow on the table, eyes bright with interest. "What's your name? My name's Lori. Lori Ann Sjokheim. I'm seven. How old are you?"

Boo took no notice of her.

"His name is Boo," I said. "He's also seven."

"That's a funny name, Boo. But you know what? I know a kid with a funnier name than that. Her name's Maggie Smellie. I think *that's* funny."

When Boo still did not respond, Lori's forehead wrinkled. "You're not mad, are you, 'cause I said that? It's okay if you got a funny name. I wouldn't tease you or nothing. I don't tease Maggie Smellie either." Lori paused, studied him. "You're kind of small for seven, huh? I think I'm taller than you. Maybe. But I'm kind of small too. That's 'cause I'm a twin and sometimes twins are small. Are you a twin too?"

Lori. What a kid Lori was. I could sit and listen to her all day long. In all my years of teaching, Lori was unique. In appearance she was for me an archetypal child, looking the way children in my fantasies always looked. She had long, long hair, almost to her waist. Parted on one side and

16

caught up in a metal clip, it was thick and straight and glossy brown, the exact color of my grandmother's mahogany sideboard. Her mouth was wide and supple and always quick to smile.

Lori had come to me through evil circumstances. She and her twin sister had been adopted when they were five. The other twin had no school problems whatsoever. But from the very beginning Lori could not manage. She was hyperactive. She did not learn. She could not even copy things written for her. The shattering realization came during her second year in kindergarten, a grade-retention born out of frustration for this child who could not cope.

Lori had been a severely abused child in her natural home. One beating had fractured her skull and pushed a bone fragment into her brain. X rays revealed lesions. Although the fragment had been removed, the lesions remained. How severe the lasting effects of the brain damage would be no one knew. One result had been epilepsy. Another had been apparent interference with the area of the brain that processes written symbols. She also had many of the problems commonly associated with more minimal types of damage, such as difficulty in concentration, an inability to sit still and distractibility. The bittersweet issue in my mind, however, was the fact that Lori came away from the injury as intact as she did. She lost very little, if any, of her intelligence or her perception or her understanding, and she *was* a bright child. Nor did she look damaged: For all intents and purposes, Lori was normal. Because of this, I noticed that people, myself included, tended to forget she was not. And sometimes we became angry with her for things over which she had no control.

The prognosis for her recovery was guarded. Brain cells, unlike other cells in the body, do not regenerate. The only hope the doctors had given was that in time her brain might learn other pathways around the injured area and

17

tasks such as reading and writing would become more feasible things for her to accomplish. In the meantime Lori struggled on as best she could.

But there was no kid quite like Lori. Her brain did not always function well, yet there was nothing wrong with Lori's heart. She was full of an innate belief in the goodness of people. Despite her own experiences, evil did not exist for Lori. She embraced all of us, good and bad alike, with a sort of droll acceptance. And she cared. The welfare of all the world mattered to her. I found it both her most endearing and annoying trait. Nothing was safe from her: she cared about how you felt, what you thought, what your dreams were. She involved herself so intimately in a world so hard on those who care that I often caught my breath with fear for her. Yet Lori remained undaunted. Her love was a little raw at seven, and not yet cloaked by social graces, but the point was, she cared.

Boo was of great concern to Lori.

"Doesn't he talk?" she asked me in a stage whisper after all her attempts at conversation had been ignored.

I shook my head. "Not too well. That's one of the things that Boo came here to learn."

"Ohhh, poor Boo." She stood up and reached out to pat his arm. "Don't worry, you'll learn. I don't learn so good myself so I know how you feel. But don't worry. You're probably a nice boy anyways."

Boo's fingers fluttered and the vacant eyes showed just the smallest signs of life. A quick flicker to Lori's face, then he turned and faced the wall.

I decided to work with Lori and leave Boo to stand. There was no need to hurry. "I'll be right here, Boo," I said. He stood motionless, staring at the wall. I turned my chair around to the table.

Lori flipped open her workbook. "It's dumb old spelling again today. I don't know." She scratched her head

18

thoughtfully. "Me and that teacher, we just aren't doing so good on this. She thinks you oughta teach me better."

I grinned and pulled the book over to view it. "Did she tell you that?"

"No. But I can tell she thinks it."

Boo began to move. Hesitantly at first. A step. Two steps. Mincingly, like a geisha girl. Another step. I watched him out of the corner of one eye as I leaned over Lori's spelling. Boo walked as if someone had starched his underwear. His head never turned; his arms remained tight against his sides. The muscles in his neck stood out. Every once in a while his hands would flap. Was all this tension just to keep control? What was he trying so desperately to hold in?

"Look at him," Lori whispered. She smiled up at me. "He's getting himself to home."

I nodded.

"He's a little weird, Torey, but that's okay, isn't it?" she said. "I act a little weird myself sometimes. People do, you know."

"Yes, I know. Now concentrate on your spelling, please."

Boo explored the environs of the classroom. It was a large room, square and sunny from a west wall of windows. The teacher's desk was shoved into one corner, a repository for all kinds of things I did not know what to do with. The worktable stretched along below the windows where I could have the most light on my work. The few student desks in the room were back against one wall. Another wall housed my coat closet, the sink, the cupboards and two huge storage cabinets. Low bookshelves came out into the room to partition off a reading corner and the animals: Sam, the hermit crab; two green finches in a huge home-made cage; and Benny the boa constrictor, who had taught school as long as I had.

Boo inched his way around the room until he came upon the animals. He stopped before the birds. At first he did nothing. Then very slowly he raised one hand to the cage.

19

Flutter, flutter, flutter went his fingers. He began to rock back and forth on his heels. "Hrooop!" he said in a small, high-pitched voice. He said it so quietly the first time that I thought it was the finches. "Hrooooop! Hrrrrooooop!" Both hands were now at ear level and flapping at the birds.

"Ah-ah-ah-ah-ah-ah," he began, still softly. "Ee-ee-ee-ee. Ah-ee. Hoo-hoo-hoo-hoo-hoo-hoo-hoo. Hee-hee-hee-hee-hee." He sounded like a resident of the ape house at the zoo.

Lori looked up from her work, first at Boo and then at me. She had a very expressive glance. Then with a shake of her head she went back to work.

Boo was smiling in an inward translucent sort of way. He turned around. The stiffness in his body melted away. "Heeheeheeheeheeheeheehee!" he said gaily. His eyes focused right on my face.

"Those are our birds, Boo."

"Heeheeheeheeheeheehee! Haahaahaahaahaahaa! Ah-ah-ah-ah!" Great excitement. Boo was jumping up and down in front of the cage. His hands waved gleefully. Every few moments he would turn to look at Lori and me. I smiled back.

Abruptly Boo took off at a run around the classroom. High-pitched squeally laughter lanced the schoolroom quiet. His arms flopped widely like a small child playing at being an airplane, but there was a graceful consistency to the motion that made it unlike any game.

"Torey!" Lori leaped up from her chair. "Look at him! He's taking *off* all his clothes!"

Sure enough Boo was. A shoe. A sock. A shirt. They all fell behind him as he ran. He was a clothes Houdini. His green corduroy pants came down and off with hardly a break in his rhythm. Boo darted back and forth, laughing deliriously, clothing dropping in his wake. Lori watched with horrified fascination. At one point she put her hands over her eyes but I saw her peeking through her fingers. A goofy grin was glued to her face. Boo made quite a sight.

I did not want to chase him. Whatever little bit of lunacy this was, I did not want to be a party to it. My greatest concern was the door. Within minutes Boo had completely stripped and now capered around in naked glee. I had not enjoyed chasing him the first time when he had been fully clothed. I could just imagine doing it now. This was a nice, middle-class, sedate and slightly boring elementary school without any classes of crazy kids in it. Dan Marshall, the principal, swell guy that he was, would have an apoplectic fit if some kid streaked down one of his corridors. I would hate to be the cause of that.

Boo laughed. He laughed and danced from one side of the room to the other while I guarded the door. I longed for a latch on that door. That had been one of the small things my classrooms had always had. Locks, like all other things, are neither good nor bad in themselves. There are times for them. And this was one. It would have been better if I could simply have latched the door and gone back to my work. As it was now, Boo had me playing warden, trapped into participating in his game. It gave him no end of pleasure.

For almost fifteen minutes the delirium went on. He would stop occasionally, usually not far from me, and face me, his little bare body defiant. I tried to assess what I could see in those sea-green eyes. I could see something but I did not know what it was.

Then during one of his pauses he lifted a hand up before his face and began to twiddle his fingers in front of his eyes. A shade went down; something closed. Like the transparent membrane over a reptile's eye, something pulled across him and he went shut again. The small body stiffened, the arms came close to his sides, protectively. No life flickered in his eyes.

Boo stood a moment, once more a cardboard figure. Then a wild flap of his arms and he minced off across the room

21

and dived under a piece of carpet in the reading center. Wiggling, he slipped nearly entirely under until all that was visible was a lumpy carpet and two bare feet.

Lori gave me a defeated look as I returned to the worktable. "It's gonna take a lot of work to fix him, Tor. He's pretty weird. Boy, and I mean not just a little weird either."

"He has his problems."

"Yeah. He don't got no clothes on for one thing."

"Well, that's okay for now. We'll take care of that later on."

"It's not okay, Torey. I don't think you're supposed to be naked in school. My daddy, I think he told me that once."

"Some things are different from others, Lor."

"It isn't right. I know. You can see his thing. Girls aren't supposed to look at those. It means you're nasty. But I could hardly help it, could I? And my dad would spank me if he knew I was doing that."

I smiled at her. "You mean his penis?"

Lori nodded. She had to suck her lips between her teeth to keep from smiling too.

"I have a feeling you didn't mind it too much."

"Well, it *was* pretty interesting."

We made it through the first day, Boo and I. Boo spent the entire hour and a half we had alone under the carpet. I let him remain there. When 3:15 approached I pulled him out and dressed him. Boo lay perfectly inert, his limbs slightly stiff but still compliant, his head back so that he was looking above him. I talked to him as I put back all the clothing he had so skillfully removed. I told him about the room, about the birds and the snake and the crab, about what he and I would do together, about other children he would meet, about Tim and Brad and Lori. About anything

22

that came to mind. I watched his eyes. Nothing. There was nothing there. A body without a soul in it.

He began talking while I was, but when I stopped, he stopped. He still stared above him, although there was no focus to the gaze.

"What did you say, Boo?"

No response.

"Did you want to talk about something?"

Still looking blankly into space. "The high today will be about 65, the low tonight in the middle forties. In the mountain valleys there is a chance of frost. The high at the airport yesterday was 56. In Falls City it was 61."

"Boo? Boo?" I softly touched his face. Loose black curls flopped back onto the carpet where he lay. The picture-book beauty lay over his features like a separate entity. His fingers waggled against the rug. I was touching him, buttoning his shirt, moving slowly but certainly up his chest. I might as well have been dressing a doll. All the while he continued talking, parroting back the morning weather report exactly, word for word. Delayed echolalia, if one wanted the technical term for it. If that mattered.

"Chance of precipitation in the Greenwood area, 20 percent today, 10 percent tonight and then rising to 50 percent by morning. It looks like it is going to be a beautiful autumn day here in the Midland Empire. And now for Ron Neilsen with the sports. Stay turned. Don't go away."

Don't worry. I won't.

3

We were piloting a reading series program in the primary grades that year. For me it was not a new program. The school I had previously taught in had also piloted the program. I got to live through the disaster twice.

The program itself was aesthetically outstanding. The publishers had obviously engaged true artistic talent to do the layouts and illustrations. Many of the stories were of literary quality. They were fun stories to read.

Unless, of course, you could not read.

It was a reading series designed for adults, for the adults who bought it, for the adults who had to read it, for the adults who had forgotten what it was like to be six and not know how to read. This series was a response to the community agitators who as forty-year-olds were not fascinated by the controlled vocabulary of a basal reader. They had demanded something more and now they had gotten it. As children's books for adults, those in the series were peerless. In fact, the first time I had encountered the books, I had covertly dragged home every single reader at one time or another because I *wanted* to read them. Of course, I was twenty-six. We bought the books, the children did not, and in this case we bought the books for ourselves.

For the kids it was all a different matter. Or at least for my kids. I had always taught beginners or failures. For these two groups the reading program was an unmitigated disaster.

The major difficulty was that, in order to appeal to adults from the first pre-primer on, the series had dispensed with the usual small words, short sentences and controlled vocabulary. Even the pictures accompanying the text, though artistic, were rarely illustrative of the story at hand. The first sentence in the very first book intended for nonreading six-year-olds had eight words including one with three syllables. For some of the children this was all right. They managed the first sentence and all the others after it. For the majority of children, including mine, well . . . in the three years I had used the series, I had memorized the three pre-primers because never in all that time did any of my children advance to another book. Normally, the first three pre-primers were mastered in the first grade, before Christmas.

I was not the only person having problems. In the first year of piloting, word soon got around in the teachers' lounge: None of the first- or second-grade teachers was having much success. Traditionally, publishers of reading series send a chart outlining the approximate place a teacher and her class should be at ay given time in the term. We all gauged our reading programs around that chart so that we could have our children properly prepared for the next grade by the end of school. This publisher's chart hung in the lounge that first year, and the five of us, two first-grade teachers, two second-grade teachers, and I with my primary special education class, would moan to see ourselves slip further and further behind where the publisher predicted we should be. No one was going to get through the program on time.

After a few months of struggling we became so incensed over this impossible series that we demanded some sort of explanation from the school district for this insanity. The outcome of the protest had been the arrival from the publishing company of a sales representative to answer our questions. When I brought up the fact that less than half of all the children in the program were functioning where the chart said they should be, I expected I had set myself up to be told my colleagues and I just were not good teachers. But no. The salesman was delighted. He smiled and reassured us that we were doing very well indeed. The truth was, he said, only 15 percent of all first graders were *expected* to complete the entire first-grade program during the first grade. The other 85 percent were not.

I was horrified beyond reply. We were using a program that by its very construction set children up to fail. All except the very brightest were destined to be "slow readers." Many, many teachers not hearing this man's words were going to assume that the chart was correct and put their children through an entire year's program under the mistaken belief that all the first-grade material was meant to be done in the first grade, none in second. That was not too extravagant an assumption, in my opinion. Worst of all, however, was that as the years went on, perfectly ordinary children who were learning and developing at normal rates would fall further and further behind, so that by fifth or sixth grade they could conceivably be considered remedial readers because they were two or more books behind their grade placement, when in fact they were right where the publisher expected them to be. And of course nothing could ever be said to these children who were reading fourth-grade books in sixth that would convince them that they were anything other than stupid. It

26

was nothing more than statistics to the publishing company. For the kids it was life. That was such a bitterly high price to pay for an aesthetically pleasing book.

Lori was one of the reading series' unwilling victims. Already a handicapped student who undoubtedly would always have trouble with symbolic language, Lori was trapped with an impossible set of books and a teacher who despised both the books and special students.

Edna Thorsen, Lori's teacher, was an older woman with many, many years of experience behind her. Due for retirement the next year, Edna had been in the field since before I was born. In many areas of teaching Edna was superb. Unfortunately, special children was not one of them. She firmly believed that no exceptional or handicapped child should be in a regular classroom, with perhaps the exception of the gifted, and even of that she was unsure. Not only did these children put an unfair burden on the teacher, she maintained, but they disallowed a good education for the rest of the class because of the teacher time they absorbed. Besides, Edna believed, six-year-olds were just too young to be exposed to the rawness of life that the exceptional children represented. There was plenty of time when they were older to learn about blindness and retardation and mental illness.

Edna kept to many of the more traditional methods of teaching. Her class sat in rows, always stood when addressing her, moved in lines and did not speak until spoken to. They also progressed through the reading program exactly according to the chart sent out by the publishing company. If in the second week of November the children were to be, according to the charts, up to Book #2, page 14, all three of Edna's little reading groups were within a few pages one way or the other of Book #2, page 14, the second week in

November. She had no concept of the notion that only 15 percent of the children were actually expected to be there and all the rest behind. Her sole responsibility, she said, was to see that all twenty-seven children in her room had gone through the three pre-primers, the primer and the first-grade reader by that last day of school in June and were ready for second grade. That all her children could not read those books had no bearing in Edna's mind on anything. Her job was to present the material and she did. It was theirs to learn it. That some did not was their fault, not hers.

Lori was not doing well. The hoped-for maturation in her brain had not yet occurred. In addition to her inability to pick up written symbols, she continued to display other common behaviors of brain-damaged children such as hyperactivity and a shortened attention span. Although Lori had not been on my original roster of resource students when school convened, she appeared at my door during the first week with Edna close behind. We had here what Edna called a "slowie"; Lori was so dense, Edna told me, you couldn't get letters through her head with a gun.

So for a half hour every afternoon, Lori and I tried to conquer the written alphabet. I had to admit we were not doing stunningly. In the three weeks since we had started, Lori could not even recognize the letters in her first name. She could write L-O-R-I without prompting now; we had accomplished that much. Sort of. It came out in slow, meticulously made letters. Sometimes the O and the R were reversed or something was upside down or occasionally she would start on the right and print the whole works completely backwards. For the most part, though, I could trust her to come close. I had scrapped the pre-reading workbook from the reading series because with two years of kindergarten she had been through it three times and still did not know it. Instead I started with the letters of her name and hoped their relevancy would help.

Her difficulty lay solely with symbolic language: letters, numbers, anything written that represented something, other than a concrete picture. She had long since memorized all the letters of the alphabet orally and she knew their sounds. But she just could not match that knowledge to print.

Teaching her was frustrating. Edna certainly was right on that account. Three weeks and I had already run through all my years of experience in teaching reading. I had tried everything I could think of to teach Lori those letters. I used things I believed in, things I was skeptical about, things I already knew were a lot of nonsense. At that point I wasn't being picky about philosophies. I just wanted her to learn.

We began with just one letter, the L. I made flash cards to drill her, had her cut out sandpaper versions to give her the tactile sensation of the letter, made her trace it half a million times in a pan of salt to feel it, drew the letter on her palm, her arm, her back. Together we made a gigantic L on the floor, taped tiny construction paper L's all over it and then hopped around it, walked over it, crawled on it, all the time yelling L-L-L-L-L-L-L-L! until the hallway outside the classroom rang with our voices. Then I introduced O and we went through the same gyrations. Three long weeks and still we were only on L and O.

Most of our days went like this:

"Okay, what letter is this?" I hold up a flash card with an O on it.

"M!" Lori shouts gleefully, as if she knows she is correct.

"See the shape? Around and around. Which letter goes around, Lor?" I demonstrate with my finger on the card.

"Oh, I remember now. Q."

29

"Whoops. Remember we're just working with L and O, Lor. No Q's."

"Oh, yeah." She hits her head with one hand. "Dumb me, I forgot. Let's see now. Hmmmm. Hmmmm. A six? No, no, don't count that; that's wrong. Lemme see now. Uh . . . uh . . . A?"

I lean across the table. "Look at it. See, it's round. Which letter is round like your mouth when you say it? Like this?" I make my mouth O-shaped.

"Seven?"

"Seven is a number. I'm not looking for a number. I'm looking for either an O," and here I make my mouth very obvious, "or an L. Which one makes your mouth look like this?" I push out my lips. "And that's just about the only letter your lips can say when they're like that. What letter is it?"

Lori sticks her lips out like mine and we are leaning so intently toward one another that we look like lovers straining to bridge the width of the table. Her lips form a perfect O and she gargles out "Lllllllll."

I go "Ohhhhhhh" in a whisper, my lips still stuck out like a fish's.

"O!" Lori finally shouts. "That's an O!"

"Hey, yeah! There you go, girl. Look at that, you got it." Then I pick up the next card, another O but written in red Magic Marker instead of blue like the last. "What letter is this?"

"Eight?"

So went lesson after lesson after lesson. Lori was not stupid. She had a validated IQ in the nearly superior range. Yet in no way could she make sense of those letters. They just must have looked different to her than to the rest of us. Only her buoyant, irrepressible spirit kept us going. Never once did I see her give up. She would tire or become

30

frustrated but never would she completely resign herself to believing that L and O would not someday come straight.

The day after Boo arrived, Lori came to my room tearful. She was not crying but her eyes were full and her head down. Without acknowledging me, she hauled herself across the room to the table and tiredly threw the workbook down on it.

"What's wrong, babe?" I asked.

Shrugging, she yanked a chair out and fell on it. With both fists she braced her cheeks.

"Shall we talk a bit before we start?"

She shook her head and swabbed roughly at the unfallen tears with a shirt sleeve.

Sitting down on the edge of the table next to her, I watched her. The dark hair had been caught back in two long braids. Red plaid ribbons were tied rakishly on the ends. Her skinny shoulders were pulled up protectively. Taking deep breaths, she struggled to keep her composure. A funny kid, she was. For all her spirit, for all her outspokenness, for all her insight into other people's feelings, she was a remarkably closed person herself. I did not know her well even though she usually allowed me to believe I did.

We sat in silence a moment or two. I then rose to check on Boo. He was over by the animals again, watching the snake. Back and forth he rocked on his heels as he and Benny stared at one another. Benny was curled up on his tall hunk of driftwood under the heat lamp with his head hanging off the branch. It was a loony position for a snake, and if one did not know him, one could easily have mistaken him for dead. However, for those who did know, he was requesting a scratch along the neck. Boo just stared

31

and rocked. Benny stared back. I returned to Lori and stood behind her. Gently, I massaged her shoulders.

"Hard day?"

She nodded.

Again I sat. Boo looked in our direction. Lori interested him. He watched with great, seeking eyes.

"I didn't get no recess," Lori mumbled.

"How come?"

"I didn't do my workbook right." She was tracing around one of the illustrations on the cover of the pre-primer on the table. Over and over it her finger slid.

"You usually do your workbooks in here with me, Lor. When we get time from our reading."

"Mrs. Thorsen changed it. Everybody does their workbooks before recess now. If you do it fast you get to go out to recess early. Except me." Lori looked up. "I have to do mine fast *and* right."

"Oh, I see."

The tears were there again, still unfallen but gleaming like captive stars. "I *tried!* I did. But it wasn't right. I had to stay and work all recess and didn't even get to go out at all. It was my turn at kickball captain even. And, see, I was going to choose Mary Ann Marks to be on my team. We were going to win 'cause she kicks better than anybody else in the whole room. In the whole first grade even. She said if I picked her then I could come over to her house after school and play with her Barbie dolls and we were gonna be best friends. But I didn't even get to go out. Jerry Munsen got to be captain instead and Mary Ann Marks is going to go home with Becky Smith. And *they're* going to be best friends. I didn't even get a chance!" She caught an escaped tear. "It's not fair. It was my turn to be captain and I had to stay in. Nobody else has to do their stuff all right first. Just me. And it isn't fair."

After school I went to talk to Edna Thorsen. For the most part Edna and I got along well. I did disagree with many of her methods and philosophies, but on the other hand she had a great deal more experience than I and had seen so many more children that I respected her overall knowledge.

"I'm taking your advice," she told me as we walked into the teacher's lounge.

"My advice?"

"Yes. Remember how I was complaining earlier about how I never could get the children to finish up their work on time?"

I nodded.

"And you suggested that I make the ones who did finish glad they did?" Edna was smiling. "I did that with the reading workbooks. I told the children they could go out to recess as soon as they finished their pages. And you sure taught this old dog a new trick. We get the work done in just fifteen minutes."

"Do you check the work when they're done?" I asked. "Before they go out?"

She made an obtuse gesture. "Nah. They do all right."

"What about Lori Sjokheim?"

Edna rolled her eyeballs far back into her head. "*Hers* I have to check. Why, that Lori has no more intention of doing her work carefully than anything. The first few days I let her go with the other children, but then I got to looking at her workbook and you know what I found? Wrong. Every single answer wrong. She'll take advantage of you every chance she gets."

I had to look away. Look at the wall or the coffeepot or anything. Poor Lori who could not read, who could not write and who got all her answers wrong. "But I thought she was to bring in her workbooks to do with me," I said.

"Oh, Torey." Edna's voice was heavy with great patience. "This is one thing you have yet to learn. You can't mollycoddle the uncooperative ones, especially in the first grade—that's when you have to show them who's boss. Lori just needs disciplining. She's a bright enough little girl. Don't let her fool you in that regard. The only way Lori's kind will shape up is if you set strict limits. It's modern society. No one teaches their children self-restraint anymore." Edna smiled.

"And with all due respect and credit to what you're trying to do, Torey, I can't see it myself. Giving her all that extra help when nobody else gets it. It's a waste of time on some kids. I've been in the business a long time now, and believe me, you get so you can tell who's going to make it and who isn't. I just cannot understand spending all the extra time and money on these little slowies who'll never amount to anything. So many other children would profit from it more."

I rose to wrestle a can of Dr Pepper out of the machine. The right thing to do would have been to correct Edna, because to my way of thinking at least, she was dead wrong. The cowardly thing was to get up and go fight the pop machine. Yet that was what I did. I was, admittedly, a little afraid of Edna. She could speak her mind so easily; she seemed so confident about her beliefs. And she possessed so much of the only thing I had found valuable as an educator: experience. In the face of that, I was left uncertain and questioned my own perceptions. So I took the coward's way out.

Unfortunately, the situation did not mend itself. The next day, too, Lori was kept in during recess and still she lugged her reading workbook in to me all full of errors. She was more resigned. No tears. The day after that was no different either. Or the day after that. If we did not get through the book during our time together, if mistakes still existed at the end of the day, Edna kept Lori after school also. Edna continued to perceive Lori's mistakes as carelessness. That Lori maintained a sort of gritted-teeth composure throughout Edna's disciplinary campaign and still did not get her work right convinced Edna it was a battle of wills.

The tension began to show on both sides. In with me, Lori could not concentrate at all. Everything would distract her. As the number of days lengthened, a distressful restlessness overtook her. As soon as she came into the room and sat down, she would have to get up again. Down, up, down, up. While working, she would lean back in her chair every few minutes, close her eyes and shake her hands at her sides to relieve the pressure. Edna was not escaping unharmed either. She redeveloped migraines.

The next Monday things came to a head. At Lori's appointed time with me she did not arrive. I waited. Over by the animal cages with Boo, I talked to him about Sam in his shell. Yet my eyes were on the clock and my mind on Lori.

I knew Lori was not absent; I had seen her in the halls earlier. Finally when fifteen minutes had passed and she still did not show up, I took Boo by the hand and we went to investigate.

"I sent her to the office," Edna replied at the door of her first-grade classroom. She shook her head. "That child has had it in this room, let me tell you. She took her reading workbook and threw it clear across the room. Nearly whacked poor Sandy Latham in the head. Could have put an eye out, the way she threw it. And then when I told her to pick it up, she turns around as pretty as you please, just like she was some little queen and says . . . well, let me tell you, it was a *tainted* word. Can you imagine? Seven years old and she uses words like that? I have the other children to think of. I'm not going to have them hearing words like that. Not in here. And I told her so. And sent her right down to Mr. Marshall. She earned that paddling."

I too went right down to Mr. Marshall's office, dragging Boo behind me because there was nothing else to do with him. There, sitting on a chair in the secretary's office, was Lori, tears over her cheeks, a mangled tissue in her hands. She would not look up as Boo and I entered.

"May Lori come down to class with me?" I asked the secretary. "It's her time in the resource room."

The secretary looked up from her typing. First at me and then, craning her neck to see over the counter, at Lori. "Well, I suppose. She was supposed to sit there until she finished crying. You done crying?" she asked across the Formica barrier.

Lori nodded.

"You going to behave yourself for once? No more trouble this afternoon?" the secretary asked.

Another nod.

"You're too little to be getting in all this trouble."

Lori rose from the chair.

"Did you hear me?" the secretary asked.

Lori nodded.

Back to me, the secretary shrugged. "I guess you can have her."

We walked down the hallway hand in hand, the three of us. My head was down as we were walking and I looked at our clasped hands. Lori's nails were bitten down to where blood caked around the little finger.

Inside our room I let go of both of them. Boo minced off to see Benny. Lori went directly to the worktable while I shut the door and fastened the small hook-and-eye latch I had purchased at the discount store.

On top of the worktable was one of the pre-primers I had been using with another student earlier in the day. Lori walked over to it and regarded it for a long moment in a serious but detached manner, as one views an exhibit in the museum. She looked back at me, then back at the door. Her face clouded with an emotion I could not decipher.

Abruptly Lori knocked the book off the table with a fierce shove. Around the table she went and kicked the book against the radiator. She grabbed it and ripped at the brightly colored illustrations. "I hate this place! I hate it, I hate it, I hate it!" she screamed at me. "I don't want to

36

read. I don't ever want to read. I *hate* reading!" Then her words were swallowed up in sobs as the pages of the pre-primer flew.

Tears everywhere and Lori was lost in her frenzy. She clawed the book, her nails squeaking across the paper. Her entire body was involved, bouncing up and down in a tense, concentrated rage. When the last pages of the pre-primer lay crumpled, she pitched the covers of the book hard at the window behind the table. Then she turned and ran for the door. Not expecting it to be locked, she fell hard against it with a resounding thunk. Giving up a wail of defeat, she collapsed, her body slithering down along the wood of the door like melting butter.

Boo and I stood frozen. The entire drama was probably measurable in seconds. There had been no time to respond. Now in the deafening silence, I could hear only the muted frantic fluttering of Boo's hands against his pants. And Lori's low, heavy weeping.

4

The class was formed.

Following the incident in Edna's room, Lori was assigned to me all afternoon, along with Boo. Tim and Brad, my two other afternoon resource students, were transferred to the morning, and now I had Lori and Boo alone for almost three hours. Although officially I was still listed as a resource teacher and these two as simply resource students, all of us knew I had a class.

According to the records, Lori was assigned the extra resource time for "more intensive academic help." However, Dan Marshall, Edna and I—and probably Lori herself—knew the change had come about because we had come too close to disaster. Perhaps in a different situation Lori could have managed full time in a regular classroom, but here she couldn't. In Edna's conservatively structured program, Lori did not have adequate skills to function. To relieve the pressure on both sides, she spent the mornings in her regular class where she would still receive reading and math instruction along with lighter subjects, but in the afternoons when Edna concentrated on the difficult, workbook-oriented reading skills, Lori would be with me.

So there we were, the three of us.

Boo remained such a dream child. As so many autistic-like children I had known, he possessed uncanny physical beauty; he seemed too beautiful to belong to this everyday world. Perhaps he did not. Sometimes I thought that he and others like him were the changelings spoken of in old stories. It was never inconceivable to me that he might truly be a fairy child spirited from the cold, bright beauty of his world, trapped in mine and never quite able to reconcile the two. And I always noticed that when we finally reached through to an autistic or schizophrenic child, if we ever did, that they lost some of that beauty as they took on ordinary interactions, as if we had in some way sullied them. But as for Boo, thus far I had failed to touch him, and his beauty lay upon him with the shining stillness of a dream.

Our days did not vary much. Each afternoon Boo's mother would bring him. She would open the door and shove Boo through, wave good-bye to him, holler hello to me and leave. Not once could I entice her through that door to talk.

Once inside Boo would stand rigid and mute until he was helped off with his outer clothes. If I did aid him, he would come to life again. If I did not, he would continue standing, staring straight ahead, not moving. One day I left him there in his sweater to see what would happen since I knew from his disrobing episodes that he was capable of getting out of his clothes when inspired. That day he stood motionless until 2:15, nearly two hours. Finally, I gave in and took off his sweater for him.

The only definite interest Boo had was for the animals. Benny particularly fascinated him. Once he thawed from his arrival, he would head for the animal corner. The only time Boo gave any concrete sign of attending to his environment or attempting any communication was when he stood in front of Benny's driftwood and flicked his fingers before the snake's face and hrooped softly. Otherwise, Boo's time was spent rocking, flapping, spinning or smelling things. Each day he would move along the walls of the classroom inhaling the scent of the paint and plaster. Then he would lie down and sniff the rug and the floor. Any object he encountered would first be smelled, sometimes tasted, then tested for its ability to spin. To Boo there seemed to be no other way of evaluating his environment.

Working with him was difficult. Smelling me was as entertaining to him as smelling the walls. While I held him he would whiff along my arms and shirt, lick at the cloth, suck at my skin. Yet the only way I could focus his attention even for a moment was to capture him physically and hold him, arms pinned to his sides, while I attempted to manipulate learning materials. Even then Boo would rock, pushing his body back and forth against mine. The simplest solution I found was to rock with him. And every night after school I washed the sticky saliva off my arms and neck and wherever else he had reached.

Boo's locomotion around the room was generally in an odd, rigid gait. Up on his toes he moved like the mimes I had seen in Central Park. However, on rare occasions, usually in response to some secret conversation with Benny or the finches, Boo would come startlingly to life. He would begin with ape laughter, his eyes would light up and he would look directly at me, the only time that ever occurred. Then off around the room he would run, the stiffness gone, an eerie grace replacing it. Stripping down until he was completely nude, he would run and giggle like a toddler escaped from his bath. Then as suddenly as it started, that moment of freedom would pass.

Aside from the occasional hroops and whirrs, Boo initiated no communication. He echoed incessantly. Sometimes he would echo directly what I had just said. More frequently he echoed commercials, radio and TV shows, weather and news broadcasts and even his parents' arguments—all things heard long in the past. He was capable of repeating tremendous quantities of material word for word in the exact intonation of the original speaker. A supernatural aura often settled down among us as we worked to the drone of long-forgotten news events or other people's private conversations.

The first days and even weeks after Lori arrived full time in the afternoons, I was perplexed as to how to handle these two very different children together effectively. I could sometimes give Lori something to do and go work with Boo. However, there was no reverse of that. To accomplish anything at all with Boo, one had to be constantly reorienting his hands, mouth, body and mind. Still there was a certain magic with us. Lori interested Boo. He would steal furtive glances at her while all the rest of him was robot stiff. Occasionally he would turn his head when she mentioned his name in conversation. He would give very, very soft hroops every once in a while when he was sitting near Lori and not near Benny at all. As I watched them that first week that Lori had joined us full time in the afternoon, I was pleased. This would never be an easy way to spend an afternoon, but likewise, it would never be dull. I was glad we had become a class.

One result of Lori's entrance into my room half-days was meeting her father. We first came face to face in the meeting with Edna and Dan over Lori's placement. I liked

Mr. Sjokheim immediately. He was a big man, perhaps not as tall as wide, although it was a congenial plumpness mostly around the belt area, as if he had enjoyed all his Sunday dinners. He had a deep, soft voice and a ringing laugh that carried far out into the hallway. Even in that early meeting as I listened to him, it became apparent where Lori had acquired much of her caring attitude.

After the first week passed with Lori in my room, I invited Mr. Sjokheim in after school to get acquainted. By profession he was an experimental engineer. He worked in the laboratory of an airplane company and dealt with aspects of environmental impact of airplanes. He derived great pleasure from talking about various programs he had implemented locally to cut down on both air and noise pollution by the company.

Tragedy, however, had marked Sjokheim's personal life. He and his wife had had an only child, a daughter, several years before. When the girl was four years old, she fell through a plate-glass window. The glass had penetrated her throat and she had nearly bled to death. Quick action by paramedics saved her life; however, she suffered severe brain damage from loss of oxygen and became comatose. Yet the child did not die. For three years after the accident she remained hospitalized and on life-support equipment before finally succumbing. She never regained consciousness in all that time.

With their finances drained and their lives left empty, the Sjokheims had moved to our community a few years later to try to start over. Soon after, Lori and her twin sister Libby were placed in the Sjokheim home as foster children. They were four years old. Very early, Mr. Sjokheim said, he and his wife realized that they wanted to adopt the twins. Yes, they knew of the brutal amount of abuse the girls had suffered and of the possibilities of complications from it, both physically and emotionally. That did not matter.

After all, he said to me with a smile, they needed us and we needed them. What more did it take?

Apparently not much more. The twins were cleared for adoption soon after their fifth birthday and the Sjokheims started proceedings. Then suddenly Mrs. Sjokheim became seriously ill. The diagnosis was simple. Too simple and too swift for its impact. Cancer. She died before Lori and Libby turned six.

There had been no question in Sjokheim's mind that he would keep the girls. If they had needed one another before, they surely did now. However, the proceedings became complicated. He was over the usual adoptive-parent age limit. Allowances had been made before because his wife was younger and because the twins themselves were old for adoption, and because there were two children. Now the agency balked. The twins were in a single-parent home and that parent was the father while they were female. Much legal rigmarole followed. In the end because of the twins' generally unfavorable prospects for other adoptions and because the Sjokheims had nearly completed the procedure at the time of Mrs. Sjokheim's death, the state allowed Mr. Sjokheim to go ahead.

The last year and a half had not been easy. At forty-five he was unused to being the only parent of two young children. The twins were coping with the second loss of a mother in two years. He had had to move to be nearer their regular baby-sitter; he had had to make some career decisions he had never anticipated. He was no longer head engineer in his lab. It had simply taken too much time. Now he was living in a smaller house and making a smaller salary, and his main job was raising Lori and Libby. Some days, he said with a weary smile, he seriously questioned the wisdom of his choice to be a single father. For the most part, however, there could have been no other life for him.

The problems with Lori showed up early. Even before the

twins had started school, Mrs. Sjokheim had tried to teach them to write their names. Libby learned immediately. Lori never did. The first year of school had been chaotic. Between her inability to recognize or write any written symbols and her mother's increasing illness, Lori did not cope well. She was hyperactive and inattentive. At home she developed enuresis and nightmares. Because both Libby and Lori were marked by that traumatic year and because they had September birthdays, making them younger than most other children in their class, the school personnel and Mr. Sjokheim had decided to retain both girls in kindergarten for an additional year. Libby profited from the retention. The more introverted, less expressive of the twins, she grew. The next year she became an excellent student, more confident and outgoing. Lori had no such luck. The second year in kindergarten was no less disastrous than the first. About midyear everyone began to realize that there must be more wrong with Lori than simple immaturity or poor adjustment to family crisis. Some things she could do with great ease, such as count aloud or even add verbally, a skill Libby had not acquired. Other things such as writing her name or identifying letters seemed impossible. The final blow came when she suffered a grand mal seizure in class one day.

Mr. Sjokheim took his daughter to the doctor. From there they were referred to university facilities on the far side of the state. Lori was admitted to the university hospital and given a complete neurological workup. When X rays revealed the fracture line and later the brain lesions, a search was instigated through the adoption agency for old medical records. The abuse incident and the surgery to remove bone fragments and repair the skull came to light.

The doctors were hesitant to give pat answers. The epilepsy, which had probably been going on in the form of petit mal seizure for years, was undoubtedly a result of the abuse damage. The small unnoticed seizures alone could have accounted for much of Lori's school failure. But as to her other problems, in the areas of symbolic language, there was no way of knowing. Too little about the operations of the brain was understood, and there were too many other possibilities. She was the younger twin, had been born prematurely; perhaps there might have been a birth injury or a congenital defect. Who could tell? Yet that evil crack running so squarely over the lesions on an otherwise normal-appearing brain gave mute testimony to what even the leading neurologist on Lori's team admitted believing the answer to be.

Following the hospitalization and testing, Lori was placed on anti-convulsant medication and sent home. The seizures were controlled but back in kindergarten the struggle with learning continued. Lori left in June to go on to first grade, able to jabber off the alphabet and count up to 1000 but not even recognizing the letters of her name.

Still there remained a little encouragement from the doctors that she might improve. She was so young when the injury occurred that her brain might be capable of learning new pathways to circumvent the damaged area. If it was going to occur, it would most likely happen before she entered adolescence.

Mr. Sjokheim expressed relief that Lori had been moved half-days from the first grade. She needed more specialized support and he had seen the pressure building when she could not meet Edna's demands.

He spoke to me about Lori's actions and reactions over the past weeks. Then he paused, pinched the bridge of his nose and wearily shook his head. "I worry so much about her," he said. "Not about the reading really. I figure if that's meant to happen, it will. But . . ." He stared at the tabletop. "But sometimes I wake up at night . . . and before I can get back to sleep, well, she creeps into my head. I think about her. I think about all the little things she does to convince herself that this much failure does not matter to her. And I think how it does matter." He looked up at me. His eyes were a soft, nondescript hazel color. "It's worst at night for me. When I'm alone and I get to thinking about her. There's no way to distract myself then. And you know . . . you know, it sounds stupid to say, but sometimes it makes me cry. I actually get tears in my eyes."

I watched him as he spoke and thought about what it must be like to be Lori. That was difficult. I had always been a good student who had never had to try. I could not imagine what it must be like to be seven and to have known failure half my life, to get up every morning and come spend six hours in a place where try as I might, I could never really succeed. And by law Lori had at least seven more years ahead of her of this torture, as many years left as she had lived. Men murdered and received shorter prison terms than that. All Lori had done was to be born into the wrong family.

5

Once long ago when I was a very little girl I told my mother that when I grew up I was going to be a witch and marry a dinosaur. At four that seemed a marvelous plan. I adored playing witch in the backyard with my friends and I was passionately interested in dinosaurs. There could be no better life than one in which I could do what I loved doing and live with one I found immensely fascinating.

I haven't changed a lot in that respect. Somewhere deep inside there is still a small four-year-old looking for her dinosaur. And there was no denying that the single hardest task as my career progressed had become synchronizing life with the kids with the remainder of my life outside school.

The task did not seem to be getting any easier. I know I did not help things much. I loved my work profoundly. It stretched me to the very limits of my being. The time spent within the walls of my classroom had formed fully my views of life and death, of love and hate, of justice, reality and the unrestrained brutal beauty of the human spirit. It had given me my understanding of the meaning of existence. And in the end it had put me at ease with myself. I had become the sort of person who got home Fridays and waited anxiously for Mondays. The kids were my fix, the experience a spiritual orgasm.

That kind of intensity was hard to compete with. I tried to step back from it and appreciate the slower, less rabid hours I spent outside school but I knew my appetite for the extreme, both mentally and emotionally, made me a complicated companion.

Joc and I had been seeing each other for almost a year. The old adage had been true in our case: opposites attract. He was a research chemist at the hospital. He worked only with things. Indeed, he loved things: cars that handled well, old rifles, good wine and clothes. Joc was the only man I had ever dated who actually owned a tuxedo. And perhaps because things so seldom needed talking to, Joc was never a talker. He was not a quiet type; he just never wasted words beyond the concrete. He could not comprehend their practicality in some areas. Why talk about things if one could not change them? Why discuss things that have no answers?

Fun for Joc was getting dressed up and going out to eat, going to a party, going dancing. Just plain going out.

And there I was with my wardrobe of three pairs of Levi's and a military jacket left over from student protest days. When I came home from work I wanted to stay home, to cook a good meal, to talk. I sorted my life out with words. I built my dreams with them.

We made an unlikely pair. But whatever our differences, we seemed to get around them. We fought incessantly. And we made up incessantly, too, which made most of the fighting worthwhile. I loved Joc. He was French, which I found exotic. He was handsome: tall, rugged-looking with wind-blown hair, like those men in perfume advertisements. I don't think I had ever dated such a handsome man and I knew that fed my vanity some. Yet there were better reasons too. He had a good sense of humor. He was romantic, remembering all the little things I was just as likely to dispense with. And perhaps most of all he stretched me in a way different from my work; he kept me oriented toward normalcy and adulthood. He could usually keep my Peter Pan tendencies under control. It was a good, if not always easy, relationship.

As September rolled into October and an Indian summer stretched out warm and lazy across the farmlands, Joc and I were seeing more of each other, but increasingly he began to complain about my work. I was not leaving it at school, he said, which was true enough, I suppose. I had Boo and Lori to think about now and I wanted to share it. I wanted Joc to see Boo's eerie otherworldliness and Lori's tenderness because they were so beautiful to me. On more practical levels, I wanted to bounce ideas off someone. I needed to explore those regions of the children's behavior that I could not comprehend. My best thinking was always done aloud.

All this talk of crazy people depressed him, Joc replied. I ought to put it away at night. Why did I always insist on bringing it home? I sat by quietly when he said that to me and I was filled with sadness. It was then I knew that Joc would never be my dinosaur.

I had meant to fix supper. Joc was coming over. We had not made plans because the night before when we had discussed it, Joc had wanted to see the newest Coppola movie and I had wanted to fix something on the barbecue. Like so many other times when we ended up unable to agree on anything, Joc just said he would be over.

When I came home from school in the evening there was a letter in the mailbox from an old friend who was teaching disturbed children in another state. She related how her kids had made ice cream one day in class. Instead of using the big, cumbersome ice-cream maker with all its messy rock salt and ice and impossible turning, she had used empty frozen-juice cans inside coffee cans. The children each had their own individual ice-cream makers. The ice cream set up in less than ten minutes.

My mind ignited as I read the letter. Ideas were coming so fast I could not catch them in order. This was just the thing for Boo and Lori and me to do. The class had been disjointed while I tried vainly to juggle them into some sort of academic program. This would make us as class. Lori would be thrilled about doing something of this nature, and what a good experience for Boo. I could make it into a reading experience, a math lesson.

When Joc found me I had my head in the deep-freeze trying to locate a second can of frozen orange juice. I already had the first can thawing on the counter.

"What are you doing?" he asked as he came into the kitchen.

"Hey, listen, would you do me a great big favor, please? Would you run over to the store and buy me another can of orange juice?" I said from the freezer.

"You have one here."

I straightened up and shut the lid. "I need three and I only have two. Be an angel, would you please? There's money on top of the dresser. And I'll get dinner started."

Joc looked at me and his brow furrowed in a way I could not interpret. He stroked the lapel of his sports coat. "I thought we might go out. I made reservations for us at Adam's Rib for supper."

I let out a long, slow breath while I considered things. Glancing sideways, I saw Candy's letter lying open on the kitchen table. Back to Joc. He looked so handsome in his tweed coat. I noticed he was carrying an eight-track tape in one hand, undoubtedly a new one he had bought for his car stereo and brought in to show me.

Candy's letter called to me like a Siren. I knew there was no way I could explain that to Joc. The scant six feet between us was measurable in light-years. Joc was not going to understand.

"Not tonight, okay?" My voice was more tentative-sounding than I had meant it to be. "I'll fix something for us. Okay?"

His brow furrowed further giving him an inscrutable look.

I glanced at the letter again. It sang to me so loudly. "I wanted to make ice cream. My girlfriend just sent me a new way. . . ."

"We can *buy* ice cream, Torey."

A pause. A pause that grew to be a silence. I was watching him.

"This is different, Joc. It's for . . . Well, it's to do tomorrow with . . . You see, my girl friend Candy in New York, she teaches kids like I do."

Briefly he put a hand up to his eyes as if he were very, very tired. Pressing his fingers tightly against his eyes, he gave a slight shake of his head before dropping his hand. "Not this again."

"Candy was telling me about doing this with her kids." There were still big pauses between my sentences as I spoke. Mostly because I had to stop to judge his reaction after each one. Yet I kept hoping that if I explained enough he would understand why I just could not go to Adam's Rib tonight. Some other night perhaps, but not tonight. Please. Please?

I kept watching his eyes. He had green eyes, but not like Boo's eyes at all; kaleidoscopic eyes were what Jocco had, like looking at the pebbles on the bottom of a stream. His eyes always said a great deal. But I kept trying anyway. "I

51

was thinking maybe we could try out the ice cream tonight. I need to try it out before I can use it with my kids, and I thought . . . well, I was hoping . . . well . . ." Cripes, not saying a word, and he was still cutting me short. I felt like a little girl. "Well, I was thinking that if it worked and . . . I could try it at school tomorrow, if it worked for us." Another pause. "My kids would like that."

"Your kids would like that?" His voice was painfully soft.

"It wouldn't take much time."

"And what about me?"

I looked down at my hands.

"Where the hell do I come in, Torey?"

"Come on, Joc, let's not fight."

"We're not fighting. We're having an adult discussion, if you can understand that. And I just want to know what it is those children have that no one else in the world seems to have for you. Why can't you put them away? Just once? Why can't something else matter to you besides a bunch of fucked-up kids?"

"Lots else matters."

Another pause. Why, I wonder, are all the important things so easily strangled by small silences?

"No, not really. You never give your heart to anything else. The rest of you is here but you left your heart back at the school. And you're perfectly glad you did."

I did not know what to say. I did not even fully understand how I felt about it myself much less how I could explain it to Joc. We were still standing there in the dimly lit kitchen. Jocco kept shifting the tape back and forth in his hands. I could hear his breathing.

Finally Joc shook his head. He looked down at the linoleum floor and shook his head again. Slowly. Wearily. Bad as I felt about him, there was an almost painful longing to try out Candy's ice-cream recipe. He was right. My heart

52

was there and it never would be at Adam's Rib, no matter where my body went. Like so many times before, I ached to please both him and myself.

"Joc?"

His eyes came to me again.

"I'm sorry."

"Just get your jacket and let's go."

I never did try Candy's recipe that night. After Jocco brought me home, I went to an all-night grocery store and bought another can of orange juice. With 144 ounces of juice mixed up in six jars in my refrigerator, I set out at 1:30 in the morning to make ice cream. Then I discovered I had no ice cubes. It did not matter too much. I was far too tired to care. So I went to bed.

The next day, armed with Candy's letter, half-a-dozen cans and the makings for vanilla ice cream, I headed for school.

"What's this?" Lori asked as I began setting out the materials toward the end of the afternoon.

"We're going to do something fun," I replied.

"Something fun," echoed Boo behind me.

"Like what?" Lori asked. Skepticism tinged her voice. Too many people had tried to pass off work on her under the guise of fun. Lori was not falling for that ruse anymore.

"We're going to make ice cream."

"Ice cream? I never seen ice cream like this before." She was standing very, very close, leaning against my arm, breathing on the little hairs and making them itch. She wanted a good look at what I was doing as I shook up the mix. Boo had commenced twirling on the far side of the table.

"Have you ever seen ice cream made?" I asked Lori.

"Well . . . no. Not exactly. But I didn't think it was like this."

"Boo! Take that off!" He had the big mixing bowl on top of his head like a helmet.

"Hee-hee-hee-hee! Hoo-hoo-hoo-hoo-hoo-hoo!"

"Oh no," Lori wailed and smacked her forehead with one hand. "He's gonna take his clothes off now. You shouldn't oughta have said that, Torey. Now he's going to take everything off."

"Lor, get that bowl from him. He's going to break it. Boo, come back here. And for crying out loud, leave that shirt on. Boo? Boo!"

Both of us took off after him and oh, what fun Boo thought that was! Never before had we chased him during one of his deliriums. "Hoo-hoo-hoo-hoo-hoo. HOO-HOO-HOO-HOO-HOO-HOO!" The bowl on his head went sailing to the floor. It did not break but rather went careening off into a corner with Lori after it.

The bowl recovered, I let Boo run. There was no point in chasing him; it appeared only to make him wilder. I called Lori back to the table and we resumed preparations for the ice cream. Together we washed the bowl. Boo, meantime, stripped down to total nakedness. Gleefully he rubbed his round little belly and hopped up and down. For the life of me, I could not help but think how much like a little monkey he looked—and sounded. We could have been spending a day at the zoo.

I chipped ice into a pan over the sink while Lori put the ice-cream mix into the bowl. Boo danced around us, laughing. Near me on the counter I lined up the three coffee cans and set the orange juice cans inside them. Carefully I layered salt and ice.

"Here, Tor, I'll bring over the ice-cream stuff," Lori called.

"No, Lori, please wait. I think that's too heavy for you. Wait. I'll bring the cans over to the table."

"No sir, it ain't too heavy. I'm strong. See?"

"Lori, wait, would you?"

She would not. Hefting the wide mixing bowl in both arms, she struggled around the table. I could not make it from the sink in time. I saw the entire disaster coming but I could not prevent it. Halfway around the table Lori dropped the bowl. It did not survive this time. The bowl nicked the table corner as it fell and glass and cream went everywhere, pouring down the front of Lori's clothes, across the tabletop, out in a huge white puddle on the floor.

Lori froze. Indeed, I did also. Even Boo was momentarily motionless.

"I didn't mean to," she whispered. Impending tears made her voice tiny and high-pitched.

That thawed me. I came over. It was hard not to say I had told her to leave it alone, so I took a deep breath. "Look, I know you didn't. Those things happen."

"I didn't mean to. I'm sorry."

"Yeah, I know, Lor. It would have been better if it hadn't happened, but it did so the best thing is to clean it up."

"I didn't mean to."

"Lori, I *know* you didn't. Don't cry about it. It isn't that important. Come on."

Still she did not move or even look at me. Tears rolled over her cheeks but she did not brush them away. Her eyes were fixed on the broken bowl. Boo walked around to stand near me. The crash had knocked the silliness out of him. Kneeling, I began to collect the glass shards.

"I'm sorry. I didn't mean to," Lor said again.

I stared at her. "Lor?"

"I didn't mean to."

"Are you all right, Lor? Lor, look at me."

"I didn't mean to."

Concern pushed my heartbeat up. I rose, broken glass still in my hand, and looked at her carefully. "I know you didn't mean to, Lori. I heard you. And I'm not angry. It's okay. Now come on, snap out of it."

"I'm sorry," she said again. Her voice was still the tight, high voice of a frightened child. She did not look at me yet. In fact she had not moved at all since the bowl broke.

"Lor? Lori? What's the matter?" She was scaring me. It was becoming apparent that something more had happened to her than simply dropping the bowl. A seizure? That was my instant thought, although many of my children had had seizures before and none had ever looked like this. With one hand I touched her shoulder. "Are you okay?"

She refused to move from the oozing puddle at her feet. Over and over again she whispered how sorry she was, how she had not meant to do it. This unusual behavior frightened me so much that I was totally without confidence as to how to handle it. Finally I went to the sink for a bucket and sponges and began to clean up the mess myself. Lori never moved an inch. She remained paralyzed by some force of which I had no perception.

Boo seemed as scared as I was. Warily he moved around the periphery of the action. Gone was the earlier delirium but also gone was his usual rigid inwardness. He watched us with concern.

Desperate to relieve the mounting tension, I began to sing the only song Boo knew. Willingly he joined me.

"Was a farmer had a dog and Bingo was his name-o," I sang in shaky a cappella.

"B-I-N-G-O!" Boo shouted, his eyes riveted on Lori. "B-I-N-G-O!"

Twelve choruses of "Bingo." The tension was still palpable.

With a wet rag I knelt before Lori and sponged the ice cream mix off her dress and knee socks. From where I was on the floor in front of her I could hear her raspy, fear-strained breathing. Having never been wiped away, tears had dried along her cheeks. Now she was watching me, yet her eyes were vacant. It was like looking into the eyes of a ghost.

I sat back on my heels. We were very close, she and I. In that position I was lower than she and she had to look down on me. For a long, wordless period we gazed at each other. Gently I brought my hands up to touch her cheeks, to encompass her face.

"What's wrong, Lor? Can't you talk to me?"

"I didn't mean to. I knowed you tole me not to." She spoke as one in a dream.

"What happened? Tell me what happened."

"I know you tole me not to. I didn't mean to. It wasn't on purpose. I'm sorry."

"Lori?"

"You gonna wup me?"

She was not talking to me. I do not know who else she thought was there. This abrupt aberrancy in her behavior scared me so much that my hands shook as I held her face. I could feel the soft, warm skin of her cheeks beneath my fingers and the tightness of her jaw. We were so close her breathing was hot on my face. Yet she continued to stare through me to whomever else it was she saw.

"Don't wup me, okay? Please? Please, don't."

Boo joined us. He came very near, his hands fluttering, making soft slapping sounds against his bare thighs. Every few moments he would reach out to touch Lori, to touch me, but never quite make contact before jerking his hand back.

"Lor, it's just me. Just Torey. We're here in school."

What the hell was going on? When she still did not respond, I rose and lifted her into my arms. On the far side of the room was a small, not quite adult-size rocking chair. I sat down in it with her in my lap. At first she was stiff and I had to physically move her limbs into a reasonable position. Then unexpectedly she relaxed, melting into the form of my arms. I rocked.

Whatever had happened to her I did not know. Nor, as it turned out, would I ever know. A seizure of some bizarre kind? A psychotic episode? A stress reaction? I had no idea. Lori never gave me a clue. But it was one of the most frightening episodes of my career.

Not knowing, I simply rocked and held her close against me. Back and forth. Back and forth. She was large for the chair and for me, her long legs coming nearly to the floor. Boo watched us. Then he came over. On his heels, he rocked too, swaying back and forth to our rhythm. Yet he watched me intently. No tuning out this time; Boo was fully alert. Next, he did something he had never done since joining me. Boo touched me voluntarily. He put his hand on my cheek, explored my lips and my chin, all the time observing me with the rapt scrutiny a scientist gives his new discovery. Then he climbed into the rocker with us.

There we sat, the three of us, one on top of the other in that small rocker. Lori was pressed against my breast. Boo sat mostly on the arm of the rocker, his bare legs across Lori's. He reached over and took my free arm and pulled it around himself. Gently he leaned forward, his head resting atop Lori's, under my chin. With one hand he clutched his penis, with the other he tenderly stroked Lori's cheek. "B-I-N-G-O," he began to sing in a soft, clear angel voice, "B-I-N-G-O, and Bingo was his name-o."

I was struck by the poignant absurdity of the moment, of what someone would have thought who might have ventured in on us, crammed together as we were in that chair. Bare Boo, lost Lori and me. Unexpectedly, it made me think of Joc. I pitied him for what he would never understand.

6

I needed the parents. I always needed the parents. To fill in all of the missing pieces. To let me know what happened the other eighteen hours of the day. To reassure me that someone else was just as perplexed about this little person as I was.

I had no children of my own. Because of that I knew I did not fully understand the life of a parent, regardless of how much I wished I did. Having four children six hours a day works out mathematically to the same as having one for twenty-four. But mathematics and emotions do not spring from the same well.

For this reason I wanted to catch Boo's mother. I wanted to talk to her, to find out about life at home with Boo. I needed to know for Boo's own welfare as I made plans for his program. And I simply wanted her to know I cared.

Each day she brought Boo but would not come inside. If I waited outside for her she always had an excuse to hurry off. If I called her at home, she never could talk. By mid-

October it was no secret that Mrs. Franklin was avoiding me.

Parent-teacher conferences occurred the last week in October just before Halloween. The children were excused from school for the last two days. Because of all the resource students, I had a huge number of conferences. I did not worry about squeezing Lori's father into one of the fifteen-minute conference slots; he and I communicated regularly. But with Mrs. Franklin it was a different matter. If I could get her there at all, I did not want to scare her off by giving her only fifteen minutes to tell about seven and a half years. So I slotted her in the last place on the second day, about 3:00 P.M.

She did come.

A small, delicate-boned black woman, she had wide fear-stricken eyes. I wondered, as she took the chair opposite me at the worktable that afternoon, who else had talked to her about her dream child. And what they had said.

"How's my boy been doing?" she asked, so quietly that I had to ask her to repeat herself. "I want him to learn to talk. Like other boys. Have you been able to teach him to talk right yet?"

"I think Boothe is doing nicely in here, Mrs. Franklin." I tried to sound reassuring. "We have a lot to do, Boo and I, but I think we're working hard on it. I'm glad he's in my class."

"You ain't getting him to talk straight either, are you?"

"I think perhaps it's a little premature for that just yet."

"You ain't getting him to talk straight either, are you?"

"No," I said. "Not yet."

Her head dropped and she fidgeted in her chair. I feared she might leave.

"I—" I started.

"I don't want them to take him away," she interrupted, still looking down at her hands. "I don't want them to put

60

him in no insane asylum. I don't want them to take my boy away."

"I can't imagine anyone will, Mrs. Franklin."

"Charles, that's my husband, he says so sometimes. He says if Boothe Birney don't learn to talk straight like other boys, they're going to lock him away in an insane asylum when he grows up and we can't take care of him no more. Charles, he knows those things. He says Boothe Birney's sick and they don't let no sick boys stay with their folks."

"Boo isn't sick. He's just different."

"Charles says they're gonna take him away. The doctors, they'll do it. They told Charles. If Boothe don't learn to talk straight."

I found Mrs. Franklin difficult to reason with. She was so frightened.

"They ain't good places, miss, them insane asylums. I seen one. My mother's brother, they put him in one once in Arkansas. And I seen it." She paused and the silence stabbed through me. "There was this big boy there," she said softly. "A great big boy, 'most nearly a man. With yellow curls. Big curls, like my Boothie has. And he was standing naked in his own piss. Crying. A great big boy. 'Most nearly a man." She brought a hand up to stop a tear. "And that boy there, he was some mother's son."

Her fear was so intense and perhaps so warranted that I could not easily calm her. We talked a long time. She had come at three and now the October dusk was settling. Outside the partly open window behind me, the wind blew, startling up brown, fallen leaves and carrying them high as the roof. Autumn freshness pressed through the opening to dispel the heavy, humid weight of emotion. As twilight came, the brilliance of the fall foliage in the schoolyard muted to a rosy brown. And still we talked. Back and forth, quietly. I pushed us off into tangential conversation because it was still too scary to speak the truth. I learned of her favorite hobby, quilting, of how she had won a ribbon at an Arkansas state fair, of how her grandmother had left her a one-hundred-and-fifty-year-old Lone Star quilt made in a slave cabin. In turn I told her of my haunted love for far-off Wales, my homesickness for a country not my own. At last the conversation turned back to her son.

Boo had been an unplanned and initially unwanted child. His parents were not married. That Mr. Franklin was white and she black had been a major issue with their families and in the small Southern community where they had lived. She and Charles eloped and finally fled north to our community in an attempt to build a better life together. Charles's family had ceased all communication with their son. Mrs. Franklin had never seen her mother since the day she had left eight years before; her father had since died. However, her siblings had all resumed a positive relationship with her.

During the early months of Boo's life, he had seemed normal to the Franklins. He had been an inordinately placid baby but their pediatrician had told them not to worry. Boo was a little slow to learn to sit up and to walk but he still did so within normal limits. He never did crawl. During those first years he even learned to say a few words. Doggie. Bye-bye. Cracker. A few nursery rhymes. Yet never once did he say mama or daddy. Then at about eighteen months of age, the changes first began. He started to cry incessantly. No one could comfort him. He rocked in his crib at night and banged his head against the wall. Lights, reflections, his own fingers began to hold more fascination than the people around him. He ceased talking.

The Franklins never knew how wrong things really were until Boo was over three. Up until then they were still taking him to the same pediatrician, who continued to reassure them it was all "just a stage." Boo was a slow developer. He would outgrow it. Then at three, prior to the birth of his sister, Boo was enrolled in nursery school. There someone recognized the earmarks of autism.

The years between the first diagnosis and Boo's arrival in my class had been ones of heartache and financial devastation while the Franklins searched for a miracle cure. Selling their small house and possessions, they left with Boo and a newborn baby for California where they had heard of a special school for children like Boo. After nine long months of no improvement, the school gave up. Back home they came, this time armed with vitamins. Then off to Pennsylvania to a school for the brain-damaged that programmed children so that they might reexperience the womb, birth, growth. Back home again, broke. Three years had passed. Mr. Franklin had worked at twelve different jobs, often three at a time to meet family expenses and keep them together. The marriage, the emotions, the finances all were sapped. Boo still showed no improvement. Indeed, now more than ever he perplexed them. At every new school it had been a new label, a new method, a new diagnosis of why they failed. And the same old blame. For all that effort the Franklins did not know any more now about their dream child than they had known in the beginning. Exhausted and discouraged, they had come home for the last time and enrolled Boo in the public school system. That had been the year before.

Poked and prodded and racked, the marriage which had gotten started on such shaky ground still survived. Neither of the Franklins was well educated; neither knew how to cope with the problems this boy had given them. When things got bad, Mrs. Franklin said wearily, it was hard not to blame someone for this child. Especially when everyone else was willing to blame too. Yet . . . yet, they loved him. To be sure.

I think I hated these stories worst of all. Worse than the ones of brutal abuse, worse than the ones of neglect and suffering. I loathed these stories where there were no answers. Innocent people in innocent circumstances, where little more had happened than the day-to-day agonies of being human, and a child like Boo was produced. My sense of fair play was always badly bruised when I heard such tales, as I did all too frequently. What sense was there to it? Why such suffering given to those I could not see as deserving it? It always left me feeling angry and impotent against a world I did not understand.

"It's so hard," Mrs. Franklin said as she stared down at the shiny tabletop. "My sister has a little boy just four months younger than Boothie. She always writes me about what Merlin is doing. He's in second grade. He got picked to sing in the children's choir at church." She looked at me. "And all I want is for Boothe to call me mama."

Halloween came on a Friday. In the time left to us between the parent conferences and the holiday, Boo, Lori and I made dozens of construction-paper decorations, carved a pumpkin, mulled cider and hung honeycomb-bellied bats that I had purchased at the five-and-dime. Traditionally at our school, children attended regularly scheduled classes in the morning. In the afternoon they returned to school wearing their Halloween costumes and each room had a party. Lori and I had discussed the matter throughout October. She wanted to wear a costume too. I thought perhaps she would have more fun if she stayed in her other classroom for the party rather than with Boo and me. After talking it over with Edna, we agreed Lori would spend the afternoon there.

The other matter of great importance to Lori was her costume. In the two days before Halloween, she considered and discarded dozens of ideas.

"I could be Supergirl. My friend Tammy's gonna be

Supergirl. Do you think I could be Supergirl too?" Suddenly she blushed and a silly smile came over her face. "You know what?"

"What's that?" I asked.

"I could be Wonder Woman. You know why?" She cast a sidelong glance at Boo to see if he was listening, then leaned close to whisper. "'Cause I got on Wonder Woman underwear. Here, see." She pulled up her dress to show me. "See, I got Wonder Woman underpants. and here, I got a Wonder Woman T-shirt. See, they're made out of that slippery cloth. Feel it. My daddy says it's *sexy*." She giggled.

"I don't think you can wear just your underwear to school for Halloween, Lor."

"No, I guess not. Hmm." She was thoughtful for a moment.

And so the discussion went on both days. Finally Lori decided to be a witch. Not as exciting as running around in your Wonder Woman underwear I suppose, but I was so thankful that this long, hard decision had been made that I patiently bore through the recital of all the costume parts Halloween morning.

"My daddy helped me make a dress," she told me while stopping by on her way to recess. "It's real long and black and I got this shawl thing to wear over it. And long black hair. My daddy dyed a mop last night for me. With Rit dye. That you buy at the supermarket. So I'm going to have long black hair and a big pointed hat. And guess what else?"

"What, pray tell?"

She exploded with giggles. "I'm gonna have *warts*!"

"You aren't!"

"I am! I boughted this stuff at the store last night. It makes you fake warts. And I boughted it with my own money, even." A hand slipped over her mouth as she laughed devilishly. "And guess what else besides that?"

"What?"

"I'm going to scare my sister. I got a better costume than her. She don't got any warts 'cause she spends all her allowance on candy."

"Oh Lor, she better watch out, huh?"

Boo and I had our own plans for the afternoon. He still was not toilet trained, but I hated keeping him in diapers all the time because it made training so much more difficult; and on those rare, rare occasions when he did attempt to use the toilet, he had missed a couple times because he could not break the tape on the disposable diapers. Recently, however, my guesses had been off and there had been a lot of puddles. I found intensive work in this area difficult with Lori around. So he and I were headed for some heart-to-heart moments in the rest room. Afterward I was considering taking a trip over to a nearby grocery store with him. Boo had never been to one and I wanted to buy new ingredients to try the ice-cream recipe again someday. That would fill our time together.

It was late afternoon, after recess. Boo and I were still in the girls' rest room. With a copy of *Toilet Training in Less Than a Day* face down on a sink, a bottle of orange juice nearby to keep Boo supplied with liquids and the door propped open to warn any unsuspecting visitors we were hard at work, I had Boo on a toilet in one of the stalls while I searched the bottom of a potato chip bag for something to make him more thirsty.

"Torey!" someone wailed from the corridor. "Torey!"

I came to the door of the rest room and looked out.

Lori in her witch's costume was struggling down the hall. "Torey," she cried when she saw me.

I could see tears coursing down through witch makeup, leaving big black smudges on her cheeks. "What's wrong, honey?"

"I got scared when I couldn't find you." She pressed her face into my jeans.

66

"What happened? You were going to be in Mrs. Thorsen's class all afternoon, remember? Even after recess. Did you forget?" I pulled her chin up. A fake wart was left sticking to the waistband of my jeans. Boo came hopping out, his pants around his ankles.

Lori would not look at me even as I held her face. She jerked her head from my hand and leaned back against my side. Finally I bent to pull up Boo's pants and fasten them. "Do you want to come back with us, babe?" I asked her.

She nodded.

In the room Lori went over to the worktable and flopped into a chair. I was still unsure what had happened to upset her. The black witch's hair was skewed to one side, the pointed hat was too large and came down almost to her eyebrows. I found the incongruity between her costume and mood pathetic. Coming over, I sat on the tabletop next to her. "What's wrong? Did it just scare you not finding us here? Was that it?"

She paid me no attention. Another wart loosened by her tears dropped onto the table. Lori smooshed it with a fingernail.

"Did something go wrong in class?"

She nodded.

"Maybe if you told me about it, that would help."

She shook her head.

"You don't think so?"

Another shake.

Across the room I saw Boo begin to unbuckle his pants. I rose to see what he was planning to do.

"Stay here with me," Lori said.

"Okay," I sat back down and gave Boo the evil eye to leave his clothes on. He flapped his hands at me.

"Mikey Nelson says I'm retarded," Lori muttered. "He says this is a retard class."

Her head was still down; she twisted a strand of mop around one finger.

"He said I was the retardest kid in the whole school. He

67

said I couldn't even read baby books like the kindergarteners have. I'm that retarded."

"You know that old saying, Lor? That one about sticks and stones can break my bones but names can never hurt me?"

"Yeah."

"Isn't very true, is it? Names do hurt. A lot."

She nodded.

Another stillness.

"I guess it don't matter so much," she said softly. "I guess maybe he's right. I flunked kindergarten. And I'm probably gonna flunk first grade too."

Across the room near Benny's driftwood, Boo had sat down on the floor, his legs crossed Indian-style. He looked like an elf. A deep seriousness rested over his features as he watched us.

Lori looked up at me. "Is he right, Torey? Am I a retard kid?"

I put my fingers under her chin and lifted her face to see it more clearly in the gray afternoon light. Such a beautiful child. Why was it all these children looked so beautiful to me? I thought my heart would burst some days, I was so overwhelmed by their beauty. I could never look at them enough. I could never fill my eyes up fully with them the way I wanted. But why was it? Surely they were not all physically attractive. I knew something must happen with my eyes. Yet no matter how I tried to see them right, they seemed so unspeakably beautiful. This kid was. So very many of my kids were. I was troubled because I could not answer that question for myself. Were they that beautiful? Or was it only me?

"Torey?" She touched my knee to bring me back. The question she had asked had gone beyond words and now rested in her eyes.

No answers for my questions. No answers for hers. I looked at her. What could I say to her that would be

68

honest? That would satisfy her? No, she was not retarded. Her brain did not work for a different reason. Mikey Nelson just had the wrong label. I could have told her that. Or perhaps I could have told her it was all a lie. To me it was. Mikey Nelson did not know what he was talking about. But what a laugh. In this world that prizes accomplishments so highly, I would have been the liar then. For Lori there might never be enough teachers, enough therapies, enough effort, even enough love to undo what had happened to her in one night's anger. And then Mikey Nelson's word would seem truer than mine.

Gently I pushed back her hair from her face, smoothed the mop strands, straightened the pointed hat. She was so beautiful.

"There's nothing wrong with you, Lori."

Her eyes were on my face.

"That's the truth and you believe it. Don't ever let anyone tell you otherwise. No matter what. There's nothing wrong with you."

"But I can't read."

"Hitler could read."

"Who's Hitler?"

"A man who really was retarded."

7

"Good afternoon, Tomaso," I said. "My name is Torey. I'll be your teacher in the afternoons."

"You leave me the fuck alone, you hear? I sure the hell ain't staying here. What kind of a place is this anyway?"

We stared at each other. I was between him and the door. His scrawny shoulders were hunched up under a black vinyl jacket. He was tall for his age, but too thin. Lank, greasy, black hair hung over angry eyes. Angry, angry eyes. He was one of the migrant kids, no doubt. His hands were hard and calloused; he had already known the fields by ten.

I had not been prepared for Tomaso. A call in the morning from Birk and here he was. One look at him and his fearless, defiant body and I could guess why he had been brought to me. Not one to fit into the regimen of a school, not Tomaso.

"What kind of shitty place is this anyway?" he repeated a little more loudly.

Lori came around to stand between Tomaso and me. She gave him a long, appraising look. "This is our class."

"Who the hell are you?"

"Lori Ann Sjokheim. Who are you?"

"What have they stuck me in? Some babies' class?" He looked at me. *"Dios mio!* I've been put in some fucking babies' class."

"I'm no baby," Lori protested.

"Some goddamn, stinking baby class, that's what this is. And with little girls in it. Go have a tea party, sweetie," he said to Lori.

Her lower lip went out. "I'm no baby. I'm almost eight. So there!"

"Shit. I'm not staying in here." Tomaso straightened his shoulders and raised one hand up in a fist. "You get out of my way; I'm going. And I'll smack you right in the boobies if you try to stop me."

My stomach cringed involuntarily at the very thought of him doing that. I said nothing. There was not much to say that would not be incendiary at this point. Anger had flared up in his dark eyes like sparks from a green-wood fire.

As we stood there sizing one another up, Mrs. Franklin opened the door behind me and shoved Boo through. Click, the door went shut again.

"Nigger! There's a nigger in here! Let me out," Tomaso shouted. "I ain't staying in no place with a shitty nigger in it."

Lori was indignant. "He's no nigger. That's Boo. And you shouldn't oughta call him names like that." She came over to take Boo's hand.

I turned to latch the hook and eye.

"That ain't gonna keep me in," he said. "I can bust that easy. You won't keep me in here with no locks."

"It isn't for you," I replied. "It's for him." I indicated Boo. "He gets lost sometimes and this helps to remind him to stay in the room."

Tomaso glared. His shoulders pulled up under the black jacket. "You hate me, don't you?"

"No, I don't hate you. We don't even know one another."

Abruptly Tomaso jerked around and grabbed a chair. Twirling it briefly above his head, he then let loose and sent it flying across the room and into the finches' cage. The birds fluttered as the cage swayed wildly, but it did not tip over. Lori squealed in surprise. Boo dove under the table.

This reaction seemed to please Tomaso. He set off on a rampage. Tearing from one side of the room to the other before I even had a chance to move from the door, he flung books off the shelves, cleared the top of my desk with a swoop of his arm, ripped Lori's work folder into quarters and threw it into the air like confetti. Another chair went flying. Luckily it only grazed the west wall of windows and fell harmlessly to the floor. Once he started, I remained against the door and did not move. I was fearful of inciting him further. Or letting him get loose outside the room.

Tomaso stopped and turned back to me. "There. Now you hate me, don't you?"

"I'm not precisely in love with you for doing that, if that's what you mean," I replied. "But I don't hate you and I don't like your working so hard to make me do so."

"But you're mad, aren't you? I made you mad, didn't I?"

Cripes, what did this kid want? I had no idea what to say to him. I was not mad. I did not hate him. Terror was more along the lines of what I was feeling right then, but I was not going to admit that either. My palms had gotten cold and damp and I wiped them on my jeans. Birk did not prepare me at all for this one.

"I bet you think I feel sorry I done that," he said. "Well, I don't. Here, let me show you." He grabbed a potted geranium off the counter and crashed it to the floor. "There."

Still with my back to the door to keep him contained in the room, I did not move. My mind was going at the speed of light, trying desperately to sort out viable alternatives before the kid wrecked my entire room. Or worse, decided to hurt someone. My inaction was not so much from indecision as it was from fear of consequences if I made the wrong move. I did not reckon this boy gave much opportunity for replay.

"Jesus, what's wrong with you?" he said. "Cat got your tongue? Why don't you do something? Why don't you get mad? Aren't you normal or something? Are you some fucking kind of crazy teacher?"

"I'm not going to let you make me angry, Tomaso. I don't want to feel that way."

"You don't? You don't?" he sounded outraged. "What's the matter with you? Why don't you go ahead and hate me like everybody else does? What makes you think you're so special?"

"Tomaso, sit down. Take off your jacket and sit down. It's time we got started on the afternoon's work."

Reaching down for a piece of the broken pot, he lofted it at me. Not a serious throw in my opinion. I imagine if he had meant it, he would have hit me. We were not that far apart, and I doubted that he missed when he aimed.

"What are you going to do about me? Are you going to suspend me? Are you going to get the principal?"

"No. I'm just going to wait until you decide it's time to work."

"Hey man, I ain't never gonna decide that, so you might as well just give up."

I waited. Sweat was running down along my sides and I pressed my arms tight against my body to stop it.

"At my other school they called the police. They took me to juvie. So you can't scare me."

"I'm not trying to scare you, Tomaso."

73

"I don't care what you're trying to do. I don't care about anything."

"I'm just waiting, that's all."

"You can send me to the principal, if you want. And he can give me whacks. You think I haven't had whacks before? I've had a million of them. And you think I care?"

I waited without saying anything. My stomach reminded me of the price I was paying for a calm exterior.

"I could bite your titties off."

My back against the coolness of the glass in the door, I waited.

"Hmmf. Mmmmmph. Pphuh." Tomaso was full of noises when I would not talk back to him. He was not ready to give in yet. Still too much pride at stake. And God only knows what else.

My gut feeling was that Tomaso did not really want to leave. No single thing I could put a finger on told me that, but I felt it. I studied him carefully.

Sometimes I think I missed my calling. I should have been a swindler. In the end, my best defense always seemed to come down to the good con game I play. My gut told me this boy was hot air. That was enough to go on. I pushed myself off the door and walked by him to the other side of the room. Righting chairs and slinging papers back on my desk, I sat down at the worktable. Reaching under, I pulled Boo out and sat him down in a chair. Then I beckoned Lori over and took her L and O flash cards. My stomach was doing the cha-cha, a surefire clue to me of the extent of my concern for winning this game of psychological bunco. If he chose to walk out the door I would have no alternative but to go out and physically drag him back in. That would be a really lousy way to start any relationship. All I was operating on was a hunch. A hunch about a kid I did not even know.

Boo was upset by the disruption in our routine. He

rocked his chair back and forth and twiddled fingers before his eyes. I reached over to reorient him and he grabbed my arm. With noisy sniffs, he smelled up the length of my exposed skin.

Tomaso approached us. He stood behind my chair as I prepared the flash cards and struggled with Boo. I could hear him but not see him.

"Do you speak Spanish?" he asked.

"No. Not very well."

"Hmmph. White honky. I don't want to go to no room with a white honky teacher in it."

"You wish I spoke Spanish?"

"I could kick you in the ass."

I swallowed. "Do you speak Spanish?"

"Of course I do. I *am* Spanish. What's the matter with you? You blind or something? My father, my real father, his grandpa came from Madrid. In real Spain, not Mexico. My father's grandpa, he fought bulls."

"Is that right?"

"It's true. I ain't lying. My father's grandpa fought real live bulls."

"He must have been brave."

"He was. He coulda got killed, but he wasn't. He was real, real brave. Braver than anyone here." A pause. "Braver than you."

"Probably so."

Tomaso was still behind me so that I could not see his face. I was instead looking at Lori and Boo as I talked to Tomaso. Lori watched us, first one and then the other. Boo was again fluttering his fingers in front of his face.

"What's wrong with that kid?" Tomaso asked. He had come closer. I could sense him just inches off my right shoulder. "How come he does that with his hands?"

"Sometimes he does that when he's frightened or unsure about things. It makes him feel better or something, I

75

guess. I don't really know. He doesn't talk yet so he can't tell us."

"It makes him look weird. What kind of freaky place is this anyway? What's wrong with her?" He indicated Lori.

"Nothing's wrong with me!" she replied hotly.

"Lor," I said.

"Well, nothing is."

"I know it. But Tomaso is new. He doesn't know us yet and he has questions."

"Well, he shouldn't ask them. They aren't polite." Anger gave a petulant edge to her voice. "He comes in here and calls us names and then he goes and wrecks our stuff and you don't do nothing. He called Boo a nigger and that's nasty, don't you know? And he tore up my folder and it had all my good work in there to show my dad."

"Lor," I said softly but firmly. "Not now. I'll get to you later on it, but hang on to things for the moment, okay?"

She slapped the tabletop.

A tremendously long silence loomed up. I had no idea where it came from but all of a sudden we were in it looking at one another. My mind was blank. Tomaso came around and sat down in one of the chairs. Boo dropped his head to the table and loudly sniffed at it. I put a hand out to stop him.

"Boo. Here," I said and tried to distract him with the flash cards.

"Boo?" Tomaso said. "What kind of crappy name is that? No wonder the kid is crazy. He sounds like a goddamn ghost. Shit."

Lori was angry still. She glared across the table at Tomaso.

"What are you staring at, kid? Jesus, you look at me like I got three heads or something. Didn't no one tell you it ain't polite to stare?"

"How come your dad lets you say words like that?" she asked. "My dad would spank me if I talked like that."

76

A strange expression changed Tomaso's features. "I could pound you right into the bloody ground. Smash your dumb-looking little face right in, I could, if you don't shut up."

"Don't your dad care?"

A fragile pause.

"Fuck off, would you? Sheesh, you're a nosy kid." He turned his chair so that he would not have to look at her. "She's wrong, you know," he said to me. "My father cares. My real father. He's down in Texas. When he finds out they got me in a foster home up here, and now they stuck me in some fucking baby class, he'll come take me away."

I nodded.

"I don't really belong in a class like this. My real father, he'll come get me pretty soon. He knows I'm waiting."

Over the recess period I had two aides take the three children out to the playground while I went down to the office for a quick look at Tomaso's folder.

Not much of a file. Tomaso was one of the hundreds of migrant children who pass through our part of the state every year. His schooling had been sketchy. No one had made a serious attempt to find out what had happened when he was elsewhere, or for that matter, what had happened here.

The only notable thing in the folder was his family history. Even that was all too similar to the stories of many other children who had worked their way to me. He had been born down south, Texas, it said, although in truth it was probably Mexico. His mother had died when he was an infant. His father had remarried. A million little details clouded my mind as I read, the agonies I had come to know lives like Tomaso's held. When he was five, his stepmother had fatally shot his father and older brother in a family argument. I stopped. Reread: Fatally shot his father. Tomaso had witnessed the occurrence.

After the father's death, the stepmother was imprisoned, and Tomaso, the sole surviving member of the family, was placed in the custody of the state. Seven foster homes followed. All this had happened in the Southwest. Then a paternal uncle showed up and took Tomaso off to live with him. Authorities in Washington state found Tomaso at age seven picking strawberries in the fields. He had never been in school. Then child abuse in Colorado, and Tomaso was removed from the uncle's care. Into foster homes again. Three of them this time. He never stayed very long. "Antisocial personality," "unable to form attachments" was scrawled over and over again along the way. Back to the uncle's care after a four-month separation, north to our state. The next time Tomaso was heard from, he had been sold to a couple in Michigan for $500. Finding him unmanageable, the couple tracked down the uncle to get their money back. Unable to get it from him, they contacted authorities. The uncle was arrested. For some reason I could not determine, Tomaso was returned to our state. Back into foster-home placement.

His school career, to say the least, had been erratic. Between the late starts and the frequent moves, Tomaso had never been in any school longer than four months. Nor did anyone seem to know in what grade to place him. In Washington they put him in first grade, second and third in Colorado, second grade here, third in Michigan and fourth here again. An IQ test administered in Colorado gave Tomaso a full-scale IQ of 92. The group test in Michigan gave him an 87. All his academic skills were delayed. In math he was more than a year behind the rest of the children in his class. His reading skills were hardly above that of a first grader.

However, it was not his IQ or his attendance or his lack of skills that had brought Tomaso to my room that November. What had was obvious. After numerous attempts to keep him mainstreamed in a normal classroom in his home school, the teacher had finally given up after coming across Tomaso strangling a younger pupil on the playground. The routes of suspension, whacks and even being sent to juvenile hall with a parole officer did not markedly affect Tomaso's behavior. Having no full-time classroom for severely disturbed children in the district, the authorities placed him on homebound instruction. However, at this the foster parents protested. They would turn Tomaso out if he were made to stay home all day. The only alternative had been my room. Still on homebound in the mornings, Tomaso became my new student in the afternoons.

The after-recess period resumed much as the earlier had left off. Boo, still nervous and unsettled, twirled and twiddled despite my efforts to divert him. Lori grudgingly started her work. Tomaso remained wary. The strain of such fragile control was beginning to tell on me. I felt immensely tired.

"What letter is this, Lor?" I was tracing in the salt box with my finger. I made an L.

Lori shifted uneasily in her seat and checked to see if Tomaso was watching. He was.

"Look at it. Down and over. What letter is that?"

Much hesitation. Tomaso rose up to see what I had made.

"Can you help her, Tomaso? Can you give her a hint so she can guess what kind of letter it is?"

"What kind of hint?"

"Something that will help her figure it out. But don't tell her. Just a hint."

His forehead wrinkled.

"Down and over, Lor. What letter goes down and over?"

"R?" Very softly said.

"R!" Tomaso shouted. "R? *Dios mio!* The girl's an idiot! Can't you read or something? Look at it. That ain't no R."

"Tomaso, that wasn't exactly the type of hint I had in mind. Maybe if you told her some words that began with that letter, that would help. That sort of hint."

"R," he giggled under his breath. "Shit."

Lori regarded him angrily. "I'm not going to work anymore if he stays here," she said to me.

Tomaso smiled. Or at least the closest thing I had seen to a smile thus far. Shaking his head, he chuckled. "You can't read, can you?"

"Tomaso," I said, "you know, that doesn't go over in here, your putting people down. There aren't many rules in this room but that's one of them. You don't put people down."

"I'm not. Shit. I'm just stating a fact."

"You are not!" Lori shouted. "You're just trying to make me mad at you. Just like earlier. You like to have people hate you."

"I do not. Just shut up before I smash your ratty little kisser in."

"Hey, hey, hey, you two. Cool it," I said.

Lori jumped out of her chair and stomped off across the room to stand near the animal cages. She flopped down on the floor after a moment.

"What did I do? What did I do?" Tomaso asked in a high-pitched, petulant voice. "What a fucking little baby. That's all she is."

Hopeless. If even Lori rejected this kid, what chance was there for him? Here was a loser. Wearily I got up and went over to Lori. I sat a moment and talked to her, leaving Boo and Tomaso on the far side of the room. Shortly, Boo came mincing over and plopped down beside us. Tomaso remained alone.

The afternoon wore on with excruciating slowness.

80

Tomaso would not work and I was in no mood to push him. Lori remained angry. Boo might as well have been on another planet. At last I enticed Lori and Boo into working together on a plastic loom to make a hot pad. With them occupied, I went to have a private chat with Tomaso over some ground rules. I must have been giving off very heavy teacher vibes because when he saw me coming he got up and went over to the cupboard under the sink. Opening it up he climbed in and shut the doors behind him. I felt like kicking the door in but instead I went back and joined the others.

"When my father finds out they put me in this mean class, he'll come get me out!" Tomaso hollered from his hideaway.

No one answered and that forced him to open one door.

"He's gonna take me away. When he sees they put me in a foster home and now they got me in this fucking class, he'll come take me to live with him."

Lori looked over. There was a long moment of thought, and I could not tell what she planning to do. She paused, looked back at the loom and chose a bright strand of yarn from the pile before looking back at Tomaso's cubbyhole. "You know what," she said, "I was in a foster home once."

"I'm just in one 'til my father finds me."

"Where's he at?" she asked.

"In Texas. I told you that once already. Don't you clean your ears or something?"

"How come he's in Texas and not with you?"

"I guess he's making money for me to live with him."

"Oh," Lori said. It was an odd conversation. The heated emotion from earlier was gone from her voice but there was still an edge to it I could not quite identify. She was on the floor with Boo and me about six feet away from where Tomaso lurked in his cupboard. She continued to work on the hot pad as she talked and did not look up. Tomaso remained under the sink.

"What were you put in a foster home for?" Tomaso asked her.

A pause. Lori brought up a hand and scratched the side of her head as she pondered over what color to use next. Without looking in Tomaso's direction she shrugged. "I dunno. I guess they just got tired of having me."

"Who? Your folks?"

Lori nodded.

A lot of shuffling and Tomaso emerged from the cupboard. He came to stand over us. "How'd you know? I mean, how'd you know they didn't want you no more?"

Lori shrugged. "I just did." Still she did not look up. She appeared deeply engrossed in weaving.

"Do you miss 'em?" Tomaso asked.

Another shrug. "I guess I do. I dunno. I got another family now."

"Yeah," Tomaso said. "So do I."

He wandered off while we remained making our hot pad. Several minutes were spent in aimless movement back and forth. "Hey, Teacher, you got any tape?"

I told him where to find it. Locating it in my desk, he went to the worktable. I helped Boo pull his weaving tighter.

"Here." Tomaso came back over. He dumped Lori's work folder in her lap. "I taped it together. It don't look so good but it was the best I could do."

Lori regarded it, nodded and then set it beside her on the floor.

"Do you speak Spanish?" he asked her.

"No."

"You look like you might be Spanish. A little maybe. Real Spanish. Not Mexican."

"I don't think I am." A pause. Lori looked over at me. "What is Spanish, anyway?"

82

"Shit! What an idiot!" Tomaso squealed. "Spain, dumb-head, Spain. That kind of Spanish."

"Spain's a place, Lor," I said. "A country in Europe. Some people's families come from there and that makes them Spanish."

"I don't think I'm Spanish," she said. "I'm from Buffalo."

Tomaso sat down next to us and picked up Lori's taped-together folder. He studied it. Then he looked over at Lori. "You might be a little Spanish anyway. I can sort of tell that. I think you're probably a little Spanish."

8

For Tomaso and me it was not love at first sight. He proved no small challenge. Tomaso arrived on the second of November. The weeks following were traumatic. His moods fluctuated violently. One moment he would be calm and cooperative. The next he exploded into destruction. And always with us was that thinly disguised insecurity so noticeable on his first day. For me the hardest thing was withstanding his constant testing of the limits. The kid wanted to make me angry. In every way he could think of he worked on it, always to be followed by a taunting, "Now I bet you're mad at me. Now I bet you hate me." After a few days that statement alone was nearly self-fulfilling.

He badly disrupted the class by his arrival. The first week he refused to do any work. He would float around the periphery of the action and watch us, but I could not coerce him into sitting down and working. Unlike the years when I had taught in a self-contained classroom, I was not equipped to handle severe aggressive behavior. There was no time-out or quiet space in the room because Boo and Lori never needed such measures. And in all practicality, I could not establish one for Tomaso because any interaction when he was angry quickly degenerated into a physical confrontation. With no aide, and the other children to take care of, I simply did not have the wherewithal to force Tomaso to remain in a time-out space. There were few other courses available. I refused to consider sending him to the principal for whacks. Beating him would hardly show him how to be less violent. Similarly, sending him home or to juvenile hall was not what I felt was dealing effectively with the problem. If ever a kid needed to be in school, it was Tomaso.

I settled on two approaches the first week. First, I let him float around the room uninvolved. Unlike Boo, he was not tuned out. He watched us; he occasionally joined us physically by sitting near us or talking to us. If he needed time to adjust, this was going to be it. I decided just to wait him out on the work issue. Second, I chose to control his violent outbursts in a physical manner. When Tomaso exploded and went off to destroy things or hurt people, I caught him in a tight, improvised bear-hug, his back to my chest, his arms pinned to his sides, and I hung on. Not an ideal solution, I suppose. That thought went through my mind every time I had to do it, and I cursed my inadequate facilities. But trial and error had brought me to the conclusion that a physical hold was what Tomaso needed to regain control. Forcing him to sit in a chair only escalated his anger. Ignored he would go from bad to worse. However, if I was quick and got a tight hold on him around the chest, he would calm down again. There would always be a moment of fighting, which I dreaded because he had not yet learned to fight fair, and if I was not careful, he would bite me or mash my toes or elbow me in the breasts. But the struggling against my arms would always cease;

then slowly I would feel the tension trickle out of him and I could let go.

The help I had not counted on came from Lori. It was unintentional, I suspect, because Lori was bent out of shape for several days after Tomaso's arrival. She, too, went through a few days of refusing to work. I think she did not want to expose any weaknesses to Tomaso. Yet, there was an attraction between them. It was subtle and mostly from Tomaso's side, but I could feel it. From the first day when Tomaso repaired Lori's work folder after destroying it, he continued to show her a low-keyed deference. Perhaps it was because she refused to be frightened of him and all his bluster. Perhaps it was because they had shared some similar experiences and Lori, in her characteristic manner, was willing to tell him about hers. Or maybe it was no more than that Lori, with her long, dark hair, really did look a little Spanish. I never knew. Lori, for her part, could not remain angry long. When it became apparent that Tomaso was not going to go away, she accepted him. This seemed to calm Tomaso. A pecking order was established in which I had no part. In small ways he tried to initiate friendship with her—sitting near her at the table, listening raptly when she talked, helping her with her work without too many provocative comments. I was thankful to see that people still mattered to this angry boy.

While Tomaso's constant testing of the limits and deep rage were difficult to contend with, I found those nothing compared with some of his other behavior. The kid figured out quickly that destructiveness and violence were not going to make me lose my composure. But they were not the only tricks up his sleeve. I finally decided he must have researched a book somewhere along the line on how to drive teachers crazy. He knew every angle.

One of his most effective weapons was his ability to pass wind. To me it seemed he could do it at any time he chose and at any decibel level. Up on one buttock he would rise and aim so that his victim received full benefit of the smell and sound. "It must have been the beans I ate," he would always say sweetly. My gosh, this kid had to be eating beans morning, noon and night to accomplish what he was capable of. I am sure that if sheet music were available, he could have farted "The Star Spangled Banner." The crowning touch involved pulling his pants out in back and sticking a hand down to feel. God only knows what he was checking. I never asked. In fact I tried my best to ignore the entire business: For that kind of behavior, inattention seemed the soundest recourse. However, with Tomaso it was not that simple. If the first or second or twelfth fart did not get a rise out of me, he would jump up from his seat and wave a hand in front of his face. "Whew, boy! That smelled baaaaad! I really cut the cheese that time, huh? Whew. I can't sit here anymore. I need a new chair." Then he would turn around to get out of his chair and fart right in my face. And of course, there was Lori. While I did my best to ignore Tomaso, Lori could not always do so. If he persisted long enough, he always found an audience.

Farting, unfortunately, was not Tomaso's only Driving-Teacher-Nuts tactic. He had plenty more. The most devastating for me personally was his mouthwash campaign.

"Whewie," he cried one day when I sat down next to him at the table. He fanned the air in front of his face with one hand. "You got *stinky breath*!" Mortally embarrassed, I immediately thought over what I had had for lunch. At recess I sneaked off for a quick chew of gum in the teachers' lounge.

Next day. A revolted look. "Boy, lady, don't you ever use a mouthwash? *Dios mio!* You stink."

This went on for better than a week and I became positively paranoid. I brought a toothbrush to school and brushed after lunch. Next came a bottle of Scope. Not strong enough. A bottle of Listerine took up residence in the coat closet with my lunch box, comb, adhesive bandages and aspirin. Every day I would breathe into a cupped hand before class to see how my breath smelled. I even considered making an appointment with my dentist. And of course this all had vast effect on the remainder of my life. I began talking to people with my hand to my mouth because I figured if I was offending a brash boy like Tomaso, I was bothering everyone and they were just too polite to tell me. Jocco and I got into one of the worst arguments we ever had when I refused to make the garlicky aïoli for a dinner party.

Not until much later did I get wise. Dan Marshall had come into the room one day and was strolling among the kids. He leaned over Tomaso to see what he was doing.

"Hoo-ee, you got halitosis," Tomaso said.

Dan straightened up abruptly, his face turning red.

"You know what that is, mister? That's bad breath."

From then on I was suspicious. Tomaso, however, did not give up easily. Once he'd figured out that I no longer fell for the bad-breath trick, he had to become more creative.

We were all together at the worktable making Thanksgiving decorations one afternoon. Tomaso was sitting next to me. He sat back and put his scissors down. Slowly he took several deep, evaluative snorts of air. Then he turned to me. "You know what you need, Torey?"

"What's that?"

"Feminine hygiene spray."

Never a dull moment with Tomaso. If it was a gross or outrageous act, he had thought it up along with twelve variations. A favorite involved sticking his finger down his throat. Although he never actually made himself vomit, it always produced this horrific retching sound. By instinct I would jump. Every damn time. And then there was the nose-picking. Tomaso never had much to pick from his own nose. Boo, however, turned out to be a gold mine for this activity. I would turn around and there he would be, bent over with one hand on top of Boo's head, the other drilling up Boo's nose. "Boy, Torey, look at this!" he would holler and stretch a long booger out. "Sure is a good thing I'm cleaning Boo's nose out for him, huh?" And when I would come screaming, Tomaso always would look at me innocently. "Sure lucky you got me, huh?"

Yeah. Sure lucky all right.

The funny thing was that as November wore on, I did begin to think I was lucky. I grew to love the kid. Love him with that potent, irrational sort of love that some kids brought out in me, a love with no clear reason, yet so strong. I loved Tomaso's scandalous approach to life, his outrageous ability to hang on in a world that had been anything but kind to him, and indeed even to extract a few laughs from it. I would sit in class and watch him some days, watch his scrawny body hunched up under the vinyl jacket he refused to remove, his dark, dancing eyes so full of fear. In the beginning I had thought only anger lived there, but I had grown to know fear was really the master and anger only the slave. Perhaps because of that most of all, I loved him. He was such a scrappy little fellow. Even fear could not dominate him completely. For all his problems, Tomaso was not a quitter.

9

December came. A rowdy month full of snowstorms and Christmas carols and all our undisguised dreams. Lori, I think, still believed in Santa Claus. Or at least she wanted to. Tomaso, in an uncharacteristic show of sensitivity, did not fall into hysterics at the thought. And Boo, of course, gave us no clue at all as to his thought. Or as to whether he even had any.

"I went to see Santa Claus last night," Lori told us as we sat around the table making paper chains to decorate the room. "My dad took me and Libby up to the shopping center and I seen Santa Claus there and my dad let me go talk to him."

I saw Tomaso look over at her without raising his head from his work. Then his eyes came to me. There was a silent question shared between us.

"Did Libby go talk to him too?" I asked.

"No." Lori was not watching me. She was struggling mightily to get her chains to stick together with our dried-out library paste. She paused a moment and sat back, surveying the mess on the worktable. "I asked him to bring me this here doll I seen on TV once. You know what it does, Torey?"

"No, what?"

"Do you, Tomaso?"

"How the hell should I know? Do you think I play with dolls or something?"

"Well, anyway," she leaned back over her chain and took another strip of construction paper to add to it, "this doll drinks and wets, but that's not the good part. Guess what is?"

"*Madre Maria*, Lori, would you get to the point of your story?" Tomaso snapped. "You always go on and on and on."

Lori ruffled her chain indignantly. "Well, anyhow, she eats. She really does; I've seen it. You get this special food that comes in packages and the baby eats it all by herself. Just like real. And she chews it and everything. No kidding. So I asked Santa to bring me one. And if I get it, I'll bring and show you guys."

Tomaso was watching her. Boo sitting next to him began to spin scissors on the tabletop. Reaching over to stop the noise, Tomaso still did not take his eyes from Lori. "Lor, do you believe in Santa Claus?" he asked. His voice was quiet and without emotion, yet there was a crusty tenderness about it which kept the question from coming out derisively.

Lori looked up. "Yeah." A note of challenge in her reply.

No answer.

"Well, there really *is* a Santa Claus," Lori said. Still the defensive edge to her voice. "I even seen him last night, so there, Tomaso."

Tomaso nodded and looked down at his work. I loved the kid. All that armor plating and yet he never did come off quite as hardboiled as I think he wished in his heart he were.

"Santa Claus is real, isn't he, Torey?" Lori asked.

91

I dreaded getting drawn into the conversation. This was one of those topics I had not really come to terms with myself. I had a harder time talking about Santa Claus than I ever did about sex. There were no facts to fall back on with Santa Claus. Just so very many meanings. Especially, it seemed, for my kids. A good man who brought you anything you wanted was a dream to be cherished, no matter how impractical. Yet every situation was different. One child needed to believe in the reality of Santa Claus because he also shared reality with a mother who beat him with a board and burned all his toys. Another needed to believe in the spirit of Santa Claus because all her life things had only been taken from her, never given. And a third needed no part in any sort of fantasy because for her as yet, there was no reality whatsoever. Thus Santa Claus brought me only worry. Such a complicated issue.

Lori, I think, needed a Santa Claus. She was stripped daily of all the millions of little dignities that failure alone can grab away. She needed to know that there were those who did not judge a person's value by the direction her letters faced. She needed the bigger-than-life splendor of the Christmas dream. Nothing less would compensate for Lori's deficiencies.

Tomaso too must have felt as I did. He rescued me from my floundering silence. "I believe in Santa Claus too, Lor," he said.

"You do?" she said in surprise.

"Yeah, I do."

"My sister don't. She laughs at me. But I tell her he's real. I know he is."

Tomaso nodded. He was involved in his work again, not looking at either of us. "A lot of things are real but we just don't know it."

"Libby says if there's a Santa Claus, where's he at? She says the one in the shopping center, he isn't real. He's just some man dressed up in a red suit. And so's the Santa downtown at the Bon Marché. He's just dressed up too." Lori shoved away the chains in front of her with an angry push. "I know that. Why does she keep telling me? Like I'm some baby. I know they're just dumb old men." Her eyes to me now, huge and resentful. "But there is too a Santa Claus, just the same."

I nodded.

"But Libby, she says, well, if there's a real Santa Claus, how come you never see him? She says nobody even lives up at the North Pole. There's just a bunch of ice up there. And Eskimos. And none of them are Santa Claus. Our folks, that's who gets us the presents. And Santa Claus is just for babies to believe in. Libby says."

"But there's lot of things you can't see and people believe in them just the same," Tomaso said. "I never seen Jesus but I believe in him. And Mary. Every night when I say my prayers, I know Jesus and Mary are listening to me, but I ain't never seen either one of them. And I don't know where Heaven is, I never seen that." Tomaso leaned an elbow on the table and thoughtfully braced his chin while he watched Lori working. "But I know Mary and Jesus and Heaven are real. Even grown-ups know that. I think maybe Santa Claus is the same sort of thing. You know, a kind of spirit."

Lori looked at me. "Is he right?"

"I guess that might be a way of looking at it," I said.

"And," Tomaso continued, "I think he gives people good feelings inside and makes them love other people and want to get them presents. He doesn't really come down and do it himself, he makes us do it for him. Sort of like Frankenstein and his monster."

"Then how come all of them men dress up in the stores?" Lori asked. "How come they want to trick you?"

"I don't think they want to trick you, Lor," I said. "I think they do it because it usually makes people feel good. It makes them happy to see a Santa Claus."

"Libby doesn't believe in him at all."

"Libby's stupid," Tomaso said flatly.

"She doesn't quite understand yet, Lor," I added. "Sometimes when we find out that things are not just the way we wished they were, we get upset and then we won't have anything to do with them for a while. But feelings change if we give them a chance. I imagine it'll be that way with Libby. She doesn't want to believe in Santa Claus because he isn't really a nice old man in a red suit, but pretty soon when she's older, she'll see the real Santa Claus is much nicer. She'll believe then."

Lori paused. "Is it okay to believe in that guy at the shopping center? I mean, is it okay to go tell him what you want, even if he isn't for real?"

I smiled. "Yeah, I imagine it's all right. Don't you, Tom?"

He nodded. "Yes, I think it's okay too. The real Santa, he won't mind."

And then there were those who knew very little about Santa Claus.

During the second week of December I had the kids outside for recess. It was a sunny day that Wednesday, brilliant in a way only winter days seem to be. Perhaps I should not have let them go out. It was still cold and a thin glaze of ice from the last thaw polished the concrete playground, the swings and the monkey bars. I told the kids to stay on the grass and off the slippery equipment, and because the day was such a jewel among the winter's damp, dark weeks, I let them run.

Lori and Boo were galloping around while Tomaso and I leaned against the wall of the building in the sunshine and talked. Tomaso was telling me about a television show he especially liked, about the actor who starred in it, how he was considering writing that actor a letter to see if he would write back. I was engrossed enough in the conversation not to be watching Boo and Lori as closely as I should have. They managed to get over onto the playground equipment without my noticing.

A piercing scream cut the air.

Boo. I looked up in time to see him fall from the monkey bars in that stop-frame clarity of accidents. The scream had been Lori's. Boo made no sound at all.

"Boo!" I shrieked as I ran. Tomaso ran behind me. "Boo! Boo!" I touched his face. He lay crumpled in an awkward lump. Very, very cautiously I moved his head back. Blood oozed out the right side of his mouth.

Lori was crying. Tomaso hovered nervously behind me. "Why isn't he moving? Is he dead?" At this Lori howled even louder.

"For pity's sake, Tomaso, of course he isn't dead. How can you say that?"

"Maybe we ought to pray," Tomaso suggested and sank to his knees beside me.

"*Tomaso!*" I cried in exasperation. "Go get some help, would you? For pete's sake, get up. Go get somebody."

He was a bundle of flighty nerves, springing to his feet but not knowing what to do next. I pointed to the door and he took off.

Boo stirred. I had him half-cradled in my arms, half in the sand under the monkey bars. I could feel no broken bones. My worry was of a concussion. Boo opened his eyes, blinked vacuously. Then the pain registered and he began to moan.

Dan Marshall and a whole covey of office staff came running out the door behind Tomaso. Dan dropped down beside me and probed Boo with steady hands while I held him. Boo was crying softly now. Blood spilled over his lips.

"Did you see him fall?"

I nodded. "I didn't see him hit anything but the ground."

95

Gently Dan pried Boo's mouth open. Blood poured over his hand. "It's his tongue. Look."

About an inch back from the tip, Boo's tongue was deeply gashed. In back of us Lori let out a new wail.

"We're going to have to get him stitched up," Dan said. And to one of the aides behind us, "Mary, call his mother to meet us at the hospital.

"Let's go," he said. "I'll drive."

"What about my other kids?" I asked.

"Don't worry about us, Torey," Tomaso said. "We can be good. Me and Lori, we'll be okay."

Dan drove while I held Boo in my lap. At first he cried but after a while even that stopped. I had a bowl under his chin to catch the blood or in case he vomited up what he had swallowed. Boo flapped his hands frantically against my legs and tried to rock but the bowl and my body in such a small space did not permit such movement. For the time being he would have to be satisfied with me for comfort.

Mrs. Franklin met us in the hospital parking lot. Dan had Boo now, carrying him flapping and squawking into the emergency exit. Blood stained both our clothes.

Into the emergency room we went. Mrs. Franklin was detained to fill out the interminable forms while Dan and I took Boo back to the examination table. Dan set him down. Boo dropped back like a rag doll and let a mouthful of blood ooze down onto his shirt collar. The soft, incessant movement of his palms against the white paper on the table was the only sound.

"And so, young man, how are we today?" A white-coated doctor came up and hollered heartily in Boo's face. His voice boomed over our still panicky silence.

I turned to look at Dan and found him gone. Undoubtedly he had forsaken me for a cigarette. He hardly ever smoked but I knew blood bothered him. I had seen him getting green.

The physician was an older man, in his fifties perhaps, with graying hair, broad features and the look of a doctor all over him. "Have a fall at school, did we?"

Boo flailed wildly, bringing his hands up to grab the doctor's arm and smell it.

"Here now! Stop that. What are you doing? There, put your hand down. And tell me what your name is? What's your name?"

Boo squirmed and spewed out another mouthful of blood.

"Can't you tell me your name? A big boy like you? It doesn't hurt that bad, now does it?"

"He doesn't talk," I said, since it appeared I was the only person left to speak for Boo.

"Are you his mother?" the physician asked.

"No. I'm his teacher."

"What's wrong with him?" The doctor tapped his forehead. "I mean, mentally."

"He's just scared. Here, Boo. Here, it's me. See? Now lie down. You're all right. Let the doctor look at you. Here, hold my hand."

"What is he? Psychotic?"

I shrugged. "Autistic, I guess. We don't know."

"Shame, isn't it?" the doctor replied. "And such a good-looking boy. Do you notice, they all seem to be. Such a waste."

Mrs. Franklin came in then. She took over my position at the head of the table and soothed Boo. Slowly, the doctor managed to pry Boo's mouth open.

The doctor said something about having to suture the cut on Boo's tongue. A nurse came in with restraints and tied Boo to the table. I could understand that. Mrs. Franklin's hands were unsteady. A slip one way or the other could be dangerous. And Boo was so frightened by this point that his erratic movements made work in his mouth impossible. No, the restraints I could easily accept.

It was the physician I was having trouble comprehending. I saw him take the needle out. Thread it. I saw him bend over Boo while the nurse adjusted the head restraint.

Boo screamed.

I had been standing far back in the room. I came closer. Still, I was confused.

"Aren't they going to give him any anesthetic?" I whispered to Mrs. Franklin.

Poor scared rabbit of a woman, she knew what was happening. She hid her head and began to cry.

Boo shrieked.

I remained bewildered. Boo was screaming so loudly I couldn't hear myself think anymore. I came closer still, close enough to have touched the doctor's starched white coat, if I had wanted.

"Excuse me." I was hesitant to say anything because I couldn't figure out what was going on, and after all, it wasn't really my business. But my confusion was too great. "Excuse me, sir," I said again, and I did touch his coat then, "but aren't you going to give him any sort of anesthetic? A local or something?"

The doctor turned to me. He had the sort of expression on his face that told me he thought I really should understand, so why didn't I? He said, "You know he doesn't really feel it. These people, they have no true feelings. Only what they imagine. No point in wasting good medicine on them."

And Boo's shrieks broke in his throat, gurgled and reduced to a hoarse cry before he caught his breath enough to scream again.

I was stunned. This was a situation I was totally unprepared for. I had no repertoire of responses to cover something as grotesque as what was occurring. In truth, I did not even have emotions at first. I only stared in disbelief.

Then came the anger. It roared up so white hot that my

mind erupted into a thousand cries at once, all of them hate-words. He couldn't do it, this Mephistophles in white, this graduate of Auschwitz; he couldn't get away with it. If I had to take him limb from limb myself, he wouldn't get away with it. I screamed at him, momentarily topping Boo's screams. Emotion spewed up that I never knew I owned. If I had to take him limb from limb myself . . .

I would hurt him. For the first time in my life I seriously wanted to injure another person physically. It was not even a conscious thought; I had gone beyond thinking.

A man in white, whom I had not seen come in, removed me from the room. I was put outside in the hall and told to go away.

My anger remained with me. Mrs. Franklin had been expelled from the room too and she whimpered all the way down the corridor. I wanted to slap her for her stupid, sheeplike docility. Dan was sitting in the waiting room, a cigarette still in his hands. With one finger he was trying to scrape blood off his tie. I wanted to kick him for running out on us.

The adrenaline in my blood made me shake and I could not sit with them. Instead, I rose and paced in the hallway to calm myself. Dan remained all scrunched down in a lounge chair and smoked one cigarette after another, always watching the ash burn down. Mrs. Franklin perched on the edge of a chair and dabbed her eyes with a handkerchief. I only paced.

The incident ate at me like a maggot. That devil had willingly tortured a defenseless boy and all I could do in retaliation was to fill out a complaint in triplicate.

This little moment, scarcely ten minutes long, was in so many ways the summation of my career.

Back in school with twenty minutes until dismissal, I talked with Tomaso and Lori to quell their fears. Boo was going to be all right. He had gone home with his mother but he would be back the next day, if things went okay. When I passed out papers, I noticed that my hands were still shaking. The children, if they were aware of my distress, did not comment on it. For that I was thankful. I could not have shared it with them. It was still too raw. I could not have shared it with anyone.

"You know," Lori said to me later as she was pulling on her overshoes to go home, "I didn't mean to fuss like I did on the playground. I didn't mean to cry."

"That's okay, Lor. It scared me too."

Rising, she shrugged. A half shrug really, just one shoulder. "Nah, it wasn't that. I don't know how to say it good. I wasn't scared really. It was just that . . . well, it was Boo. I didn't want him to be hurt."

She drew her upper lip between her teeth and considered some thought carefully before looking back to me. "I just wish I could explain it good. It's that sometimes I kind of wish it was me that got hurt. Then at least I'd know how bad it was and I could do something to make it better. But when somebody else gets hurt, there's nothing you can do to take the hurt away from them. Do you know what I mean?"

"Yes, I think so."

"That's sort of what made me cry. I hate that. I hate for other people to hurt."

I smiled at her. She turned away and went to get her coat. I continued smiling, an inadequate expression for what she made me feel. And I sent up a small prayer of thanks to whomever it might be by whose grace I worked here and not twelve blocks away at the hospital.

100

10

The saddest part of being human is the depth of our ignorance.

In dealing with children it is so easy to believe one is omniscient. Unfortunately, it is not so. I tried hard to remember that fact as I worked with the kids. I tried to stay alert to the comforting but often meaningless lullings of theories. I tried to fill my mind not only with the ponderous offerings of textbooks and university classes but also with the day-to-day ambiguity of life. It was not easy. I kept wanting answers. Intellectually I could accept that for many of my questions there never would be answers. Emotionally I do not think I ever did.

Tomaso continued to be a challenge to me. Just when I thought I had caught up with him and come to terms in my mind with what I needed to do, he would take off in some new direction. With him more than almost any other child I had had, it was too simple to fall back on my adult omniscience. He is acting this way because of thus-and-so.

He is doing that because of such-and-such. I was turning out theories on mental illness at a rate worthy of a young Freud, just, I think, because I did not know what was going on with him and was frightened by my lack of understanding. I had fallen back on the old educator's and psychologist's trick—indeed, the old shaman's charm—of naming a thing to obtain power over it. Then, like the sorcerer's apprentice, I, in my ignorance, touched upon the truth.

There was a sale on hyacinth bulbs at the drug store. A big wooden box of them was sitting by the door, a huge garishly colored sign above proclaiming them to be direct from Holland: GET THEM NOW FOR SPRING! ALL COLORS! 3 FOR $1. I smiled as I passed the box. I loved hyacinths. They brought back memories of my college days in Washington state where huge masses of the flowers bloomed outside the public library where I used to study. But here in our colder, drier climate they did not do well. These little bulbs would probably never see a spring.

I paused, half in the door, half out, which undoubtedly endeared me to the fuel company. Could we grow bulbs in our classroom? Could we force them to bloom early during the long, snowy days of January and February? Lori would like that. Boo would too, I thought. I did not know about Tomaso. Backing up, I let the outside door close while I felt in my pants pockets to see how much money I had. $3.28. I bought us nine bulbs in three colors.

What a glorious mess! Pots and dirt and newspapers and spoons were scattered about on the floor. A book with pictures was propped up in front of us. I had read to the kids about bulbs, about hyacinths, then about potting, growing and forcing things. I explained that we had to put the plants into flowerpots and then stick them into the refrigerator for six weeks while the bulb grew roots.

Lori listened raptly to all I had to say. She had a bulb in her fingers, rolling it around and around as she studied the pictures in the book intently. "I'm gonna do this at home," she said. "I'm gonna ask my daddy to buy me and Libby some of these, so I better listen close." She turned to Boo beside her. "Here, Boo, you look too. See these flowers? No, no, don't look over there. Look here. See? We're gonna do that."

Boo with his poor swollen tongue permitted Lori to turn his head with her hand.

"I want to do four," Tomaso said.

"We're doing them together, Tom," I explained. "We only have two pots."

"I want to do my own. I don't like to put my flowers in some shitty pots like those. I want to make my own pots."

"That's a really good idea, Tomaso, about making pots and maybe we can do it soon, but for right now let's just plant them in these pots. They're all I have. Besides, it doesn't really matter what they are in just to sit in the fridge."

"I want to do two. I want them in my own pots." He picked up a spoon and waved it threateningly at me. "I want one pot for me and one for me to give my father."

"We're just planting them for the room, Tom. To put on our windowsill in January." I still never knew quite how to handle the issue of his murdered father. "No one is taking them home."

"No!" An explosion of limbs and cursing and he was on his feet. He threw the spoon at me. I ducked and it flew by my left shoulder. "No! No! No! I want my own flowers, you fucking bitch. Can't you hear me? I want one for myself!"

"Tomaso," Lori said, "you can have mine."

"Go to hell!" With a mighty kick he sent the clay pots across the room and into a hundred pieces. "I hate you!"

"Hey, hey, hey." I was on my feet and had him around the chest. Clutching him to me, I held on while he fought. For a long minute or two we struggled, as we had struggled so very many times before. He tromped my tennis shoes and I gritted my teeth to register no response. Lori and Boo sat wide-eyed and watched us. If they were afraid, as I suppose they must have been every time Tomaso and I had one of our savage little dances, neither of them showed it much. However, their eyes were on us and Lori was poised to run in case she would have to move herself and Boo out of the way.

It was while we were locked in mortal combat that my mind went tiptoeing through theories. Why was he doing this? What bogey from his past loomed up so impossibly when denied hyacinths? What complex, what unfulfilled desire kept that dead man living in this young boy's head? Whence came the immense anger? I was a shaman pleading with unseen gods. That my gods were named Freud and Maslow and Skinner in no way decreased their perceived godliness at that moment. And like all good agnostics, now in the time of need, I was a much more willing believer. *Come on, somebody, explain this kid to me. Don't let him scare me so.*

Then, as always, I felt Tomaso's anger fade. His muscles relaxed; he sighed; his body became heavy. I loosened my hold slightly and we sat down, me on the chair, him between my legs, not quite on my lap, not quite off it.

"I think I could fix that pot," Lori said softly into the great stillness about us and pointed at the pieces.

I shook my head.

"My dad, I think he's got a couple pots out in the garage at home. I could bring them," she said.

"No, Lor, it's okay. Don't worry. We'll get milk cartons

from the kindergarten. We'll plant our hyacinths in those. That'll be better anyway."

I had let go of Tomaso and he had slid off the chair to sit at my feet. He turned to look at me. "Can I take one to my father?" His voice was nearly inaudible. "When we're done with them maybe?"

What could I say to him? What should I? Tiredly I shrugged. "I guess so, Tom. If you want to then, I guess you can have one."

"Okay."

I sent Lori down to get the milk cartons while Tomaso, Boo and I picked up the shards of clay pots and put them in the garbage. Within a short time we were busy again, spoons in hand, putting bulbs into dirt. Tomaso remained subdued.

"Lor, be careful not to bury them too deep. Here, like this," I said.

"All right."

"Tom, how are you coming?"

He looked up. "How come you always call me that?"

"What?"

"Tom. My name's not Tom; it's Tomaso. And you don't even say it right. It's To-MAH-so."

"I thought that's what I was saying."

"No, you weren't. You were say it wrong. And calling me Tom. My name isn't Tom."

"I did that without thinking. I just do sometimes. I seem to shorten names."

"Yeah, like she calls me Lor all the time instead of Lori. Unless she's mad at me. Then she calls me Lori."

I had not noticed that fact.

"Well, I don't like it, so stop. Tom's an American name. I'm Spanish. So don't do it anymore."

"Okay, I'll try not to," I said.

"You better not do it. I don't like you calling me some white honky name." That sharp edge of anger was in his voice again.

Lori and I continued to discuss the hyacinth bulbs and the planting process as I helped Boo with his. He hrooped softly to himself, his sounds slurred by his oversize tongue. Yet through the normalcy of our chatter I could keenly sense Tomaso's rage rekindling. I watched him carefully, if not with my eyes then with my mind, because I could feel another explosion imminent.

Boo reached over to get another spoon and accidentally tipped over a milk carton of potting soil.

"Watch out, you little fucker. I'll kick your goddamn brains in if you do that again."

"Tomaso," I said in a voice he could not mistake.

"Shut up."

His anger was making him clumsy. He could not get the dirt around the bulb in his carton. In one vast movement he knocked the container away. "I don't want to do this! What a stupid thing to have to do. It's your fault it won't turn out. My father would have known how to make it come out right."

I looked at him. "Your father really makes you angry, doesn't he?"

A stupid statement. A statement that belonged in a psychiatrist's office or a textbook on how not to screw up your kids. It did not belong in my classroom. That it was most likely correct made it no less inappropriate.

Tomaso froze when I said that. His eyes were wide and horror-struck. Immediately I knew I had said too much. I saw the tears form. Tomaso brought his hands up and clamped them over his ears. The explosion I thought surely I had precipitated did not materialize. Instead he fell over on his side as if in agonizing pain and squeezed his eyes shut. "Goddamnit," he wailed, "why is it always so noisy

106

in here? It hurts my ears. It's killing me! I can hear the blood running in my ears. Make it stop!"

Then before I had time to react, he bolted up, ran across the room, undid the latch and left.

The three of us sat paralyzed. For several moments none of us flexed a muscle in the utter, motionless silence. Then Lori turned to me. "What happened?"

"I'm not sure I know."

Boo looked at us, his green eyes round and fathomless. "Oh, oh, oh, oh," he said. I felt the same way.

I could not find Tomaso. Leaving Lori and Boo with one of the office aides, I went in search. I could not find him anywhere. Panic that he had left the building rose as bile in my throat. For some unclear reason I did not believe he would, yet I could not figure him. Up the hall, down the corridor, around the corner until I had searched all the places in the H-shaped building that I could think of. I did not call out to him. If he were hiding I would not expect him to answer. Moreover, there seemed some jungle law of dignity that made me unwilling to alert outsiders to our plight.

Again I went through the building, through the unlocked book closets, through the storage rooms off the gymnasium. I walked outside the building and checked through the cars in the parking lot. I made a fast trip through the nearby neighborhood. I wondered if Tomaso would be able to find his way home from here. He came several miles by bus, all through city streets. With his jungle instinct for survival I figured he could. Still he would be scared. I knew that too. Back inside the school I went and searched one more time. A dead weight had formed in my stomach from the worry, the thought of having to call his foster parents and tell them he had run away.

*   *   *

Then he was there. I do not think I would have seen him if he had not stirred. I was in the back of the gym up on the heavily curtained stage where all the old school desks and play props were kept. Tomaso was among them on the floor, underneath an old table. As I was walking through I heard the rustling in the darkness and looked. There he lay, tears still streaming over his cheeks, face smudged with untold years of backstage dirt. His nose ran onto one hand.

The small place was illuminated by what must have been no more than a 40-watt bulb. Even with it on I could barely see him. I had to get down on my hands and knees and press my face to the floor. "Hi," I said.

He looked at me with great black eyes and said nothing.

"I'm sorry, Tom—Tomaso. I shouldn't have talked like that to you. I was saying things that I shouldn't have said." I could hardly make him out in the gloom. "Will you come back to class?"

He shook his head.

I lay down on my stomach in order to see him better. He was perhaps six feet away from me, back under the table and through a tangle of old, unused student desks. A few of the desks were those ancient wrought-iron ones that were bolted to the floor at one time. How Tomaso had gotten back into that spot I did not know.

We stared at one another. I felt keenly isolated from him. That moment's carelessness back in the classroom had brought us here in the dark, flat on the floor, looking very much together, in truth being very much apart.

"I'm sorry, Tomaso. I really, really am. What more can I say to you?"

"Just go away."

"People make mistakes, Tomaso. I'm sure not exempt. I'm sorry I upset you and I know I was wrong."

"Shit. Don't you ever shut up? All you do is talk, talk, talk. Jesus Christ. Don't you ever listen?"

108

There. That put me in my place. It hurt, and I shut up. We watched each other in the dusty darkness.

The minutes ticked by. What time was it getting to be? I could hear my watch but I did not dare look at it; he would misinterpret that. I worried how Boo and Lori were doing with the aide. Still we lay motionless on the floor.

Tomaso stirred and wiped his face with a hand. His tears made no noise. I looked at him through a forest of desk legs. He looked back. Somewhere in that long, slow quiet the gulf between us began to diminish.

Outside came the shuffle of kids in the corridor. Oh geez, it couldn't be time to go home already. What was I going to do? I shifted my weight slightly.

"Don't leave me," he whispered. I almost did not hear it.

"I won't." My voice too had become a whisper without my thinking about it.

More silence. More waiting. There was no doubt in my mind now that it was the end of the school day. The hallways had swelled with cheery going-home noises. I was paralyzed by the fear that someone might inadvertently come in upon us and disturb our strange sharing. It was a needless worry. I had had to go through the building three times before I thought to come in here. Apparently it was a place only Tomaso thought of.

Then came the stillness. All the children had left. Lori would be home by now, she lived so near the school. Boo's mother would have come. I missed not having said goodbye to them.

We waited. My breasts were sore from lying facedown on the hardwood floor so long. My nose tickled from the dust.

"I want to kill myself," Tomaso said, his voice still just a whisper.

"You do?"

He nodded.

"Why?"

"I hate it here."

109

"Here? Is school so bad?"

"No, not here, stupid. *Here.* This world."

"Oh."

"I know how, too. I planned it. I'm gonna take some pills. And I got some. My foster dad takes these blue pills for something, high blood pressure, I think. Anyway, I been sneaking off his pills one at a time for a long time now. I just about got enough. I'm going in my room and take them and tie a pillow over my face to make sure. I want to die."

I looked at him, all ten years of him huddled on the floor beneath that table.

"I don't want to live anymore. I just don't. I don't. It's too hard."

There were no words from me. What could I say? What words were there that I could give him?

I slid forward on my belly until I was as close to him as I could get, which was not very close. I put my hand through the legs of the desks and still my reach must have been two feet short. "Tomaso, can you touch my hand?"

A pause. I could see his still tear-bright eyes glistening.

"Tomaso, can you reach me?"

"I think so."

"Take my hand."

A rustle. The creak of an unwilling desk as he pushed against it. Then I felt his hand in mine. It was cold and wet.

"Hang on to me, Tomaso. Don't let go."

And so we lay like that, twisted around the cast-off seats, our faces smudged with dirt. Minutes passed. I could feel my heart beating against the floor.

"My father's dead," Tomaso whispered.

"I know."

"I want to be dead too. I want to be with my father. I want to get away from here."

"Hang on to my hand, Tomaso."

"It's too hard here. Living's too hard."

I did not speak.

110

"My foster dad hates me. My foster mother, she hates me too. They don't care if I live or die. I'm nobody's kid. Everybody hates me."

"Lori doesn't."

"Huh?"

"I said Lori doesn't hate you."

"Pph. Who cares? She's just some little kid. A baby."

"Yes. But she's somebody."

"Yeah." A pause. The pause extended into a silence. "I don't hate her either."

"I know you don't," I said.

"You can't hate Lori. Even if you want to."

"No, I guess you can't."

Another long pause. I let out a breath of air. Tomaso's hand tightened around mine.

"Do you hate me, Torey?"

"No."

"Yes, you do."

"No." I smiled at him. Softly. Sadly. Again I felt the inadequacy of words. What could I tell him that he would believe?

We continued staring at one another, like survivors of a disaster, our hands still clasped to keep us together. Abruptly my own emotions welled up. I thought I would cry myself. What I was doing was so hard and I did not feel equal to it.

"No, Tomaso, I don't hate you. I don't know how to tell you so you'll believe that. You know, you're making me cry because I just don't know what to say but I want you to believe me."

No answer.

"You . . . you're a special guy to me. And I love you for it. That's the truth." It was so hard to say.

He did not respond. All he did was watch me. Tears, renewed, rolled down the side of his face and onto the floor.

111

"Come out here, Tomaso. Come here, would you?"

He shook his head.

"Please?"

Again he shook his head.

"I need you, Tomaso. Come here so I can put my arms around you."

He came. In a way which was neither slow nor fast, neither silent nor noisy. There he was standing over me after crawling out over the desks. I was still on my knees on the floor and he towered above me. For a moment neither of us moved. His face was still wet, his hair rumpled. Then he bent and hugged my neck. Because he never came down to my level I had to hug his legs.

"You won't tell them I was crying, will you?" he asked at last, his face still in my hair.

"No."

"You won't tell Lori?"

"No."

"I didn't mean to cry. I'm too big. A man doesn't cry."

"That's okay. We all need to sometimes. Even men."

He stepped back and broke the embrace. He gazed down at me. Then very gently he knelt and put his hands on either side of my face as if I were a little child to be comforted. His slight smile was enigmatic. "You can call me Tom, if you want."

11

Christmastime. There were carols from every store, bell tower and elevator. Snow was half a foot deep. Candles flowered in windows; a rainbow of lights twinkled around door lintels. Cheeriness came from strangers and friends alike.

All the fun of the season gave me enormous pleasure and not until January did I ever realize how glad I was to get back to ordinariness. The kids and I did all the usual Christmas things. We bought a tree from an eighty-year-old man who still cut his own and hawked them from a corner of the shopping center parking lot. Choosing the biggest, fattest, bushiest tree we could find, I stuffed it into the hatch of my tiny car and the four of us rode back to school with pine needles and the intoxicating green smell of the forest. We strung popcorn and cranberries until our fingers were stained red; we sang Christmas carols until I, at least, was hoarse; we baked gingerbread cookies while Tomaso regaled us with his own version of *The Gingerbread Man*.

The magic of the season wrapped itself around us. For a brief time we shared sheer, undiluted joy. Then came Christmas break, ten days of vacation.

Joc and I had a party. I was planning to leave for Montana two days before Christmas, and so the preceding Friday night we held a large but informal party for all our friends. Not much of a partygoer, much less a partygiver, I had been a little intimidated by the guest list of forty. But here, as in so many other situations, Jocco was confident. He ordered the food, the candles, the wine, the extra chairs, arranged the furniture and borrowed additional tableware. I got to do all the unfolding, the setting up, the cutting of eight pounds of cheese.

Despite my misgivings, the party turned out to be a warm, cheery affair with lots of Tom and Jerry, and half a dozen kinds of cookies on the buffet, compliments of Joc's sister in Massachusetts. The cat climbed on the table and nibbled the cheese, Josh Greenberg danced the hora and Joc taught everyone Christmas greetings in French. I was left with a glowing, almost nostalgic feeling, unable to remember any time when things had ever gone badly.

On the following day Jocco came over to help me clean up. After we emptied the ashtrays into the garbage, scraped all the bits of food out of the carpet and washed a small nation's worth of dishes, we settled down in the living room to wrap Christmas gifts. Jocco had brought over his presents, all of which seemed to be huge and unwieldy, and made a tower of them in the middle of the floor. We tumbled them onto the carpet between us and hauled out rolls of wrapping paper, ribbon and cellophane tape.

I had put up a tree. Normally I was not much one for decorating, I think perhaps because I got too much of it at

114

school. Joc, however, had insisted we have a tree for the party, and he had bought one and a box of lights and brought it over for me to set up.

Now, the next afternoon, he turned the tree lights on, turned off the overhead light and stoked up the fire in the fireplace. Darkness had come early with a snowstorm, shrouding us in that deep, purple, winter-twilight color. I was aglow with the same mellow feeling the party had given me the night before. Jocco was full of funny little stories and he would pause, gift half encircled by paper, one hand poised to pull off tape, and tell them to me. The firelight was captured in his eyes and it made them dark and shiny. How very good he looked to me. Especially when he laughed. I thought that consciously and it made me feel happy.

"I liked the party," he said after a lull in the conversation.

"Yes, so did I."

"I think everyone had a good time, don't you?"

"Mmm-hmm." I could not get a ribbon tied right and most of my attention was on that.

"Even Gary Stennett had a good time, I think," Joc said. "Don't you think he did? He looked like it to me."

"He was drunk, Jocco."

"Well, yes, but he was having a good time."

"Yes, that's probably true."

"It wasn't so bad as you thought it would be, was it?"

"What do you mean? I didn't think it would be bad."

He smiled. "I mean, I know the party was for me. I know that isn't the way you like to entertain. I just want you to know I liked it. And I think it went well. *I* had a good time."

I returned the smile. "Me too."

Another pause in the conversation. A small one. We were eating tortilla chips left over from the night before. I could hear Joc crunching. If I had been doing anything less mindless than gift wrapping, I doubt I would have noticed, but since my mind was in no way occupied, I felt the munchy silence. I looked up. Joc was watching me. Again I saw his laughing, shiny eyes. I bent back over my box.

"Tor?"

"Yes?"

"Let's get married."

I had been unrolling a very noisy roll of paper, great big old Santa Clauses all over it. Maybe I had not heard him right. "Huh?"

"Let's get married."

That time I knew I had heard. I rocked back on my heels. "What did you say, Joc?" I asked just once more to make sure there was no mistake.

"I said, I want to marry you."

Bang.

He could have slapped me. That would not have shocked me more. We had never, never discussed even the remote possibility of marriage. Truthfully, it had never crossed my mind. At this point in my life I was not ready to marry, a fact I had told Joc. There had not been any indication to me that he thought our relationship would go beyond where it currently was. But apparently I did not have a good idea of where it had managed to get to.

The silence was substantial. Joc's eyes were on me and all I remembered was looking beyond his shoulder to the window and seeing the deep blue darkness outside.

"I want this to continue," he said, his voice gentle. "Nights like this, like last night. I want us to be this way all the time. This is good, Tor. I want to share my life with you."

I was still without words. So much was in my head, but none of it broke through to the surface.

Joc watched me. The stillness in the room stretched out to make us universes apart. I wanted to say yes to him. Right then and there, and more than I would have ever believed possible, I wanted to say yes. But I knew I was not

116

ready. Not now, not yet. Sometimes I feared I never would be.

And not with Joc. Even as I sat there, I knew that immediately. I always had. Not only were Joc and I different in so many fundamental ways, but we were also so much alike. Both of us were restless, outspoken, driven individuals. We could never make it together long, not on a daily basis. We'd kill each other first. As I watched him in the firelight, I knew that when the time came for me, if it ever did, the man could not be Jocco, no matter how much here in the winter darkness I wished it to be.

Joc sat waiting, a half-wrapped gift in his hands. Tenderly he leaned across the paper and package between us, put his hand on my face and kissed me. I could feel the sturdy warmth of his fingers on my cheek, the crushing pliancy of his lips, and was very aware of it. I did want to marry him. Just for once, I wanted to be like everyone else. But the matter was so complicated, so much more than the witches and dinosaurs of my childhood. The complexity brought me to tears.

Jocco sat back. "You don't need to answer now. If you need time to think, that's okay. I understand."

I could not stop the tears.

He watched me intently. The fire crackled and a spark flew out over the screen. Joc stretched a toe to crush it into the carpet. My fingers and my palms and the backs of my hands were wet. Finally I had to get a tissue.

"It's your kids, isn't it?" Joc asked as I came back into the room with a box of Kleenex. He caught me unawares. The children had been the last thing on my mind.

I shook my head.

"It's those damn kids of yours. I'll never be able to compete, will I?" His voice was still soft.

"Jocco, the kids have nothing to do with this—"

"You're married to that job. I don't know why I fight it so."

"Joc, you're wrong. This issue has nothing to do with my work. I wasn't even thinking of it. I just need to sort things out. I mean, this *is* kind of sudden."

An edge had come to both our voices. I could tell he was becoming angry and I had no idea how to prevent it, short of agreeing to marry him. The thought of ruining this idyllic afternoon with an argument hurt almost as much as the more serious issue at hand.

"I'm not wrong," he said. "That job is part of every issue for you, Torey. And someday you're going to have to decide which is more important to you because no man is ever going to want to share his life with half an insane asylum."

More than ever, I knew the end was coming for Joc and me.

He looked away to the fire momentarily before turning back to me. "For you, that work is more than just a job. It's a love affair. I'd have no objections to your working or to your finding fulfillment in whatever career you wanted, but I can never be just a paramour."

"You don't understand," I protested.

"Don't give me that shit, kid. I understand. Better than you do, I think. And what I'm saying plainly is that there just cannot be the three of us in bed together any longer."

"The three of us?"

"Yes. You, me and your job."

"Joc, there aren't three of us. Only two. That's all part of me."

We argued. It was a low-volume argument for us, but I think the intensity of it kept it that way. We were both too afraid to let it get out of hand. In the end Joc left. He kicked the wrapping paper out of the way, stomped over to the closet and pulled on his jacket. Shutting the door softly behind him, he left me in the ruins of our Saturday afternoon.

Again, I wept. Softly. In the low light of a fire in embers

and a lighted Christmas tree, I let the tears come to soothe away the injustices of both dreams and reality.

Jocco returned. It was about 10:30 that evening. I had just gotten out of the shower and was sorting through things in the linen closet to put away clean towels. He opened the door and came quietly down the hallway.

"Look, Tor, I'm sorry."

"So am I."

He had a sad smile for things never to be recovered. "I guess I knew we'd never make it. We never would. I just had to try, that's all. You understand, yes? I asked because I had to know I tried."

I nodded and managed a smile myself.

"No hard feelings?"

"No hard feelings." I opened my mouth to say more but nothing came out. Jocco was standing perhaps ten feet down the hallway from me, his gloves in his hands, his dark hair dusted with new-fallen snow. Neither of us spoke. We had gone beyond the simplicity of words.

12

January came in full of surprises.

The first was Claudia, who became my fourth student in the afternoons. She appeared the first day following Christmas vacation with little more warning from Birk Jones than he had given me on Tomaso.

Claudia was twelve, Birk told me. She was atypical of my kids. An honors student from a parochial school on the far side of town, she had been a quiet, well-behaved sixth-grader. She came from an upper-class family; her father was a dentist and her mother an art instructor at the community college. To Birk's knowledge, Claudia had always been a good kid with no history of trouble or school problems. Except, of course, for one thing. She was pregnant.

"Pregnant!" I had screeched over the phone at Birk. What in heaven's name was he thinking of? The mere thought unnerved me. Over the years Birk and I had worked together he had sent me psychotics, garbage-eaters, screamers, fighters, inmates and one kid who had been

armless, legless and had a hole in his head. I thought I had seen them all. But I guess I hadn't. I had no idea what I was going to do with the girl.

Unfortunately, neither did Birk. Until Christmas no one had known Claudia was pregnant. To a family not expecting pregnancy, she had managed to explain away quite a lot. When the truth was finally revealed following a trip to the doctor, Claudia was immediately withdrawn from the rolls of the private Catholic school she attended. In our district there were no educational programs available for pregnant girls. In fact there were not any anywhere in our part of the state. In desperation, Birk had placed Claudia half-days with high school students at the Career Center to learn baby care and vocational skills. My class was chosen as the likeliest place for Claudia to complete her academic requirements for passing sixth grade.

Not to worry, Birk said again and again to me on the phone. She would be no problem. The former school was sending all her books and work over; I needed to do virtually no planning for her. She was a very nice girl, he assured me, very quiet, very mannerly—absolutely no problem. All that was necessary was for her to attend school where she would not be noticeable.

It made my room sound like a hideout.

"Okay?" Birk asked.

Pause.

"Okay?"

Pause. "Okay."

The hard part for me was not so much Claudia herself but rather explaining her presence to the other children.

"*Pregnant!*" Tomaso shrieked in the very same tone of voice I had used with Birk. "You mean she's going to have a baby in here?"

Before I could clarify, Lori broke in. "A *baby?* I thought you said she was a kid like us."

121

"She's twelve," I said.

"But that's still a kid, isn't it?" Lori asked.

Tomaso's eyes were wide. "Oh Torey," he said with great seriousness, "maybe we better not have Lori and Boo around while we talk about this. They're too young."

"Too young for what?" Lori cried indignantly.

Tomaso grabbed me by the arm. "I mean, she had to do it. You know. *It.*"

"What are you guys talking about?" Lori asked. She turned to me. "What's he talking about anyway? What am I too young for?"

"Tom, if you're talking about her having sexual intercourse—"

"Torey! *Torey!* They're just little kids!" He turned red to the very roots of his hair. I was amused that Tomaso should find the words for the reality so embarrassing when he cursed with them so freely.

Lori for her part was indignant that a conversation was going on around her that she did not fully understand. Quickly, the entire experience degenerated into Babel.

Claudia's actual arrival did much to dispel all our concerns. She was an inordinately shy girl with an eager smile. For twelve she was tall, a whole head taller than Tomaso, not much shorter than I was. She was angular about the face with high, prominent cheek bones, heavy dark brows and large eyes. Her hair was more than shoulder length, thick, not quite blond but not quite brown either, with adolescent greasiness. Her eyes were some color I could never settle on. Yet for all her lines and angles, Claudia had a soft look about her, soft in an innocently provocative way, as a very young child has.

Lori and Tom were hardly models of etiquette upon Claudia's arrival. Tomaso stayed half a room away from her, as if he might catch her condition, and stared at her stomach. Lori bordered on downright nosiness and I had to pull her aside more than once and make vile threats. However, Claudia bore through it all. She was polite to Lori far beyond what good manners would have considered necessary. She asked Tomaso if he missed his old school since he had had to come here. She was afraid she would miss hers.

I watched from afar when I wasn't policing Lori. Claudia seemed so shy that it hurt to watch her in conversation. Her face would redden, she would bite her lip, draw her shoulders up, duck her head. I wondered how she had ever gotten close enough to a guy to get pregnant.

The other surprise in January was Boo.

All the time I had had him, all through September, through October, November and December, I tried relentlessly to get communicative language out of him. I tried programming it, forcing it, bribing it and coaxing it. Nothing worked. He spoke only at random moments, always meaninglessly. Most of his language was delayed echolalia—days and days of maddening repetition of television commercials and weather reports and conversations between other speakers. Sometimes he would parrot back obscure conversations I had had with Lori or Tomaso days or even weeks before. It was like constantly having small auditory hallucinations.

Along with the echolalia went the simple repetition of selected phrases. One, apparently picked up from my old sessions with Lori's letters, was "What letter is this?" Some days he got stuck on that like a broken phonograph record, and the entire time all we would hear would be "What letter is this? What letter is this?" Over and over and over he would repeat it, half under his breath much of the time and in my exact intonation. "What letter is this?" in the bathroom. "What letter is this?" while he rocked and stared at Benny. "What letter is this? What letter is this? What letter is this?" And never, never any answer.

Yet despite all that vocalization, not once did there appear to be any communicative value to his words. The most impersonal of all his sounds, the small hroops and whirrs, seemed to be the only ones he ever made directly to someone, usually to Benny, sometimes to Lori. And none of us understood those.

My spirits had flagged during December. While I continued my attempts to elicit speech, most of our energy turned away from that to self-help skills—toilet training, dressing, keeping clean—whose mastery seemed more feasible.

"For pity's sake, Boo, sit down, would you?" I hollered. Lori and I were taking down the remnants of our Christmas decorations. She was up on the window ledge and I was standing on a table trying to reach our paper chain pasted to the light fixtures. It was Friday afternoon of the first week back and almost time to go home, so I was not being too particular about what the kids were doing. Tom had some small racing cars and was playing on the floor. Claudia was reading. But Boo persisted in spinning, arms out like a ballet dancer, eyes closed in self-stimulated ecstasy. I had gotten down to stop him once. I was more afraid of his running into something and hurting himself or stepping on Tomaso's playthings than of the spinning itself. However, it had persisted so long and had forced so many interruptions that I was losing patience. So I hollered.

Lori climbed down from the ledge and went over to him. She reached out to envelop him in her arms, the way I did with Tomaso.

"Lor, leave him alone, please. He can hear me and I'd like him to get used to listening to words. Boo, come on, *now*, stop and sit down."

Still he spun.

Sometimes he would hear me. Despite his lack of useful speech, he had developed quite good receptive language, if only he would use it. But when he got into persistent self-stimulation, we often as not had to reorient him physically.

Suddenly Boo spun into the corner of Claudia's desk and knocked the book from her hand. He tumbled over onto the floor. I leaped down from the table and grabbed him.

"You're going to be the end of me yet, Boothe Birney," I said and pulled him to his feet.

"You're going to be the end of me yet, Boothe Birney," he said back in a high singsong. Both Lori and Claudia giggled.

I groaned and lugged him over to the toy box. Lori came too and pulled out a top for him as I pushed him into a sitting position. "Here, he likes this," she said and started the top. Yes, he did like it. It was another type of self-stimulation. He would bend over and watch the spinning colors with great fascination. But not now. He was on his feet the instant I let go of him. His arms went out to spin.

"I said, sit down, Boo." My no-nonsense teacher voice.

"What letter is this? What letter is this?"

I grabbed him firmly. "Sit *down!*" I shouted right into his face. One hand under his chin, the other tangled in his curls, I started to push him down into a sitting position again. "Sit down," I said more softly as I did it, and put my face up close to his and looked deeply into vacuous green eyes. "I mean it, Boo. Sit."

All the other kids were watching us. Lori hovered around

the edges. Boo was still her baby. "I'll get him something to play with, okay?"

"Not okay, Lor. He's gotten himself a little too excited already. I want him to just sit and get a hold on himself again." I still had a hand on top of Boo's head and I had shoved him down, cross-legged on the floor. We stared at one another like a snake charmer and his cobra. "Sit," I said. Carefully I lifted my hand. It was like adding the last card to a card house. "Sit, Boo."

He stayed on the floor and continued to watch me. I was unable to tell if he was alert or still spacey.

"Sit there, Boo. Here, here's a magazine. Can you look at pictures?"

He let the magazine fall through his hands and continued to stare. I backed away and prepared to climb back onto the table to take down the decorations.

Not a very unusual interaction between us, those few minutes. Countless times before he had become over-stimulated by his spinning or flapping or something else. Always, if I could get him to sit down and be quiet a few moments, he would calm down. For a while.

Lori and I went back to work. She was chattering to me. In the background I could hear Boo mumbling. I did not think much about it. Boo always mumbled. It was Lori who was listening.

"What's that, Boo?" she asked right in the middle of an involved conversation with me over her sister and a shared bedroom.

I turned to look at Boo.

"Leave that alone, Boothe," he said. "I told you once, I told you a million times now, leave that alone. Now you do it!"

"He's just talking," I said to Lori.

Lori jumped down from the window ledge. "Leave what alone, Boo?"

Boo had cocked his head as if he were talking to an

invisible person. Over and over he scolded himself. He lifted one finger and flapped it expansively. "Leave that alone right now! You're going to be the end of me yet, Boothe Birney. Now I mean it, leave that alone!"

"Leave what alone?" Lori persisted. She had come over to stand in front of him. Wearily I climbed down from the table again, my intention being to get Lori back on the job, but as I came around in front of Boo, he looked up at me. The familiar vacant glaze was on his eyes.

Lori knelt down. "What you supposed to leave alone, Boo, leave *what* alone?" She shouted in his face as if she were talking to a deaf person.

"Don't bug him, Lor."

Then Boo raised his head to her. Recognition seeped into his eyes. "The plug places. Boothe Birney, leave them plug places alone."

"Plug places?" Lori's nose crinkled in confusion.

I came down on my knees beside her. I touched his face, although he needed no reorientation. He was watching us, his eyes squinted slightly, as one trying to see a great distance.

"Leave what alone, Boo?"

"The plug places. Leave them plug places alone, Boothe Birney," he answered. Slowly, as one sleepwalking, he rose to his feet and pushed past us. Going over to an electrical outlet on the wall, he touched it cautiously with one finger. "Leave them plug places alone, Boothe." He turned to us. "They bite if you put your finger in."

I was immobilized. Not a very brilliant conversation, this. To be technical, it probably could not be considered a conversation at all. Mitigated echolalia, a purist might call it, the ability to echo an appropriate answer to a question. But still, Boo had spoken to us. For the first time since he had come into the classroom, he had responded to us verbally. He had communicated an idea.

Then Boo turned around and put his back to the wall and

the outlet. He fluttered the fingers of one hand at the fluorescent light overhead.

"Mostly sunny days are forecast for the region. Daytime highs in the low thirties. Overnight lows 15 to 20. Fog in the low-lying areas. Windy at times along the east slopes of the Rockies."

13

Santa Claus had not overlooked Lori. During the second week of January, after the excitement of Claudia's arrival and Boo's talking had died down, Lori felt obligated to show us all her loot. She staggered in one afternoon with a big box. Her doll.

It was Baby Alive, a masterful creation which drank from a bottle while moving its lips and ate a vile-smelling gelatinous goop from a plastic spoon. Lori had to demonstrate every one of its marvelous accomplishments right down to the evil truth that the goop came out a big hole in the doll's rear end onto a disposable diaper.

Tomaso was inordinately patient with the exhibition. He sat at the worktable with the rest of us and did not once make a sarcastic remark, a groan of ridicule, or a fart. This pleased me, particularly in light of the fact that Lori had gotten long-winded and was telling us details none of us wanted to know. I mentioned it to him.

Tomaso shrugged off my compliment. "You know, once

I had this teddy bear and I liked him a whole lot. I was always showing him around and junk. So I know how it is. Little kids are like that. I was myself."

Touched by his sensitivity, I smiled. "Well, I appreciate your being thoughtful about it and not making fun of her."

Lori was listening now. She pulled out a chair and sat down, the doll cradled maternally against her breast. "Do you still got your bear? You and me, we could play dolls sometime, if you brung it."

Tom gave a tolerant smile. I knew he would have decked anybody else who might have suggested that. "No. I ain't got my bear anymore."

"What happened to it?" Lori asked.

"Well . . . well, back at this other place I used to live a long time ago, it got tooken away from me. This bigger kid who lived there, he took it and threw it out the window. And me and him got in a big fight over it, so when my foster dad got home, he said I was too old to have a bear anyway and so he threw it in the garbage and burned it."

Lori's brow furrowed with concern. "How old were you?"

Tom shrugged. "Just little."

"Littler than me?"

Another shrug. "I don't remember."

Shivers ran down Lori's back and she clutched her doll close. "Nobody better try and throw *my* toys away in the garbage can!"

A paternal smile from Tomaso and he patted her shoulder. "Don't worry, Shrimp. I wouldn't let 'em. I'd smack 'em for you, if anybody tried."

"I'd smack 'em myself!" Lori paused while considering the matter. Cocking her head to one side, she scrutinized Tomaso's face. "But don't you got any other bears or anything? Was that the only one you had?"

Tomaso nodded. Not looking at her, he studied his fingers instead.

130

"But don't you got nothing?"

"Well sure I got things," he replied. His voice was a bit indignant. "I got me a game of Sorry! And some Lego toys. And where I live now, they have kids about my age and sometimes they let me go in their kidses' rooms and look at their stuff. Once, this one kid, his name is Barry, he even let me try on his baseball glove. And he even said maybe someday he'd let me play with it."

"But don't you got no bears or stuffed things?"

"Aw, Lori, shut up, would you? Jesus, those are girls' toys, don't you know? What do I need anything like that for? He was right, my other foster dad was. I'm too old for things like that. Quit being dumb."

"But what you got to love?"

"Jesus Christ, Lori, you're bugging me. Tor, make her quit, would you? Jesus. But this, but that. But I don't know, Lori Sjokheim. Does that satisfy you? I got plenty of junk to love. I got me my game of Sorry! Didn't you hear me say that? Your ears full of wax? And I got my Lego toys. And I bet I can build a hundred million times more betterer with it than you can do. And I got me Barry's baseball glove to love. What more does a guy need? So lay off me before I get mad."

"But don't you ever get lonesome in the dark?" she asked softly. Her voice was so quiet after Thomaso's that it went in smoothly and deeply like a fine-edged blade.

"Shit!" Tomaso jumped up and knocked his chair across the floor. "You damned little bitch, all you do its ask questions. Jesus Christ and Mother Mary, you make me want to strangle your stupid neck sometimes." Then to me: "Why the hell don't you ever make her shut up? She's got diarrhea of the mouth." He darted to the far side of the room. Although he did not knock anything else over, his running was tight and tense. On the far side of the room he hoisted himself up on top of a desk and sat there. He swore at us from that safe distance.

Lori turned back to the table, lay down her doll on the floor beside her and reached for her folder. She said nothing more. From looking at her I was unable to discern her thoughts. I took up the remaining folders and handed Claudia hers, set Tom's in front of his place at the table and opened Boo's to start work with him.

We worked in silence. Tomaso remained apart from us. His swearing had quickly degenerated into little noises: huffs and puffs, snorts and pphumphs. I found the silence about us poignant, in part because no silence should have been there, in part because we all knew something had happened and it hurt, yet no one knew quite what.

At last Tomaso slid down from his perch and returned to the table. He stood behind me a while and watched me work with Boo. I did not turn to acknowledge his presence because something in me made me shy. Then he walked around behind Lori and leaned over her shoulder. "I know all those words," he said softly about what she was copying. "You want me to read them to you?"

She nodded. He read the sentence. Finally he went over to his own chair and sat down. Pulling over his work folder, he opened it. He looked at us. First at Lori, then at me. I raised my eyes to him.

Tiredly he braced his forehead with one fist. "You know," he said, "I do get kind of lonely sometimes. I do get real, real lonely."

I nodded. "Yes, everybody does sometimes."

"Yeah. Everybody does."

Claudia remained a puzzle to me. Not so much, I suppose, for anything she did. More for what she did not do. She did not do much. From the time she arrived until the time she left, if I got three complete sentences out of her, it was unusual. She seldom looked me in the eyes. Her favorite way of looking was down. The girl must have memorized the pattern of our linoleum by the time she had been there a week.

She was an excellent student. The parochial school sent over all her books and the work she needed to do to complete her grade. Each afternoon after school I would sort through them and pick out assignments and place them in her folder for the following day. Claudia would come in the next afternoon, pick it up, take it to a desk away from us and for the remainder of the time completely absorb herself in finishing the assignments, without ever saying a word to us. Her shyness created an almost tangible wall around her. The puzzle to me remained how she ever managed to get pregnant.

The second week she was with us, the file arrived from her former school. By and large it was an unremarkable folder. Her grades had always been excellent. Her IQ, although not in the gifted range, was well above average. She read at the tenth-grade level; her other skills were not far behind. If anything, Claudia was an overachiever.

Little was said about her family. She was the oldest of five children, all girls. Three younger siblings also attended the parochial school. The youngest sister was not of school age yet. The family was characterized in one small paragraph as being cold, distant and competitive.

According to the notes, Claudia was three months pregnant with a predicted delivery date in early July. Apparently there had never been any consideration of abortion in this strict, Catholic family. In any case, from what was written, it was not clear if the family had discovered the pregnancy in time to consider abortion. The school had not been notified of the situation until Christmas vacation. No information about the father of the child was available.

All the reports in the folder mentioned Claudia's unusually shy and reserved behavior. After each grade, the

133

teacher had remarked on it. Claudia would participate in groups only if coerced. She became physically ill when made to speak in front of the class. Her skin would mottle with red blotches when interacting with adults. Although other children did not seem to avoid her, she was never observed to have any close friends. Her only noted interest was reading. She escaped into books.

I closed the file and pitched it over from the worktable to the top of my desk. It slid off the far side with a satisfying thud. This kind of child made me so damned frustrated. Why didn't anyone ever see them? How could they sit and rot for years in classrooms without someone noticing them? They were invisible kids. Claudia was in as much trouble emotionally as Tomaso was. Yet, in the current state of the art, if one were bothersome, one usually gained attention and subsequently treatment. On the other hand, one could kill oneself quietly and as long as one did not disturb anybody else doing it, no one noticed. Or cared.

Then as I sat looking at the folder and its scattered contents, I had doubts about myself. Was it only I who saw her as having a problem? Was my being in these special classrooms so many years beginning to skew my judgment of normalcy? I felt that way sometimes. It seemed no matter how normal a child given to me was reputed to be elsewhere, the kid always ended up acting crazy in here. Maybe it was just all my perception. Maybe it was the air in my classroom. I laughed at myself and rose from the chair to go home. I felt like the Typhoid Mary of the disturbed.

Tomaso and Lori were quite willing to include Claudia in the class. I don't think their curiosity had ever been fully satisfied regarding her pregnancy and they were trying to put her enough at ease to continue the interrogation I had interrupted the first day.

We were painting one afternoon. I had laid out newspapers and large sheets of art paper on the floor along with paint and an assortment of brushes. Tom, however, very quickly decided that he wanted to finger paint and before I could stop him, he had poured paint onto both his and Boo's paper. Rolling up his sleeves, he plunged into it. Lori, of course, had to join them. Claudia did not. She just sat and watched, not even picking up a brush. Only after I had given in and joined the others, did she hesitantly pour a little paint on her paper and push it around with one finger.

The episode led to a lot of good-natured camaraderie. I had not planned to paint for the rest of the afternoon after recess but that was what happened. The kids really got into it, laughing and squealing over their work. So, continuing seemed more beneficial to me than the other activities I had planned.

Tomaso was the first to discover that removing one's shoes and putting paint on the bottom of one's foot resulted in footprints. Lori experimented with other parts of her body: elbow prints, knuckle prints—and before I caught her—nose prints. I could see Claudia loosening up. She began to laugh with them. She willingly painted their feet. Finally she volunteered to show Tomaso how to make prints by cutting designs into erasers. When next I turned from the art cabinet, she and Tom had painted themselves clear up to their elbows with red and purple paint. What a worthwhile mess.

When I finally called for cleanup, I found Tomaso and Claudia together at the sink, laughing and splashing each other with dirty water. They had a puddle going around their feet that stretched clear back to the newspapers. The moment of frivolity put Tom at ease.

"So how come they put you in this class anyway?" he asked. "Just because you're going to have a baby?"

She nodded.

"Boy." He shook his head. "That's really something." A pause while he stuck his entire arm up to the elbow under the running tap. "Tell me, did you do it? *It?* You know. With a boy?"

"Yeah."

"Wow." His voice was serious, not joking. A hint of respect. "Wow. Was he a big kid?"

She shrugged.

I was coming up behind them with the mop and I thought perhaps I had better step in before the conversation got out of control for Claudia. "Tom, I think that's enough. No one has a right to pry."

"I wasn't prying. Was I, Claud? I was just asking."

"I know it. But some things are pretty personal business and people often like to keep them private. We don't want to put Claudia on the spot."

"Oh," Tomaso replied. "Don't you want to talk about it, Claudia?"

Again she shrugged.

After the dismissal bell rang and the other children had gone, Claudia lingered and helped me clean up the mess of newspapers and paint that remained. She was on her hands and knees scraping at the linoleum with her fingernail.

"Here, that's good enough," I said to her. "We can leave the rest for the janitor. I don't want you to miss your bus."

She jerked one shoulder, a half shrug. "It doesn't matter. I can walk. It isn't that far."

"Yes, but you don't need to worry about the floor. It'll have to be damp mopped anyhow. And we don't want to worry your family, if you're late."

"No one will be worried," she replied.

Finally I gave in and left her to her paint chipping. I went across to the worktable and started sorting through things

136

to be corrected. Claudia rocked back on her heels and looked in my direction.

"You know," she said, "I don't really mind talking about it."

I looked up. My mind had been on other things and I was confused. "About what?"

"The baby." Red blotches came out along her neck.

"I'm glad," I replied. "I know the other children are sort of curious. I don't want them to make you uncomfortable with too many questions. That can be hard."

She shrugged. "There isn't even so much to tell. I was just seeing this guy. Randy. He's fifteen. And I got pregnant. That's all." She made it sound like going to the movies.

I regarded her. In an odd way, Claudia made me uncomfortable. My experience with adolescents was limited, and what little I did have had been with kids so severely disturbed that they functioned as much younger children might. But the discomfort was more than simply lack of experience on my part. I felt sometimes as if my soul had been frozen somewhere in middle childhood, that the rest of me had grown, but that part of me which was I, myself, had never reached adulthood. I worked so well with the children not because I had any special gifts but simply because I was one of them; my only advantage was extra experience of life. Their thoughts were no mystery to me, nor were mine to them. Then would come the older children, Claudia's age and up, and I could not understand them, I think simply because they were in fact older than I was. This lack made me uncomfortable.

Claudia rose from the floor and went over to the trash can to dump her handful of paint chips. Then she came to where I was sitting on the edge of the table and sat next to me. It was the closest she had ever been physically. Only a small space remained between us.

"I like your jeans," she said and gingerly touched my leg. She gave me a very quick smile before dropping her head back down. I noticed the mottling was along her arms now.

"Thank you."

"I asked my mom to get me some like that. They make you look nice."

"Thanks."

"I like the way you wear your hair."

She was melting my heart. I wanted to open my mouth and tell her I understood, to let her know I cared and she wasn't alone anymore. But I couldn't do it. If she had been five or seven or nine, I would have had no hesitation, but here she was, by virtue of her body, a young woman like me. The instinct on which I normally functioned was pinioned beneath etiquette and I was too shy to risk the verbal freedom I was accustomed to with the little kids. Her eager, halting attempts to bridge the gap even I could not manage touched me.

"Do you like being a teacher?" she asked. She was looking at me. Warily, though, like an untamed animal.

I nodded.

"I might be a teacher someday." She touched her stomach. "I don't know though." This was followed by a long breath, as if she were very tired. "I only did it once, you know."

"Oh?"

"Yeah. Just once. And Randy said I couldn't get pregnant. He said you had to have breasts before you could get pregnant and look at me: Even now I don't hardly have any breasts. See? Even now." She pressed her shirt to her chest.

I nodded.

"He said I couldn't get pregnant. And we only did it once." She lifted her head and looked beyond me. I could see the odd, indescribable color of her eyes; the bitterness was plain too. "A lot of truth that was." She looked down again and traced around a red blotch on her arm. "I didn't even like it. It hurt."

We sat together, not talking. The silence communicated what I was unable to say with words. Hesitantly I reached over and put my arm around her.

"I'm scared," she said.

"Yeah."

"What am I going to do with a baby? I'm just a baby myself."

14

Subtle changes that bothered me were beginning to occur in Lori. I could not quite pinpoint when the changes started. To be honest, I could not even pinpoint what they were exactly. Still I was aware of them. And while they were small in and of themselves, they seemed to bode a greater transition. Like the shadowy movements of a northern autumn into winter. She seemed less resilient to me, less full of humor. Small things upset her more; she could be moody in a low-key but enduring way.

I think the time I felt these changes most distinctly was when we were playing games. Among the many things I had resorted to in teaching Lori reading was the use of little homemade card games. Anything to make letters go down more palatably. Most of them were simply matching letters, L to L, S to S and so on, even when the letters were of different colors or sizes or styles. She did not have to know the actual letter itself.

At first the games were fun for both of us. The goal was

to see who got stuck holding the last card, who could match up her hand first. Being a game of chance we both had an equal opportunity to win, although years of teaching had given me a cardsharp's ability to cheat so that those times I felt I needed to throw the game, I could.

Lori was delighted with the activity. She kept track of our score in a little chalked-off corner of the blackboard. Every day she would add on who had won what and our scores had accumulated for over a couple of months by this time. The scorekeeping itself became an exercise.

Almost daily we played one or two hands. From time to time I had made new cards to keep the learning aspect of the game alive, but Lori continued to enjoy it. She still clamored for it if I tried to delete the activity, and some days she would come in early from lunch to get in a couple of games. Yet despite her interest, the ambience of the game was changing. For a while I did not notice exactly what it was. Then one afternoon it occurred to me that I was letting her win on purpose. Often. Looking at the score on the chalkboard, I realized "often" had been happening a long time. I felt vaguely afraid of having her lose.

We were in the middle of a game when that occurred to me. Instantly I wondered what had made me realize it. I watched her. Lori was bent over her cards with great concentration. Matching the letters was still a hard task for her. Her eyebrows were pulled down, wrinkling the skin over the bridge of her nose; her eyes were intent.

"I'm going to win," I said softly, the mocking note of fun clear in my voice.

"No, you're not." No mockery in that statement.

"What if I do?"

A little pause. Lori raised her eyes to me and I could see the nameless difference then. Only a flicker of it but I saw it just the same. Then she smiled disarmingly, a regular old Lori-type smile. "You better not."

I did not win the game. She did. As the game drew to its

close I almost did draw the winning card. I knew where it was; I just did not want to think I did. I chickened out. Whatever the change that was taking place, I did not want to know about it.

As the days passed and I continued to play games with her or watch her at other times with the kids, I kept intending to challenge her and bring this nameless thing out where I could get a good look at it. Yet every time I meant to do it, I didn't. Something always came up that I could use to rationalize losing my nerve. Right down to the final card in our games I would plan on winning. I even stacked the deck before school so that my cheating to lose would be more difficult. Still I would chicken out in the end.

The truth, I think, was that I already knew what was happening, but I did not want to accept that. I kept wanting to believe that things were better for Lori. My hard, dedicated work with her was helping. My having her in the room afternoons was enough to reduce the pressure. Just simply my love for her was making the difference. Things were improving. She was feeling better about herself. She was going to make it, even with the reading problem. She was too strong, and I was trying too hard for it to be any other way. I wanted to believe that so desperately, even when I knew deep down it was not true. It was like living with a cancer victim.

"I'm going to win this time," I said.

"Mmmm-mmm," she replied not even looking up. All week she had not bothered to tally our score on the board. She had just played. It was like a drug fix for her. She was obsessed with getting in a couple of games.

"I haven't won in a long time now. Don't you think I deserve to win?"

"Nope." Still not looking up. She laid out an M matched with an N. "Your turn."

"Lor, those don't match. See? Look at them."

"Yes, they do."

I pointed out the problem. Up and down the letters I went with my fingers until I finally convinced her they were not the same letter.

She frowned. "But I don't got any others that match it."

"Here." I handed the cards back to return to her hand. "Hold them until you can match them."

"Nooo," she protested. "I don't got any others to match. I want these to match. Leave them down. They count."

"No, they don't, Lor. Take them back."

She was becoming upset with my insistence. I got a very dirty look. "Leave them down, Torey. I can't win if you don't. You got less cards than I do."

"That's cheating. It wrecks the point of the game."

"I don't care. Leave them down."

I left them down. And felt angry myself. We played several moments in silence.

Then, there it was. I drew the winning card, an X to match the X I already had. My last card. For a long second or two I held the card just as I had lifted it from the table and stared at it. Now or never.

Lori looked at me then, when I paused so long. I think she knew.

"I got my X," I said abruptly. I had to, to keep my courage. "Here, see?" I laid down my last pair. "I'm out."

A totally unreadable expression crossed her face. The silence grew so loud around us that both Tom and Claudia looked up. "What are you guys doing?" Tomaso asked.

Tears were on Lori's cheeks. Her eyes filled with a great, reproachful hurt. "You're not supposed to do that, Torey. That's not fair. I was supposed to win."

"It was just a game, Lor. We were just playing, remember?"

The pain turned to anger and she swept the cards off the table in one tremendous motion. Whoosh! Cards fluttered

143

everywhere. "How come you're so mean to me? You're supposed to let *me* win!" Then she began to sob, her head down, her thin shoulders shaking. "It isn't fair. It isn't fair. This is the only place in the whole world I ever win anything and now even you won't let me. I hate it!" And she kicked the table.

There. I had done it. I sat motionless, speechless. Not much else I could do. Like Pandora I had opened the box. Unlike her, I think I had always known what I would find when I did. And that it had to be opened. What I was going to do now that I had, I did not know.

I invited Claudia's parents in for an informal meeting. I wanted to let them know what kind of academic program I was following since achievement was such an important matter in that family. In turn I wanted to know what kinds of plans they had for Claudia and her baby so I could follow up that course during the time Claudia was with me.

Of all the parents, Claudia's were definitely the most uncommunicative. They were not untalkative. Far from it. The father was a bold, overbearing fellow who seemed to enjoy the sound of his own voice. The mother would rush in to fill even the slightest silence that crept unexpectedly into our conversation. However, nothing they said was of any value. That in itself I found thought-provoking.

I was used to dealing with a wide range of individuals concerning the children in my classes. Over the years I had had college presidents, Nobel nominees, and acclaimed artists across the table from me as well as alcoholics, prostitutes and ex-convicts. Yet they had all shared the same problem: disturbed children. Pathology in the families was unnervingly similar despite the differences in education, social standing and money. And truthfully, I think I preferred working with the poor or the ignorant.

144

The problem with the families having better education was that they were more elusive.

So it was with Claudia's family.

The father was a real stinker. For all his intelligence, he was addlepated when it came to being human. "You know," he said to me, "Claudia comes home and tells me about this class some days. She tells me that you put her in charge of some of the children." *Translation*: Can't you do your own teaching?

"She tells me she has to work with a . . . a black child." *Translation*: Now you know what I think of blacks.

I nodded. "Yes, that would be Boo."

"I understand that he is an autistic child. I've been reading on autism. Incurable, isn't it?" *Translation*: Kid's nuts.

"She said she had to work with this little black, autistic boy. That you asked her to."

"Yes, that's right," I said. "Does she object to it?"

He gave a one-shouldered shrug. "Well, no, not really. Just telling me about it." *Translation*: I object.

"And she was saying there's another boy in here. A migrant boy. Who actually works in the fields." *Translation*: Now you know what I think of Chicanos, too.

"Actually," I explained, "Tomaso doesn't work in the fields now. He never misses a day of school. He's one of the best students I've had."

The father nodded thoughtfully and ruminated a moment over the matter. Then he leaned across the table between us, his voice low, almost a whisper. "These children, they're not dangerous, are they?"

I leaned back toward him. "No," I whispered indignantly. "My kids aren't dangerous."

"Oh," he said. "Well, then, what about their behaviors? They sound pretty bad. Are we in danger of having Claudia learn any of that? I mean, if she's working with that little colored boy, she isn't going to learn any of that stuff he

145

does, is she? I mean, we've paid plenty of money to keep her in a good school up until now. I'd sure hate to have her pick up anything here."

I felt I deserved a medal for my civility. The only person who deserved one more was Claudia for living with this guy and still being such a nice girl.

"No," I explained as nicely as I could. "You need not worry. What the other children have, it isn't catching."

"Well, good. I *was* worried. I'm sure you can understand."

The mother seemed nice enough, except that she never talked other than to fill pauses. Any silences in our conversation seemed to terrify her and she loaded them with the most inane comments. She smiled a lot and nodded her head as if it were attached by a string to a puppeteer's stick. She and Claudia together must have been quite a pair.

Although she worked as an instructor in art over at the community college and had held the post for some years, she appeared to me as the stereotype of a dominated, unfulfilled woman absorbed in her children and her home.

Neither parent had given much thought to what Claudia was going to do with the baby. They had provided her with prenatal checkups but would not consider even the suggestion that Claudia might profit from psychological counseling both to cope with the baby and with her other problems. When I suggested it, the father was irate. Nothing wrong with his child! It was all the boy's fault. Well, didn't I know that Claudia was practically raped? Maybe she needed some help to deal with that, then, I suggested. He stated flatly that I had been in here with the crazy kids too long if I thought his daughter needed psychological help. And he was not thrilled as it was, to have her in this class. He had a good mind to pull her out of school altogether and hire a tutor. At that I shut up. The last thing Claudia needed was total isolation.

146

The conference ended on a slightly hostile note. My back was up and I could not bring myself to smooth over our differences completely. The father, in his turn, saw me as meddlesome and overstepping my boundaries as a public school teacher. The matter was spelled out directly for me. I knew I had better be careful in my dealings with him. If he did not withdraw Claudia from my class, I had no doubt that if I irritated him sufficiently, he would find a way to sue me.

15

"What's going to happen when the baby comes?" I asked.

Claudia and I were together after school. She had stayed to help me plan for Boo and then continued afterward to make Ditto masters for a project of her own.

It was a snowy afternoon, gray and cloudy, although not dark. Snow clouds always seem to have an uncanny brightness about them. I had gone to stand before the window and watch the large flakes drift down. My back was to Claudia at the table.

"I dunno."

"Don't you think about it?" I asked and turned around to look at her.

"Yeah, sometimes."

"Do you ever talk about it with anyone? Your folks? What do they say?"

"Nothing. We don't talk about it at home. I'm not supposed to. My father said not to. He doesn't want Corinna or Melody to get ideas."

"Your sisters?"

"Yeah. Corinna's eleven and Melody's nine. He doesn't think Caroline knows what's going on yet. She's only six. And Rebecca's just four, so I can talk to her. Rebecca's my favorite person in the family. I tell her everything."

"I see. But Claudia, what's going to happen to the baby when it comes? That's only five months away. That isn't as long as it seems."

She nodded in a way I think was meant to shut me up.

"What are you going to do with it?"

"I said I don't know. We'll see when the time comes, that's what my mom says. I'm going to keep it. Is that what you mean? Of course, I'm going to keep it."

"You want to keep the baby?" I came to the table and sat down.

"Certainly." She paused briefly and a smile slipped across her lips, an inward smile as if she were thinking pleasant thoughts. "It's going to be all mine. My baby. I'm going to fix it so that it loves just me. Just me." A pause. "And Rebecca maybe. A little. But mostly me."

"Are you planning to take care of it?"

She nodded. "Me and my mom. I'll feed it and stuff. And change its diapers. I won't mind that. And she can do the other stuff. My mom said to me once, once at night when we were talking and my dad was out at the Elks Club, she said she missed having babies around. Rebecca's hardly a baby anymore. And she said she wanted another baby."

"But your mother works, Claudia. She's gone all day."

"Yeah, I know. But . . . It'll work out."

"Babies aren't like dolls. You can't just set them up on the shelf when you don't feel like taking care of them."

"I know that. Don't worry about it so much."

"I can't help it."

A small stillness grew long. It was so quiet I imagined that I heard the snow falling. Claudia studied her fingers, ran a hand over the very slight curve of her belly, looked

149

away from me. I rose to pace back to the window again.

"It'll work out. I know it will."

I hoisted myself up onto the wide window ledge. The glass was cold against my back. When I did not speak, she fidgeted in her chair.

"It will, Torey. You always worry about things. It'll come out okay. Something will happen."

Yes, something would happen all right. For Claudia, who at twelve had left the Good Fairy and Santa Claus behind such a short time ago, there was no lack of confidence. For me there was no lack of doubt. Already three-quarters of her life was written for her, if she kept the baby. That was the way it was for 90 percent of all teen-age, unwed mothers. Dropping out of school or at least never making it to college, never finding a job that paid enough money to support her and her child, never settling the rift the baby's birth had caused in an already disturbed family, marrying to get out of a situation too unbearable, and so on and so on and so on. Perhaps most of all, though, never getting to finish being a child herself before she was forced to be an adult—something that would hurt both her and the baby. Even as I sat I could hear the doors of opportunity closing, the click of the locks reverberating in my ears.

"Claudia, have you ever thought of giving the baby up for adoption?"

Horror electrified her face. "No. Of course not!"

"I know that's a terrible thing to think about, especially after you've carried the baby all those months, but sometimes it is the right thing to think about. For both you and your child."

"No! Be quiet; don't even say that. I'd never give it up. It's *my* baby. My own, and nobody has the right to take it away from me unless I say."

"Claudia . . ."

"Be quiet!"

150

I opened my mouth to speak, but she gave me such a determined frown that I closed it again.

Claudia began to cry. "How can you even say such things to me? You've never had a baby; you don't know what it's like. I want this baby. He's going to fix things right."

Oh. My heart sank.

She rose from the table and turned as if to run. I thought she would. She did go clear to the door. There she stopped, leaned her head against the door frame and sobbed.

I sighed. Lately someone seemed to be in tears all the time in this place. It made me tired. Pushing myself off the window ledge, I went over to her. She immediately moved away from me. However, instead of going out the door she turned back into the classroom, ran to the reading corner and flopped down on the pillows on the floor.

Remaining by the door, I regarded her. I knew I had gone too far, had been too blunt. For our first discussion I should have only planted the thought and then left it. I could recognize now that it was too emotional an issue for both of us.

I did not know what to do. Claudia was a champion when it came to bringing out inadequate feelings in me. That in itself made me feel worse.

Claudia was sobbing into a pillow. Going over to the reading corner, I stood over her a few moments. I wanted to kneel and take her in my arms as I would have done with Boo or Lori, but the same shyness that I had felt before stayed me. She seemed older to me than I did myself; she had problems I did not know how to cope with. Those were not a child's tears.

I could not overcome my reticence. "Listen, Claudia," I said finally, "I'm going down to the teachers' lounge for a few minutes, okay?"

No response.

"I'll be back."

The truth was, I needed to get out.

In the lounge I bought myself a can of Dr Pepper from the pop machine. Sitting with the cold can pressed against my forehead, I paged through back-dated teaching magazines. Maybe there were some hints in there about what to do when you felt tired and confused and in water over your head.

Back in the room all was silent. January dusk was already settling into the corners. The fluorescent lights often bothered Boo, so we had gotten used to working without them except on the darkest days. We seldom noticed the gloom. Now I did.

From where I stood in the doorway, I studied Claudia. Although she had ceased crying, she remained in the reading corner, still stretched out on her side on one of the pillows. Her back was to me. This was too much, I thought, for a young girl to cope with. She should be home pinning up pictures of her favorite movie star and listening for good songs on the radio.

I came over to her. I knelt on the rug. "I brought you some pop. I hope you like Dr Pepper."

She turned and regarded me briefly before sitting up. Her eyes were red and swollen. Slowly she reached for the can of pop, grasping it in both hands, and drank deeply. Afterward she set it down on her knee, still clasping it between the palms of her hands. There came between us all the stillness of the January twilight.

"Claud, I'm sorry," I said, and then I had to stop because I couldn't explain what I was sorry for. Just for being so fallible, I guess, for having presumed the position of authority when I, too, had no answers.

She looked at me. For the first time she looked directly into my eyes. Her brow furrowed. "Why's it matter to you what I do? Nobody else cares."

I did not have an answer.

152

She continued to watch me. "I can't figure your game out. We're all just somebody else's kids in here. What do we matter? Why do you care?"

The dusk had stolen what little color I could discern from her eyes. There were tears there again, brimming but not falling. She caught her lower lip between her teeth to stop the trembling of her chin. I had reached a hand out to touch her but stopped halfway. We were trapped in each other's gaze and I felt like Alice in the rabbit hole, falling, falling, falling. So much I perceived, so little I understood.

Then Claudia dropped her head. With one hand she brushed back her hair. A long sigh, then she looked back up. She smiled very slightly. "You're weird, did you know that?"

I nodded.

And then there was Lori. For every wrong moment, for every lost chance, for every mistake I made, Lori could make it all worth the effort. I wished there was some way to bottle her spirit and carry it with me, although in truth, I did not even know quite what it was about her that I found so uplifting. I could never capture that airy, quintessential quality when describing her to someone; yet, it was so much the essence of what Lori was.

The day following my afternoon with Claudia, I was sitting at the worktable over the noon hour, finishing my lunch. Lori came bounding into the classroom, a piece of paper in hand. When I pushed my chair back from the table, she jumped in my lap.

"I brung you something," she announced.

"You did?"

"Yup." She sat, straddling my legs, her back to my chest. "You wanna see what it is? Here." She lifted the paper over her head so that it was against my nose. I took it.

The picture was of a bird, a blue bird with black wings and very yellow legs. It was a rather tottery-looking bird, because Lori's ability in art followed her ability in other things done on paper. But happiness was clearly written all over that bird's beak.

"I think this is just the best picture I ever drew. I used my best crayons, the ones with the points still on them. And do you see? I stayed in the lines this time. Pretty good, anyhow. It's just about the best thing I ever done."

"Oh, Lor, you're right. It is."

"Mrs. Thorsen thought so too. She wanted to put it up on the bulletin board even." Lori squirmed around to look at me. "But I told her I's making it for you, so she couldn't have it."

"Oh, you shouldn't have. This is beautiful. You should have let her put it on the board. This is a picture to be proud of."

"I am proud of it. But I made it for you."

"Well, I'm glad to have it. It is a good picture. Maybe I can find a place on our bulletin board to put it, so everyone else can enjoy it too."

Lori took the picture from my hands and held it out in front of her. Thoughtfully, she examined it. "You know what I was thinking when I made this?"

"What was that?"

"Well, I was thinking that it isn't as good as a real picture. You know, as a photograph. Like in a magazine or something. And I really wanted it to look just best with no mistakes. But it wouldn't come out like I was trying to make it. It wasn't perfect."

"Oh Lor, don't say that. It's beautiful. Better than any old photograph."

"No. No, that's not what I'm saying. It isn't right because that wasn't the way I wanted to draw it. It wasn't perfect, like I wanted it to be. But you know, Tor, what I was thinking about . . ." She paused, her voice trailing off while she gave the picture another thorough viewing. "What I was thinking about was: It *is* perfect. Not the part you see but what's inside you. In my head, I could see this bird perfect." She turned to look at me briefly and gave me a smile. "And that's sort of enough for me to like this picture even though it isn't really very perfect. Because . . . well, because I kind of know it could be . . ."

She turned to me again. "You know what I mean?"

I nodded. "Yes, I think I do."

"Things never really are perfect," she said. "But inside you, you can always see them perfect, if you try. That makes things beautiful to me."

"You're a dreamer, Lor."

She gazed at me, her eyes dark and round and beyond smiling. She said nothing.

"That's a good thing to be."

The blue bird picture never made it up on our bulletin board. I took it home with me. I hung it on the wall over my bed to remind me at least twice a day about beauty in an imperfect world.

16

School time is not marked off by months as is time in the rest of the world, but rather by holidays. There are Halloween and Thanksgiving and Christmas, of course, but there are also the in-between times like After-St.-Patrick's-Day-But-Before-Easter and Not-Quite-the-End-of-School, when one has to make do with kites or flowers on the bulletin boards.

We were moving into February, gearing up for St. Valentine's Day. I tried never to emphasize the holidays too much because my kids got over-stimulated if we went on too long with anything. However, after the long drag of January, I always looked forward to St. Valentine's color and was a little more lax.

Lori, of course, was our class celebrator. Before any of the rest of us was even thinking about a holiday, Lori was filling our discussions with plans for parties and presents and decorations. Valentine's Day was no exception.

*   *   *

156

February had just begun and we were still in the first week when Lori arrived one afternoon with a huge grocery sack.

"I brung us some Valentine things," she announced. "For us to put up on the walls and make it pretty." And so she had. A cupid with a honeycomb heart, three worn wall decorations from the dime store and an empty heart-shaped plastic candy dish. And cards. "These here's my Valentine cards to everybody." She lifted up an assortment of odd-shaped envelopes. "Last night, me and Libby, we made 'em. She helped me write the stuff and I cutted out the pictures." She handed them to me.

By now the others had arrived. Tomaso was leaning over Lori's shoulder to peer into the paper bag. Claudia fingered one of the wall decorations. Boo spun in ever wider circles around us.

I held the cards and wondered what to do with them. We had not yet made folders to put cards in because Valentine's Day was still so far away. I hated to put the cards on my desk. It was such a mess I feared I'd never find them when I had to.

"Shall I put these on the shelf over here?" I said to Lori. "Then when we make Valentine's folders, you can put them in. All right?"

"No." Lori put her hands on her hips. "These are Valentines for today. I want everyone to open them now. I made 'em special."

"It's only the fifth of February," Claudia said.

"I don't care. They're still for today. My dad'll buy me store Valentines for Valentine's Day 'cause I have to have 'em for my other class then to. But these are for just you guys. For today. Open them now."

I smiled and shook my head. "Okay, Lor. Help me give them out. There aren't any names on them."

"Well, of course not," Lori replied with great exasperation; "I wouldn't know how to read them." She rolled her eyes in a show of tremendous patience with me for not thinking of that. "Here. This one is for Tom and this one is Claudia's. The big one is for Boo and that's yours."

They were very personal cards. Claudia's contained a cutout of a woman holding a baby. I LOVE YOU. AND YOUR BABBY, it read in Lori's sister's broad first-grade script. For Tomaso there was a magazine picture of a dubious-looking Spanish dancer pasted on the outside of a piece of folded construction paper. Inside was an undecipherable message. Lori had written it herself.

"What's this say, Lori?" he asked.

"Well, I had to write it myself. If Libby wrote it, she woulda thought you were my boyfriend and you're not." She shrugged. "You're just a friend."

"So what's it say?" I asked.

She blushed and would not tell me. I think it said something like I love you. I mentioned that.

"Well, it's okay to say those things in a Valentine's Day card," Lori said quickly. "All Valentine's Day cards say that. It's not because he's my boyfriend, 'cause he isn't. You know that, don't you?"

Claudia giggled.

"Yeah, we know it, Lor."

My card was simply a drawn picture. Because, Lori explained to me, there were no magazine pictures that looked like us in the room. So she had drawn all five of us, arm in arm. I LOVE YOU, said a yellow balloon over the head of one of the people in the picture, YOU MACKE ME HAPPYE.

Boo's card was biggest. On several sheets of paper Lori had pasted large, simple cutout pictures of animals, toys and people. "It don't have any words on it," she said, "because Boo doesn't know how to read. Just pictures. Because I watched him look at pictures before and he likes them. So I made him that. A book with lots of good things to look at."

Immediately Boo glommed onto the homemade book and sat down on the floor at my feet to look at it.

"That's for you, Boo," Lori said to him. "I made it for you 'cause you're such a nice kid and I like you." She patted his head.

On the second page of the little book was a large cutout magazine picture of a shaggy dog. Boo lifted the book up close to his nose and scrutinized the picture. And smelled it loudly. "Doggie. Doggie."

"Hey, Tor! Listen!" Lori cried. I had moved away a short distance to look at Tom's card. Lori grabbed my arm. "He's talking! Boo likes my card."

Boo tapped the picture of the dog. "Doggie."

Tomaso dived down beside him. "That's Benji, Boo. Benji. Can you say Benji?"

"Doggie."

"Yes. But say Benji," Tomaso said.

"Doggie."

"Benji."

"Benji," Boo repeated. "Doggie. Benji."

"And what's this?" Lori pointed to the opposite page.

Boo looked over at the other picture. It was a cat from a Purina Cat Chow advertisement, chow-chow-chowing across the page.

"Doggie," Boo said.

"No," Tomaso replied. "That's no doggie, Boo. That's a kitty. Say kitty, Boo."

"Kitty."

"Now what's that?" Tom asked.

"Doggie."

"No." A note of exasperation.

"Kitty."

"Yes!" Both Tomaso and Lori erupted with a cheer.

Excitement ran through us like a prairie fire. All four of us were down on our knees, pressed around Boo. Tomaso

159

had become the leader. He was turning pages against Boo's unwilling hands. Boo still wanted to look at the dog and cat. But with a gentle firmness, Tom insisted Boo look at other pictures. In short, direct sentences he elicited the names, corrected Boo if he erred and gave him the right names.

I sat back on my heels. A miracle here. My own small miracle. I smiled as I watched them, the girl who could not read, the boy kicked out of school, the pregnant twelve-year-old, the crazy kid. Not whom you'd ordinarily cast as miracle workers.

"Wow! Wow, listen to you, Boo," Tomaso was saying. The small knot around Boo opened. "Listen to him, Tor. Just listen to him talk. And not nonsense either. He can really talk."

They continued. Lori broke away and crawled over onto my lap. She hugged my neck. "Oh, Tor, I'm so happy. I feel like I'm gonna laugh and cry all at the same time. We made Boo talk like a real person." Her voice dropped to a whisper of awe. "*I* made Boo talk. I did, didn't I? I made him the card. He talked because of me, huh?"

I nodded. "I think he did, kiddo. You're just the person responsible for this."

She was still in my arms. Closing her eyes, she let her head drop back and I thought she was going to melt from sheer joy.

Our reverie was short-lived. Within moments after the initial excitement wore down, Boo reverted to his old, wacky self and began babbling about Chuck Barris and "The Gong Show." I had known it was coming, but twice in the last month Boo had responded to us. This time had been much better than the first. What had happened was enough magic for me. I had no illusions about Boo. What had happened was a miracle of the first degree in this business.

160

Understandably, the children did not share my open-mindedness. They had expected magic of the magnitude found only in fairy tales. When Boo forsook us so quickly for his own world, they could not help feeling that everything had been for nothing.

Lori in particular was crushed. "I thought we made him better," she said, her voice crippled with unshed tears. "He was talking to us. I thought we fixed him. What's the matter with him anyhow? Doesn't he want to get better?"

I knelt beside her and put my arm around her shoulders. "Of course, he does, Lori. It just isn't like that. It isn't because he doesn't want to talk; he just can't always. But I'm sure he was very, very happy that you made it possible for him to talk a little."

"But why did he stop?"

"I don't know."

"But how come you let him? How come he isn't getting better?"

"Oh Lor," I said, "that isn't something I can do. I want him to talk just as badly as you do, but those kinds of things just aren't in my power. Boo has to do his own growing in his own way."

She lowered her head. With the toe of her tennis shoe she drew an invisible design on the linoleum, around and around. She studied it. "But we been teaching him and teaching him every day and talk to him just like you said and he *still* doesn't learn. He's never going to be a regular kid."

"Yes, it's discouraging, isn't it? Sometimes I feel bad too."

"But it doesn't do any good, no matter what you do. He's never going to be regular."

"We'll still keep trying though," I said. "What he'll be are all someday things. What's important to remember is that today he talked. That's all that matters."

She continued to maneuver her foot along the floor.

161

"All we care about's today. You understand that, don't you? It's all that matters."

"Yeah," she replied half-heartedly, still regarding the floor.

Then she paused and looked at me. She shook her head. "No. Not really. I *don't* understand. Not really."

Bringing up my other hand I hugged her to me, pressing her face into the soft cloth of my shirt. Disappointment had left her unwilling for my comfort. As I held Lori I looked beyond her to Boo, who sat alone on the floor. With the fingers of one hand he flicked his eyelashes; the other hand was suspended above, fluttering in the light. His soft baby features were drowned in distrait dreaminess.

But today you talked.

17

Tomaso's eleventh birthday was on the twenty-second of February. I gave thought to celebrating it. Should I? Shouldn't I? How big a deal should we make of it? Tomaso was a funny kid. Very unpredictable. On one hand, he wanted desperately to be the center of attention, to be loved, to be fawned over. On the other hand, he was the big macho man and desired only manly indifference. In the end I decided that I would go ahead and at least bake a cake. The rest we would play by ear.

It was Lori who thought of presents.

Stopping by my room on her way out to recess one morning early in the week of Tom's birthday, Lori came over to my desk. I still had resource students in there so she tiptoed in very, very quietly and tapped me on the shoulder. I jumped.

"I have to ask you something important."

I raised an eyebrow.

"You know, it's Tomaso's birthday on Friday. Can we give him presents?"

"No, I don't think so, Lor. We'll just have cake and maybe play some games or something. No presents."

A pause. She wrinkled up one corner of her lip. "I already boughted him something. I got it at the store last night when Daddy took Libby to get her ballet tights."

She had on her coat for recess and also a red stocking cap. The cap was pulled way down to her eyebrows giving her a gnomish look.

"I saved my money. I boughted it myself. My dad didn't even help me." A long, almost reproachful gaze through dark lashes. "Besides, I spent twenty-nine whole cents on a bow for it."

"Oh," I replied, "well, I don't know, Lor. I guess it's okay. But none of the rest of us has a gift for him. And nobody else gets to celebrate a birthday in here. Do you think it would be fair?"

An impatient frown. "Oh, Torey, birthdays aren't supposed to be fair. They're just supposed to be birthdays. So can I?"

I gave in. "But look, scoot out to recess now before Mrs. Thorsen finds out you're missing."

Lori grinned gap toothed and yanked her stocking cap down even further. "That's okay. I told her you said for me to come in." A laugh. "And she believed me." She jumped out of reach when I moved to whomp her.

"So aren't you even going to tell me what you got Tom?"

"Nope!" A giggle and she shot for the door. "It's a surprrrrrise!" And out she ran.

Friday the twenty-second. Lori and I tied crepe paper all around Tomaso's chair at the table. Claudia penned a huge HAPPY BIRTHDAY TOMASO sign to put across the door. We were ending up with a five-star affair.

164

Tomaso was delighted. "I ain't never had a party before," he said as he came in the door. His head swiveled to look at the sign from every side. "You done all this for me? For me?" His eyes were shiny.

He was thoroughly amazed. He walked around and around the room gazing wide-eyed at our feeble attempts at decoration. "For me? I ain't never had a party before. Not ever. And a cake? You made a cake for me? For me?" I had never seen a kid so incredulous over a sign, a cake, eight balloons and a roll of yellow crepe paper. Tom kept circling the room. Each time he would touch the balloons or the cake, gaze at the sign and ask us over and over again, "For me? For me?" I think at that point more than any other I understood the extent of this boy's deprivation.

"And guess what?" Lori said to him on his umpteenth circle around the room. "Guess what, Tomaso. I brang you a present."

His eyes were filled with skepticism.

"I did! Didn't I, Torey?" She turned in my direction. "Can I give it to him?"

"As much fun as all this is, I think we ought to do our work first. Up until recess we'll work. Afterward, we'll have cake and Tom can open your present."

Protests. Lori finally talked me into letting her show the box to Tomaso. Just show it to him, she promised. Then we would get to work. I folded under pressure.

It was a large box, probably two feet square, glorious by its size alone. Undoubtedly Lori had wrapped it herself, judging from the job. Livley yellow circus animals cavorted across the paper. A huge gold bow crowned it.

"For me?" Tomaso said immediately. "That's for me?" His eyes widened to the very edges of his face.

Getting Lori to put the box back in the closet and convincing everybody to come to the table was no small task. Tom and Lori continued to exchange excitement over by the cupboard.

165

"Come on, you two," I called. "Over here now. First we work, then presents. Come on."

Claudia had captured Boo and they came to the table. Tomaso remained with Lori, the bright yellow box between them. They could have been lovers, the way they stood, so much going between them without words.

At last the box was stowed and they reluctantly joined us. I gave Tom his work folder. Lori took the sandpaper alphabet. A moment's silence reigned while everyone considered the work to be done. Then Tomaso glanced sideways at Lori.

"Did you really get that for me?" he whispered. "Did *you* get it for me?"

Lori nodded without looking up.

"Because you wanted to buy me a present, *sí?*" There was a soft emphasis on the word "wanted."

As I looked over at them, I smiled. A feeble expression for the deep, bittersweet emotion brought up in me. These terrible small tragedies always hurt my heart. They always did.

The hour and a half until recess was a pocket-size eternity. Lori kept watching the clock, nudging Tomaso or Claudia for the time, since she could not tell it. Tomaso's glances were no less numerous, although he was less obvious. I even caught Claudia at it. Only Boo was oblivious. As usual.

Finally two o'clock arrived. I had an aide from the office take the kids out to recess while I cut cake, put out napkins and poured orange juice. Last of all I set the package wrapped in circus animals with its twenty-nine-cent bow right in the center of the table.

In they came. Wildly. Tomaso whooped, swung from the door lintel, leaped over a desk. Boo flew in, airplane-style, arms out, whirring loudly. Someone must have communicated to him during recess because he was definitely in a party mood now. Lori was singing. Only Claudia entered in a manner that I as a teacher could consider even close to appropriate, an expression of forbearance on her face.

"My present! Open my present first!" Lori shouted.

"Here." I was handing out orange juice as they tore by. "Boo, no! No, no!" He was holding his cake above his head.

"Open my present, Tom!"

"Torey, Boo's putting cake in his hair."

"Lori, look out, for pity's sake, would you? Sheesh. You almost stepped on me."

"Help! Help me, somebody! Somebody? I'm gonna drop my orange juice."

"Boo, would you *please* sit down? Don't put that in your ear. Claudia? Lori? Would you get that cake out of his ear? Boo!"

"Lookit, I got a flower on my cake."

"Hey? How come I didn't get no flower? Torey? I want a flower too."

"*Boo!*"

Chaos. "Okay, everybody. I'm going to count five. When I finish, everybody better be sitting on the floor with their food in front of them. Got it? One . . ."

A quick shuffle of chairs and feet.

"Two."

"Tom, here. Quick. Sit by me."

"Three."

"Boo. Boo, sit down. Boo!"

"Four."

"Stoppit! Quit shoving, Lor. Sit down, would you? We're gonna get in trouble and it'll be your fault."

"Four and a half."

Shuffle, shuffle, shuffle.

"Five."

Four bright angelic faces looking up at me. Tomaso and Claudia had Boo squashed down between them. Frosting still clung to his black curls, but he and everybody else sat.

"There. That's better," I said. "My goodness, you were acting like a bunch of savages. Now let's sit and finish our cake and juice. Like civilized human beings. Okay?"

Three nods. Boo was slurping his drink.

There is nothing that quite equals the conversations of children while eating.

"I like this cake, Torey," Tom said. "What kind is it?"

"Chocolate."

"Oh yeah. I was trying to remember that name. It was on the tip of my tongue."

This struck Lori as hilarious and she choked over her juice. Meantime, Claudia lifted her plate up. "I like the way chocolate smells." Of course, everybody had to lift his or her piece of cake up for a good whiff. Even Boo tried when he saw the others.

"Boy, it sure does smell good," said Tomaso taking a deep snort. "I could just sniff it right up my nose, it smells so good."

Lori was up on her knees with excitement. "Guess what? Guess what I know? You're attached back there."

We all looked at her in puzzlement.

"Back there." She opened her mouth wide and pointed. "Your nose and your mouth are attached back there. You know how I know?"

"Uh-uh."

"Well once my sister Libby, well, we had beans for supper and then she went upstairs and threw up. She got sick in the sink and you know what? She threw up beans through her nose."

"*Lori!*" My teacher voice.

"She did, Torey. I'm not lying or nothing. I was there. I seen her. I was standing right in the bathroom with her when she did it and beans came out her nose. So you must be attached back there."

"I didn't think you *were* lying, Lori. It's the topic. . . ."

"Well, you know what my grandfather does?" Claudia puts in. "He gargles up his nose with salt water."

This cracked everybody up. I cut my cake in half and gave part of it to Tomaso who was sitting next to me. The conversation never did get any better.

Then came the big moment. Lori ceremoniously took the yellow-wrapped package from the table and brought it to Tomaso, seated on the floor. "Here," she said, her voice hoarse with pleasure. She set the box down.

Tomaso sat a moment and simply stared at it. Then carefully, cautiously, he began to loosen the ribbon. With just one hand he worked and so delicately, as if the box at any moment might disappear. *"Leones,"* I could hear him whisper to himself, *"Leones y monos. Para meh."* The words were so soft as to be no more than a breath. *"Para meh."*

The yellow circus paper fell away to reveal an appliance box. Lori's excitement was getting the better of her. She had one braid stuffed between her teeth and she was up on her feet bouncing, legs crossed. Coming back to where I sat on a small chair behind them, she gripped my knee with one hand. Hippety-hop from one foot to the other. Every few moments she would turn to pass her excitement on to me.

The box was well taped. Tomaso was having difficulty breaking through. His own excitement had grown and he was at the box with both hands now. But his fervor was making him clumsy.

"You want a pair of scissors, Tom?" I asked.

"No." He pulled at the box top. Lori had used strapping tape to hold it down. A few more grunts of exertion. "Well, yeah, I guess I do, Tor. I can't get it."

"I'll get 'em, I'll get 'em!" Lori cried and ran for our scissors rack on the window ledge.

"No, wait, Lor. Those won't be sharp enough to cut that

169

tape." I went to my desk and found the long, pointed shears that I kept but seldom used around the kids. "Here, Tom, use these. They should do the trick."

"Yeah!" he cried approvingly and snipped away the binding of the box.

With religious care he opened the lid. Up came a wad of tissue paper. Lori was hopping against me again. Then he reached in and pulled the present out.

A teddy bear. It was brown and fuzzy, wearing a darker brown T-shirt. Not too big, not too small.

Tomaso held the bear a little way away from his body and stared at it. Lori erupted into joyous hooting. Claudia smiled at me. Tomaso, apparently stunned beyond words, simply sat. Soundless. Motionless.

"Well, do you like it?" Lori asked. "I boughted it with my own money. My daddy didn't help me even one little bit and it cost $10.98. I've been saving clear since January and I even had to use some of my Christmas money that Aunti Gert gave me. But I knew you didn't have no bear, Tom. I didn't mind."

Tomaso exploded.

Up on his feet, wrapping paper and tissue going in every direction. "What a dumb gift! What the hell you think I would do with that? What do you think I am? Some goddamn baby?" He was shouting. "What a shitty present! You're as stupid in everything else you do as you are in reading. No wonder they got you in this fucking idiot's class. You don't know nothing!"

Stricken, Lori's shoulders sagged, her mouth turned down. Tears bubbled up and flowed raplidly down her cheeks. She let out a long, low howl.

I was up and after Tomaso but I was not fast enough. He had caught me offguard.

"Here, let me show you what I think of your stinking present!" Tomaso yelled. He grabbed the shears. With one deft movement he plunged them into the bear's belly and disgorged a wad of foam. The bear fell disemboweled to the floor. The shears crashed after it. Tomaso tore off around the room in hysteria, screaming and cursing. Lori wailed.

"Tomaso, *stop!*" I sprinted over the worktable in one jump and cornered him momentarily between the window and a low bookcase. Then up he went over the bookcase and on the run. Terrified that he would get out of the room in this condition, I bolted back over the worktable again and ran for the door.

Tomaso took that moment to gain the advantage. He had not been as incoherent as I had thought. Taking a small chair he swung it hard against my shin. The whack of wood and bone hitting one another resounded in my ears. Clutching my leg in pain, I fell against the door.

When I straightened up, Tomaso was holding the shears within inches of my stomach.

Silence. Abrupt ear-splitting silence. Lori even stopped crying.

"You don't tell me what to do," he said. His voice was low and hoarse. "I'm sick of listening to you, you goddamn bitch. You just shut up or I'll run this thing right through your gut."

He would. As I eased myself up to my feet, my back flat against the door, I warily regarded the scissors between us. I knew he would do it if necessity required it. His eyes left no doubt in my mind about that.

He moved the shears closer to my shirt. A mere fraction of an inch was between the point and the cloth.

Still the unearthly silence.

I took deep breaths and let them out slowly to force myself to relax. The pain in my leg still echoed inside my head and I could not dispel it. The air around us smelled heavily of birthday cake and orange juice and fear. I could not tell whose fear it was I smelled, his or mine. Claudia, Lori and Boo stood transfixed.

"You goddamn fucking bitch. You bitch," he said again.

171

Still the hoarse, low voice, but there was another emotion under it which I could not read.

The silence.

My heart was pounding in my ears. This type of occurrence was an occupational hazard for me. I worked too close to violence not to experience it myself occasionally. The acceptance of that fact left my head clearer; however, it did not necessarily lessen my fear. Sweat had soaked under my arms and along the back of my shirt where it pressed against the glass of the door. Now I felt it trickling down between my breasts. *Don't do this to me. Come on, Tom, don't. Please don't.* Yet all around me was the silence.

We were watching one another. The scissors in his hand gave him the confidence to look me straight in the eye. Such a beautiful kid. Even now, and no matter how inappropriate the thought, that was what I was thinking, a thought more powerful than my fear.

We waited. Eye to eye in the silence.

I wished someone out in the hallway would notice me, my back to the door, and stop in the room to help. Then as soon as that wish materialized, I feared the consequences if it came true. Time alone was my best ally. If only I could outwait him without inciting him, if only I could hold out myself until his emotions ran down, that would be better. Should an outsider come upon us now, things might easily become worse than they already were. Tomaso might spook or be egged into doing something I hoped I could keep him from doing. Still, I felt so alone there on the wrong side of those scissors. And God knows how afraid I was.

The minutes edged by. One by one.

"Tomaso," I whispered, "you don't want to do this."

"Shut up."

"Come on, Tom. You don't want to hurt anybody."

"You goddamn bitch, *shut up!* You're always telling me

172

what to do! You're always making me feel things I don't want to feel. I'm tired of it. I'm not your property." After the silence his voice knifed across the room. "I'm tired of it! You make too much noise. It hurts my ears. You, especially. You make my ears hurt."

Suddenly the corners of his mouth pulled down, his chin quivered. Bringing his free hand up, he wiped his eyes on the cuff of his shirt.

"I hate you. It's all your fault," he cried.

"My fault?"

"And her fault." He gestured toward Lori.

"It's our fault that you're so angry?" I said.

"I'm *not* angry! Why do you always say that for? How many goddamn times do I have to tell you? I'm not angry!"

"Oh. I see. You're not angry."

"No." The tears were beginning to trickle down his cheeks and he brushed at them roughly. "I'm just unhappy." A small sob convulsed his body. I took that opportunity to move slightly. Tomaso interpreted the move as hostile and jammed the scissors up against my diaphragm. I froze.

"Don't you dare move."

"Okay."

I looked beyond him to the clock. I felt like I had spent half my life on the wrong side of those shears. In fact, we had only been in from recess half an hour. I sucked my stomach in and pressed even more tightly against the door to ease the point of the scissors out of my skin.

He was still trying to keep control of things. I shivered. The sweat that had drenched by body earlier was turning cold. Gooseflesh ran along my arms. In back of Tomaso, Claudia had taken hold of Boo. She pulled out a chair and sat down. The noise made Tomaso press the shears into the small space I had earned with my shallow breaths. Lori had begun to weep again. We were falling apart, to put it mildly, and all over a stupid teddy bear.

173

"Look, I'm sorry, Tomaso. Whatever it is I've done to make you feel so bad, I'm sorry."

"No, you ain't. It's your fault."

"What did I do? Won't you tell me that at least?"

"You don't even know?"

"No."

"*Parece mentira.* You are as stupid as everyone else in this class."

I nodded.

The tears came again, harder now. He looked down at the scissors. Slowly he turned them in his hand so that they rested on his palm. His tears were falling on them.

I dared not move. His hand was open flat now, and as I breathed, my shirt touched the point of the scissors and made them quiver in his palm. Or perhaps his hand was trembling.

"Why don't you just leave me alone?" he asked. His voice was very soft and he raised his eyes to me. "Why are you always looking in me?" I saw his hand close around the scissors and lower them. "I wanted to hate you. I wanted to hate you. Why wouldn't you let me? Why wouldn't you just let me be alone?"

He did not run. I had expected him to. Instead he took the scissors and with one mighty motion he slammed them to the floor. Then he simply lowered his head, covered his face with his hands and wept.

I was overwhelmed. The question of questions he had asked me. What right did I have to make him care about a world that did not care about him? For every child I saw, for every child I touched, that question was there. And he had not been the first to doubt my wisdom in it. For me the sorrow came in having no answer, in never being quite sure that the pain I gave was any better than the pain I relieved. It was an issue that made the scissors look unimportant.

"Oh Tommy." I had my own tears then. "Oh Tommy, I am sorry." I reached out for him and he was in my arms.

We comforted each other. Down on my knees, I held him to me. My residual fear made emotions difficult to control. Sitting on the floor, my back still to the door, I took Tomaso on my lap. He was a great big boy, eleven, and within sight of manhood, but there was no other way for either of us. He clung to my neck and buried his face in my hair. He wept in low, hard, body-racking sobs. I rocked us back and forth against the door and crooned soft things to him, small nonsense words only love knows. My own heart was full of things too deep for tears.

The first half hour in from recess had been endless. The remainder of the time went unaccountably fast. I sat with Tomaso on my lap for almost thirty minutes. Then the pressure of the other children forced me to rise and attempt to reconstruct our class. We all moved and spoke to one another with the abashed gentleness common to the aftermath of great anger.

Most of all I wanted a moment for Lori because I knew how upsetting all this must have been for her, but in the bare fifteen minutes left, I could not carve it out. Instead, we went about the mundane chores a Friday brings: the cleaning up, the putting things away, the making out of next week's attendance slips.

Tomaso wandered. Like a sightless man in a foreign place, he bumped into things, staggered from point to point as we worked around him. Lori, I noticed, would pause and watch him. I could not read her feelings as she did.

When next I turned, Tomaso was bent over the bear, picking up the stuffing and gently trying to get it back into the body. Meekly he came to me, the bear in his hands.

"Do you think you could fix this?" he asked. He would not raise his head to look at me. "I think maybe it could be sewed up."

I took the bear from his hands and examined it. "Yes, I think maybe it could."

"Do you have needle and thread? Could you do it?" A small pause. "Now?"

"I'm not sure I have what I need."

"Could you look? Please?"

Taking the wounded bear with me, I went over to my desk. Tomaso was behind me. As I searched, Lori approached.

A long, aching silence was between them as they surveyed one another. I would have needed words; they did not. Lori leaned over my desk. "I'll go to the office and see if they got any thread down there, if you want me to."

I looked over at her. Not for the first time I envied her for her strength. And for much more. "Okay, Lor, if you would."

The bell for dismissal rang before Lori returned from the office. Claudia helped me stuff Boo into his boots and then she took him outside to wait for his mother in front of the school. Tomaso remained beside me in the classroom doorway. The maimed bear was pressed to his chest.

When Lori came back, I took the bear from him and went back into the room. Sitting at my desk, I examined the damage more carefully. "I'm not exactly going to be able to make this look like new, Tom."

"That's all right."

I poked at the hole again.

"Tor?" he asked.

"Yes?"

"Will you do it now?"

"You have to get out to your bus, Tomaso. And this is going to take me a while. I'll have it for you on Monday. How about that?"

He watched me without immediately replying. All his defenses were down and I could see directly into his soul. His eyes began to fill again. "Can I stay? I don't feel much like going home now."

I considered, then nodded. "Okay. I can give you a ride later."

176

"Will you fix it now?"

"All right."

Lori still stood with us. "Torey?" She touched me lightly on the shoulder as I bent over the bear. "What about me? Can I stay too?"

I looked up.

"I don't feel like going home either."

I smiled at her and nodded.

They sat at my feet while I pushed the stuffing back into the bear and sewed it up. The secretary had only navy-colored thread in the office and my clumsy stitches against the brown fur were obvious. But I bent forward, held the bear up close to see and did the best I could.

The quiet around us, the absolute stillness, was lulling. My emotions had been in such high gear that coming down was almost physically painful. It was like when I was small and had played too long in the snow: When I came inside, the warmth of the house against my numbed fingers and toes was an agreeable agony. So it was now as the deep Friday-after-school tranquillity leeched out dregs of earlier feelings.

Lori and Tomaso watched me intently as I worked. Both sat cross-legged on the floor. Their eyes were on the bear. No surgeon ever performed to a more concerned audience.

About fifteen minutes into the sewing I had to take a breather. My fingers were sore from pushing the needle through the tough cloth. My back ached from leaning over it so closely. Sitting back, I stretched to loosen tight muscles.

Those eyes. Both pairs of them. They were so intense, so obvious in their belief that I was going to be able to set things straight again.

I smiled. "You know, you two are just about my favorite kids."

Lori smiled. Slightly. Enigmatically. Tomaso did not.

"You don't really care that things don't always work out so good, do you?" Lori said.

"No, I don't really care."

"See, Tomaso?" She looked back at me. "I told him that."

"Do you love me?" he asked faintly.

I nodded. "Yes. I guess that's another way of saying it."

18

What it was about Lori's teddy bear that set Tomaso off that Friday afternoon of his birthday I never really knew. Maybe the gift evoked memories of a time when he had been hurt too badly for caring. Perhaps simply Lori's kindness in selecting such a personal gift was too painful for this boy who had known so little kindness. Maybe it was something deeper, more complicated. I did not know. The bear went home with him that afternoon, blue stitches and all, never to be seen again.

The episode had an effect on Tomaso's behavior from that day on. It was a subtle effect that was difficult for me to pinpoint, but he changed. Previously, there had never been an explosion that had involved violence toward any person. For all his hostility, I do not believe that Tomaso was basically the type of individual to hurt people. Afterward, he never again threatened me or any of the others. His anger persisted, but from that time on I felt safer with it, and I think he was more secure with me. We both knew now how bad things could get between us and not damage the relationship. The test by fire had come and we had survived it.

I wish, however, I could have known what had changed, how it changed, what it affected. I did not. But that turbulent afternoon was a milestone for Tomaso, and for me. And when I caught myself looking at him in quiet moments, I felt an understanding, a deeper understanding in that unconscious part of my mind which functions without words.

Claudia's pregnancy continued to bother me. I knew that the chances of her giving birth to a high-risk infant were enormous because of her age and because of the lack of prenatal care in the first months. Worse for me I think, was that I knew the chances of her raising a high-risk child were even greater. I had little experience with birth and infants; I had far too much when it came to knowing about unwanted children raised by immature, troubled parents. What Claudia was providing was new fodder for my room. That hurt me.

All my attempts to talk to her about the future of her child had ended disastrously. She would not believe that her child could grow up anything but fairy-tale perfect. Everything was going to be wonderful after the baby arrived. It was going to be an ideal child: pink, pretty, sweet smelling. It was going to love her tremendously and make her feel like the most important person in the world. None of this in juxtaposition with girlish dreams of being a prom queen in high school, dancing in the ballet or winning a merit scholarship to Stanford seemed incongruous to Claudia. She knew that when the baby came, she would live happily ever after, just like in the storybooks. Nothing I said could disabuse her.

That was one side. There was another side Claudia

seldom gave words to, although I think it existed far more sharply for her than did her dreams. It spoke loudly to me, too, as during the times I would observe her standing alone on the playground, her back to the brick wall, hands over stomach, as she watched the other children playing. I would hear it even as she talked to me about her fantasies, her words saying one thing, her eyes saying something entirely different. And occasionally she even dared to speak it out loud: how am I ever going to survive?

I was concerned in no small way about Claudia. We had grown closer as the weeks had passed, but I still did not know her. Worse, I did not know enough about what was happening inside her head. No child ever left me feeling as powerless as she did. It was like one of those bad dreams where one tries and tries and tries and never makes any progress. I knew it was only a matter of time before reality and fantasy collided in Claudia, and I feared she would end up trying something none of us would want. With this girl it was all a race against the clock, and as the time passed and the situation did not improve, I knew I needed help. We were going to lose this kid.

I still could get no aid from Claudia's parents. I called her mother at work one morning. It had been weeks since we had spoken to one another, and I hoped that by talking to her alone I might more easily make her see things my way. We passed small talk back and forth between us for a while before I said to her that I hoped she and her husband had had the chance to reconsider getting mental health counseling for Claudia. They hadn't. It still seemed unnecessary, the mother said. I mentioned that the more I worked with Claudia, the more convinced I became that she was suffering from depression, at the very least. She escaped into books, into movies, into music, and, when these failed her, into academic work. I told her mother that I was worried that the time would come when a song on the radio might not be enough.

Depressed? Her mother laughed in a congenial way. Just

an adolescent phase. She'd been that way herself at twelve. Besides, how could Claudia be depressed? She was just a little kid.

I was left holding the phone and feeling once more like a frustrated character in a nightmare.

In the end I decided I would try to find some resources for Claudia myself. What I was hoping for was a support group of some kind, perhaps a group of other adolescent mothers and a counselor. I wanted a place for her where she could share feelings, find out alternatives, learn future behaviors, and just belong to a group of understanding people who cared. Stupid me, I just assumed such a group existed.

Telephone book in hand, receiver clamped to my ear by one shoulder, I dial the high school guidance department.

"How old is your daughter?" the counselor asks.

"She isn't my daughter. She's a student of mine. I heard you had some sort of program for pregnant girls."

"Do you have parental permission for this call?"

"No. I was just trying to find out what was available."

"I'm sorry. Why don't you tell the girl's parents to give me a call? I really don't think we could divulge confidential information over the phone, could we?"

Confidential? One look at Claudia was all it took to know what her problem was. Doesn't matter. Click.

"Hello, my name is Torey Hayden."

A nurse at the hospital this time. Rumor had it that she taught a class on childbearing. I explain what I am looking for.

"There is this excellent book. I wrote it. It's called *The Miracle of Life.*"

"What is it about?" I ask innocently.

"The facts. How the sperm grows inside the father. How the father plants the little seed in the mother. How the baby is conceived at just that moment. Just right for a twelve-year-old to read. Very up-to-date and modern. Uses teen-age language. Shows some electron-microscope pictures of the sperm and ova."

"That sounds very nice. The problem is, I think we've already figured out the part about the sperm and ovum. What I was looking for was some sort of support group for this girl. Something to help her cope."

"Oh." Another, enlightened, *"Oh"* follows. Then, a long pause. "Well, that does sound like a nice idea, doesn't it? Have you tried the Mental Health Center?"

Mental Health. I get a male psychologist on the line. "Hmmmmm," he says meaningfully. "Hmmmmmm. Ahmmmmm."

"You know," I am saying, "I feel bad about this. The girl never had any information on birth control. In truth I don't think she even knew that what she did could make her pregnant."

"Mmmmmm. Yeees, terrible, isn't it? We flaunt sexuality in front of these kids and then don't teach them how to cope with it. Hmmmm. A different age than when you and I were kids, isn't it? People don't realize these little kids are even out doing it. You know, *it.*" He sounds like Tomaso.

"Exactly," I say. "But what I was thinking of is that she needs some support in this. She's only twelve."

"Mmmmm. Mmm-hmmmm. I can see that. Therapy, do you think? Eh?"

"That would be nice. But I was just thinking of some group of girls sharing the same experience. Perhaps with a counselor. Just so she doesn't feel so alone in this."

"Hmmmm. That's a hard one."

"I'm afraid her parents wouldn't go for therapy."

"I see. Hmmmmmmmm. Hmmmmmm. That's a hard one, all right. How about Planned Parenthood, have you tried them?

Planned Parenthood, a young woman with a thick English accent on the telephone this time.

"Twelve years old, is she?" she asks me. "Oh now isn't that just terrible? A crying shame is what it is."

"Yes, but . . ." I explain for the fourth time what I am looking for. I feel like a broken record.

"Does she know about birth control?"

"Apparently not."

"Yes," the young woman replies thoughtfully. "Apparently not, huh?" This strikes her as funny and she laughs. "Well, I could send you some literature on birth control."

"What I need is to find a support group for this girl." Or for me. Ha-ha.

"I could let you bring her in and we could talk to her. Will her parents allow her to be on the Pill? Young girls aren't very reliable with a diaphragm."

"I don't really think we need birth control at the moment. She's pregnant—"

"I don't suppose we should be giving her anything without a parental permission slip. Especially with a twelve-year-old. Would the parents sign a slip?"

"Like I was saying, I'm not sure we need birth control right now."

"How about some literature? Then if they want to investigate it further . . ."

"To be frank, we don't need any birth control now."

"Oh? Oh, I suppose not, huh? Well, what can I do for you?"

"A group?"

"We don't have anything of that sort. Have you called the hospital? I understand a nurse up there has written a simply splendid book. Geared right to that age group."

From the phone book I pick out a priest's name at random, dial, recite my problem.

"Twelve years old, do you say?" He has a kindly voice.

"Yes. And I'm looking for a support group."

"I know of only one. And I don't even know if it's running anymore. Up at the high school. Through the guidance department."

Again I dial the high school guidance counselor. I raise my voice one or two steps and hope he will not recognize me.

"Yes, we do have a group," he tells me. "How old is your daughter?"

"Twelve."

"Twelve? Twelve years old?"

"Yes."

"Oh, I am sorry, but we only accept girls who are sixteen or over."

I sigh, too weary to do otherwise. "But she's still pregnant."

"I'm sorry. But in my opinion twelve would be just too young to be able to cope with the discussions. They're mature discussions."

God Almighty. She'd old enough to get pregnant but not old enough to talk about it? But I don't say that. "You couldn't make an exception? She's a very mature twelve-year-old. She has a high IQ."

"I'm sorry."

One last call. I dial the school nurse, a casual acquaintance. I know she has nothing of this sort going but I hope she can give me some ideas. I must sound desperate because she tells me to slow down.

"Dorothy, I need some suggestions at least."

"You got me stuck."

185

"There has to be a need for such a group in a community this size. More than just for those the high school serves."

She agrees. The problem, she feels, is in Claudia's age, not her pregnancy. No one wants to acknowledge that a young child can and will get pregnant. As in such areas as physical or sexual abuse of children, the issue is too shocking to allow most people to accept it as a problem to be worked on. Maybe if they ignore it, it will go away.

While I understand her philosophy and agree, this will not help Claudia. "So there aren't any groups?" I ask.

"It's just too touchy."

"Couldn't we start something?"

Dorothy laughs. "Yeah. You'd start something all right."

19

I heard the screaming.

I did not think much of it at first. It was morning, about 10:25, and I was helping Bobby Beechinor with his spelling. The three other resource children in the room were playing a game at the worktable. So when the screaming started, I noted it but went back to work.

It stopped a moment. I think. Then resumed and came closer. It was like a siren in the hallway, high and undulating. Bobby now had his head up, cocked to one side to listen. The others paused. Definitely coming down our corridor.

Slam! Something hit against the closed door. Hard. Outside it the wailing continued, although more mutedly.

Bobby gave me a questioning look as I rose to investigate. Cautiously I turned the knob of the door to open it. The door would not move at first, but when I gently put my weight against it, I managed to push it open.

Lori.

Slumped against the other side of the door, both hands locked over the knob, she had slid to the floor, sobbing. Now she remained there, shoved back by the door's opening, squeezed between the wall and the door itself. Only a low, moaning cry came from her.

"Lori? What's wrong?" I was alarmed, my heart up in my throat, nauseating me. "Answer me!"

Abruptly, she bolted to life. Up on her feet, she whizzed past me into the room. Across she went, around the table, between the desks. On the far side by the window were two large built-in cabinets in which I kept art supplies. They were slightly elevated off the floor by two supports running the depth of them. Lori pulled the rug away from the front of one cabinet and deftly slid into the small space under it.

Astonished, I remained half in, half out of the door. What on earth was going on? The resource children were just as astounded. Bobby Beechinor had risen partway from his chair but was frozen in mid-move. Carrie Weems, who had been playing a game at the table, bent down to see under the cabinet.

"Lori?" I walked to the cabinet. Getting down on my hands and knees, I tried to see her. She was there, curled up with her hands protectively over her head. "Lori, what is going on? What's wrong?"

The only response was her soft weeping.

I stood up. The resource kids stared in bewilderment. "Okay, everybody, just leave your stuff for today and go back to your rooms, all right?. We'll pick up from here tomorrow."

"But it's only ten-thirty, Torey," Bobby said.

"Yeah. We're not done with our game."

"I know. But just do as I say, okay? We'll finish another time."

Quietly they collected their belongings. Within moments the room was empty except for Lori and me. I went back to the cabinet and stooped down. She was way back under. I think I could have reached her if I had been intent on it, but I did not try. Her hands remained over her head. The sobbing was still audible, heavy and disconsolate. The sound of a world out of control.

"Lor? It's just me, babe. Everyone else left. Won't you come out now and tell me what's wrong?"

No indication she even heard me.

The door behind me opened. In came Dan Marshall and Edna Thorsen. They paused and looked around the room. I rose.

"She isn't in here? I thought you said she came down here," Dan said to Edna.

"She's here," I said. The sobbing was not audible from that part of the room, and both of them looked perplexed. I pointed. "She's over under the art cabinet."

"Oh Great Scott," Edna muttered and threw her hands up.

Dan pulled his lips back in a grimace.

"I swear," Edna said more to Dan than me, "that girl is as crazy as the day is long. She's going to end up in a nuthouse yet."

"What's going on?" I asked.

"Your guess is as good as anybody's. I think we ought to call up Mental Health and have them come cart her away. I really do, Dan. The girl is certifiably crazy. That's all there is to it."

Dan was watching over my shoulder for any sign of life under the art cabinet. He pulled at his chin thoughtfully with one hand.

"What happened?" I asked again.

"Who knows?" Edna replied. "We were in reading group like any other day of the week. She was with us as usual, and fooling around as usual too. I had just about had it with her and I told her so. And she got all upset. Vomited. All over her dress and the floor and Sandy Latham's new shoes. No warning whatsoever out of a big girl like that. Just

189

sitting there refusing to work like always and whoops! She urps all over us. Then up she bolts and goes screaming out the door like a lunatic. I tell you once and for all, the girl's mad."

Dan was shaking his head. "I'm worried about her."

"And what does she do?" Edna continued. "She comes down here. Well, I naturally thought she was in the girls' rest room. Here I am running up and down the halls chasing after the little stinker. If I hadn't gotten Dan, I probably still would be. I told her she'd get the paddling of her life if she didn't stop tearing up and down the halls screaming like that."

For a brief moment all of us gazed in the direction of the cabinet. I had no idea what to do. In truth I was not even exactly sure I knew what had happened.

"Well, shall we get her out or what?" Dan asked. The question was as much to me as to Edna. Dan was a big man, in his late forties perhaps, and with the sort of gentleness many men about that age seem to have. He appeared genuinely perplexed by this untoward behavior on Lori's part.

"No, wait, Dan. Don't." I put a hand on his sleeve.

He paused.

"Couldn't we just leave her? She's upset, whatever the reason. Let's not aggravate it now."

"Oh, Torey." Edna's voice was heavy with condescension. "Don't play into her so. I know you mean well by Lori, but you just let her wrap you around her little finger sometimes."

"The girl is upset and hiding under my cabinet, for gosh sakes. Whatever reason she thinks she has for doing that, I think she needs to pull herself together before we attack her. She'll get upset all over again if we drag her out."

Edna shrugged. "You're too soft."

I shrugged back.

"Even you have to admit that is not normal behavior,"

Edna said. "That child is not behaving normally. She is definitely . . . what can you say? Disturbed? Even you have to agree with that."

Wearily, I nodded.

"Well, see there?" Edna turned to Dan. "See, even Torey thinks she's crazy. I don't know why they persist in keeping her at this school with normal children. She can't read, she can't write, and now she's nuts. Even Torey with all her degrees can see that. It's time somebody does something about it."

My opportunity. "So let's just leave her here for now. This would be the best place for her anyway, wouldn't it? In here? Let's just all go back about our business and let her be. I'll take care of it later."

Edna tossed up her hands again and turned back to the door. "You can have her. Good riddance. That's what I say. Good riddance to bad rubbish."

The snick of the latch as Dan closed the door behind them was a very finite sound. I looked over my shoulder at the art cabinet. I had not the faintest idea what to do.

"Lor? Lori? Are you all right?" Down on my hands and knees again, I peered under. Releasing the resource kids early had brought me about fifteen minutes in which to talk her out. "Come on, babe, won't you come out and sit with me? We're all alone and nobody's going to hurt you." I came closer so that my forehead was against the edge of the cabinet. I could smell the stale sourness of vomit.

There was no response at all. The crying had stopped and now there was nothing to indicate she was any more alive than the lint under there.

Rising into a sitting position, I pressed my cheek against one knee and felt the rough cloth of my jeans. "Lor? Come on, Lor, come out." Silence. I was feeling terrible, not only because she was so upset but also because I had not seen it coming. This behavior was an earmark of serious problems. Not having wanted to recognize Lori's descent into disturbance, I had waited too long to intervene. And now here we were. I felt awful.

"Listen, Lor, I've got to get up now and do my work. The other kids will be here soon. You can stay there as long as you want, I guess. We won't bother you. Nobody will make you come out. And I'll be here. I won't go away and leave you."

The remainder of the morning went quietly. The resource children did not even know she was there. Lori never stirred.

I did not go down to the teachers' lounge for lunch as was usual. Taking out my peanut butter sandwich, I ate it at the worktable.

Billie, the speech therapist, came into the room about halfway through the period. "Hey, hey, what is this, Hayden?" She laughed in a carefree infectious way. "I was looking all over for you. Weren't you coming down to the Burgerteria with us for the salad bar?"

I loved Billie. She was one of those marvelous, one-of-a-kind people one encounters so rarely. A black woman from South Carolina, she had moved clear across the country to the Northwest almost ten years before, newly divorced, with five kids under twelve and virtually no skills. Those who had said she would never make it, however, did not know Billie. Now with a master's degree in speech therapy nearly completed and three of her five kids in college, she still sought new frontiers. She headed a local program for battered women; she had written a grant for funding of a child-abuse hot line; she was chairwoman of the Mother's March for the March of Dimes. And even with the two dozen things Billie forever had going, she would always manage to make each one of us lucky enough to know her feel like the only person in the world she really cared about.

Yet for all my love of Billie, I could not bring myself to tell her why I sat alone, choking down a dry peanut butter sandwich. For no reason I could identify, I did not want to give Lori away. Even to Billie. So I made some feeble excuse about having to work.

Then the door opened again. Dan Marshall. Billie rolled her eyes. "Here comes Trouble."

Dan was not up to Billie's good humor. Brushing past her he came to me. "Is she still there?"

I nodded.

A long silence followed, uncomfortable because Dan said no more and I could not find any words either. Billie looked from one to the other of us trying to discern the problem.

"Are you just going to leave her there?" he asked. A genuine question, no challenge in it.

"I guess so. She'll come out in time," I said. I hesitated, weighing the advisability of talking in front of Billie. "Dan, what really happened down in Edna's room?"

He shook his head. "I don't know, Tor. I honestly don't."

"Sometimes I don't think she's fit to teach," I said. "She kills some of these kids."

Wearily he shrugged. "I'm sure she was a little hard on Lori, but what can we do? She's going to retire next year anyhow."

Silence again.

"This really concerns me, Torey," he said, jerking his head toward the cabinet. "No joking. I wonder if we shouldn't call someone or something. I really am worried."

"So am I."

We gazed at each other across the expanse of the worktable. Finally Dan nodded and turned. "I'll catch you later. Keep me posted."

"I will."

He left.

Billie's eyes widened. *"Honey*, what is going on?" She sat down in a chair next to me, and I told her.

12:40. Boo arrived first. What was I going to tell the kids? I thought frantically when I saw him. When last I looked,

Lori was still hiding, body drawn up in a fetal position, head hidden.

Like Dan, I was worried. I did not even dare acknowledge how very worried I actually was. What were we going to do? What should we do? Dan wanted to get someone to help. Who? Mental Health? Did they have some brigade that would come out and extract a little girl from under my art cabinet, like firemen rescuing a stranded kitten? I was in a moment of failing faith. I knew the Mental Health people had no answers. Good people, but without answers. How about Lori's father? Would he understand more than we what had happened to his daughter? Cripes. I was lost.

Tomaso came bounding in, a bundle of energy. "Hi, Tor. Hi, Boo." He did a little dance around the worktable and picked up his assignment folder. When Claudia arrived, he hopped in her direction. "Hi, Claud."

A huge pause. Tomaso spun around. "Where's Lori at?" All year long, Lori had never missed a day. Tom spun around again. "Where is she?"

"You want to come over and sit down, please?" I asked.

"Where's Lori?" he persisted.

"That's what we're going to talk about."

Fear darted through his eyes. "What happened to her? Is she sick?"

"Sort of."

It was a hard discussion. Hard solely because I did not know what to say. "Lori's not having a good day today. Something happened in her room and she's very upset."

"But where is she?"

What was I going to say? This was just not coming out right. Letting my shoulders drop, I spread my hands out on the tabletop before me. "This is hard, guys."

They watched me. Their faces were so open, so guileless that I smiled. "I guess she needed to hide a while because she's so upset. She came in here. She's under the art cabinet."

Tomaso and Claudia both turned to look. Then before I could stop him, Tomaso was up from his chair and on his way over.

"Tom!" I shouted. "Get back here and sit down." He stopped in his tracks.

"I just want to see her."

"Sit down. Now listen, I don't want you bothering her. No going over, no peeking under, nor any other way of being trouble. Lori is upset. I want you to just leave her alone."

"Maybe she doesn't want to be left alone," Claudia said.

"I think she does."

"But how do you know?" Tom added. "You're not her."

A heavy sigh. I put my hand over my eyes and rubbed them. The day seemed endless. "I know I'm not. And I don't know. But just trust me for once, would you, and don't give me such a hard time."

The afternoon dragged by. All three children were upset. Claudia kept starting her work and stopping it, whining to me about not being able to understand the assignment when she had been doing the same sorts of problems for days. Every little thing irritated her. Boo was uttering to himself too loudly and too much. Tomaso, when I pressed him for answers on his math, became angry. The minutes loitered by mercilessly.

I honestly thought I would strangle Tomaso as the time progressed. He would not stay in his chair. Up and down, up and down, around and around, nervously pacing back and forth. Down again, up again. He was a tinderbox waiting to be touched off. I feared a major explosion. Yet he would not help me in any way. Every single answer on his math work was wrong, all of them. My own worry was making me impatient. I yelled at Boo because I was afraid to yell at Tomaso, and Boo made the mistake of getting in my way. I finally yelled at everybody.

195

Recess came. I had to get out. My own sanity revolved around leaving that room for the weak March sunshine. Kneeling before the cabinet, I told Lori we were going for recess and would be back. She was sobbing again, or still, I did not know which. Her face was buried in her arms now. A small pool of fluid spread out to one side of her. I could not tell if it was vomit or urine or something else. Again, I told her we were going out. Again, I reassured her we were coming back. Then I left.

That final moment's look under the art cabinet depressed me further: three hours since she had crawled under there and still no sign of change. Edna's diagnosis was all too correct. However Lori had managed to maintain her mental health over these last months, it was gone now. Lori was broken.

I leaned against the wall of the school building and watched the children play. My mind was half a million miles away. At least.

"Tor, can I go use the bathroom?" Tomaso asked. He stood beside me and I had not even noticed him come up. One lank lock of hair hung over his left eye. He shook it back.

"Go ahead."

What was I going to do? What if the school day ended and she still did not come out? I would have to pull her out. *Oh Lori.* I was feeling very guilty. I should have seen this coming. There were the little changes in her: the breakdown last fall, the slow deterioration in her ability to cope with even mild competition. Why hadn't I faced it? Why had I let it go on? I knew better. I had been in the business too long for such foolishness. *Oh Lori, I'm sorry.*

Brusquely I was brought back to the real world by Boo throwing a ball against the wall next to me. I looked at my watch. The recess period was almost over. "Where's Tomaso?" I called to Claudia.

"I don't know. He went in and never came out."

196

"Oh geez. Watch Boo a minute, would you? I'll be right back."

I trotted into the building, half afraid my carelessness had cost me another kid. "Tom?" I whispered into the boys' rest room. "Tomaso?" Then on down to the classroom.

There he was. Legs crossed, sitting on the floor, bent forward so that his chest was between his knees, almost flat on the linoleum, he looked like a yoga master. He spoke softly into the space under the art cabinet.

Irritation frothed up in me and I grabbed him by the shirt collar. "Tomaso, get up off that floor this instant! I mean it. I told you to leave her alone and I wasn't kidding. Now get up and get over to your chair and sit down before I really get mad. And don't you move until I get the others. I mean it. Don't you move an inch!"

Because I knew he had been explosive all afternoon, I half expected him to come back at me in full force, to be as angry as I was. In fact, I was in such bad humor by that time, I was almost picking a fight with him. Worry and fear had made me senselessly short-tempered and I wanted blood. It was the only thing that would release the tension built up inside.

Instead, Tomaso burst into tears.

"Oh good God, Tom," I muttered at him and left to get the other children.

When we returned he was still sitting in his chair, just as I had commanded. His tears had stopped but when he saw me, they started all over again. "I was just trying to make her feel better. I wasn't hurting nothing. Honest."

There was Claudia standing beside me. "Can't we even talk to her?"

"Sit down. All of you, just sit."

Claudia drew up a chair. Boo sat on the table itself.

"Now look, this is a hard time. I'm not in a good mood myself. I'm just as worried and scared as you are. And I

197

want to help Lori just as much. But nothing will work out if you drive me crazy first."

"This sure isn't much of a democracy," Claudia muttered.

"Right now it isn't."

Tomaso blubbered, like some damn little kid. His voice went way up in a howl. "But she needs me!"

I melted. Worry was making us all a little goofy. Slumping into a chair across the table from him, I covered my eyes with one hand. Finally, spreading my fingers a little, I looked at him. He was watching me. Snot ran over his upper lip. His cheeks glistened. I had to smile.

"You foolish kid, you're going to be the end of me yet."

The last twenty minutes of school Tomaso sat on the floor in front of the cabinet and talked to Lori. I could not hear what he was saying most of the time; some of it was not even in English.

Dan Marshall came by. He stuck his head in the door and when I saw him I went over and slipped outside into the hall.

"How's it going?"

I shook my head.

"I think we're going to have to call her father to come get her," he said. "This has gone on too long."

I had a terrible sinking feeling in the pit of my stomach. Mr. Sjokheim was such a good man. I hated to return his daughter to him in this condition. Yet she needed more than we seemed to be able to give her. I nodded. "I guess so."

"Okay," Dan replied, turned and went down the hall, leaving me alone.

After the dismissal bell, I leaned against the door frame and watched down the corridor. I did not know how soon Dan would be able to get Mr. Sjokheim to come. Finally, I went back into the room and closed the door.

198

Alone. The classroom was heavy with undispelled tension. Going over to the cabinet, I sat down and leaned forward to look under. Lori had never moved. The space beneath was warm and humid and reeked of sickness and urine. Quietly, I went to the sink and dampened a washcloth. Then I returned.

"Lori? Can you hear me? It's time to come out now."

She was no longer crying or making any other noise. There was no response to my words.

"Lor? Come on now. Come on, love. Please? Everyone is gone. It's just you and me."

No sound.

"Love?"

I sat in silence and watched her. Beyond the window a cold March rain slapped the pane. Afternoon darkness surrounded me.

"Your daddy is coming to take you home, sweetheart. School's over already. It's time to go home."

Silence.

I found myself rocking. Legs crossed, arms folded, I rocked back and forth. A lulling motion. I could understand why Boo enjoyed it. For a moment or two I closed my eyes. The day had been far harder on me than I had realized. My muscles were quivering in the same way they did some days before dinner when I had eaten poorly at lunch.

"Lori. Loooori. Lori-Lori-Lori," I said. It became a little song toward the end. Rather tuneless, but a gentle little song. Comforting. "Lori. Lori-girl, where are you? Lori-Lori-Lori."

I began to sing to her. Sang as I watched the clock, the minutes slipping by. Sang to the tune of whatever came into my head. Nursery rhymes, television commercials, hymns, folk songs. Sang them with her name and whatever other words fit. All the time I rocked myself back and forth to soothe my own fears.

A small sound came from under the cabinet.

"Lori, Lori, Lori's coming out," I sang to the tune of "Hark, the Herald Angels Sing."

A shuffling. Her head appeared. The small space under the cabinet was forcing her to come out on her belly, like a snake crawling. I kept singing. She slithered out, and without even rising up from her stomach, she pushed herself forward until she could lay her head in my lap. With a tremendous sigh, she sank down again and closed her eyes.

I sang. She was still on her stomach, her head on my crossed legs, her hands clutching the cloth of my jeans. All her hair was damp, whether from urine or vomit or sweat, I did not know. She looked like some newly hatched creature emerged from an egg. Gently I took the washcloth, now long gone cold, and wiped her face. Still I continued singing, my voice sounding foreign and far-off to my ears.

When I finally ran out of tunes and my throat went dry, a total silence dropped down on us, but for all its vastness it was not uncomfortable. I stroked her hair, the soft skin of her face.

The clock read nearly four. I wondered when Mr. Sjokheim was coming, what I would say to him when he did. Lori never moved from her position on the floor with her head in my lap. Her eyes were still closed, her fingers white from gripping my knees.

"How you doing, Lor?" I whispered. "Are you okay?"

No answer.

I reached down and lifted her up. She fell heavily against me as I cradled her in my arms. A powerful feeling swept over me, maternal, instinctual, raw. It clutched at the deep, most secret parts of me with a savage, almost sexual force. The sensation was too primitive to be called an emotion and it overwhelmed me with a desire to protect her.

"I wet my pants," she whispered into my shirt.

"It doesn't matter, love."

Outside, March rain had turned to snow. The room was dim. Lori began to cry, almost noiselessly.

"Hush, hush, baby," I put my face down until I could feel her warm, wet skin against my cheek. "I love you, Lor, and we're going to get out of this. You'll see. I won't ever let anything happen that we can't handle. I won't ever let there be such a time."

And still she cried.

20

I was completely beyond any feelings by the time I reached my car in the parking lot that evening. Absolutely every ounce of energy was used up. Snow continued to fall, really more of a solid rain now than snow, leaving a slush on the roads. Although it was not even five yet, late winter dusk had combined with the storm clouds to make it almost as dark as night. The trauma of the day had drained me, but, as so often happened after a rough day, I was filled with a crawly restlessness. Going home to a dark house, supper from a can and the boob tube just would not do it for me tonight. Instead, I turned the car down a side street and headed for the highway.

I loved to drive. The faint vibration under my fingers as I held the steering wheel was an intoxicant. Out on the highway I went through all the turns and twists, dips and rises of the hilly farm country near town. There was little traffic on this inclement evening. The cold air had settled into the valleys, and when I climbed higher, I left the snow behind to drive in a misty spring rain. About eight miles out of town I turned off onto a gravel road that led toward the mountains. Rolling down the windows on both sides of the car, I let the cool night air pour in around me.

There were no thoughts in my mind as I drove. Only the misty cold made an impression. That and the dark road ahead. The heaviness of the afternoon dissipated into the rain, and I was left with a giddy, almost lighthearted calmness. Still I drove.

At almost 7:30 I looked at my watch for the first time since leaving school. I had gone clear up the road into the mountains, swerving around narrow, gravelly curves pockmarked with mudholes from the rain, and down the other side into a small town about 60 miles away, 74, if one took the highway on the flatlands. On the way through town, I pulled into a drive-in. I still was not hungry, but my head hurt from not eating. After reading over a weather-beaten menu painted on the wall, I settled on a hot fudge sundae, a true extravagance since it cost as much as a hamburger and fries would have. In a burst of sheer, self-indulgent reverie, I sat on a small, white, paint-peeled picnic table in the cold rain and savored every bite.

Still I did not think of the day. I was even aware of not thinking about it, viewing the entire thing in an abstract way, as if it had happened to someone else. I climbed back in my car and drove home.

"Where the hell have you been?" Joc was standing silhouetted in the doorway between the garage and the kitchen. His hands were on his hips.

"Driving."

"Driving? What the fuck? Do you know what night this is? Where the hell is your head?"

"Jocco, calm down, would you?"

"Calm down? You know what night this is? This is

Carol and Jerry's anniversary. We were supposed to be at their house two hours ago."

Oh geez. I slammed the door to the car and came on in the house. Apologetically I smiled. "Oh well."

"Oh well?"

"Cripes, Joc, do you have to repeat everything I say?"

"Oh well? Is that all you have to say for yourself, oh well? Honestly, Torey, Carol fixed a whole goddamned dinner for us. And here you are off on some toot. For four and a half fucking hours. Is that all you have to say for yourself?"

"Holy Toledo, Jocco, will you lay off me? *Jesus!*"

We were arguing in the kitchen, still. I had not even taken off my coat. Joc stomped into the living room and I followed.

"If you want to know the truth, I had a hell of a day. My whole class is falling apart. One of my kids went right off the deep end. I should have seen it coming but I didn't and I feel like hell. I had to get out. You wouldn't have wanted me at any party anyhow."

"Oh get off your God trip for once. You're not so goddamn important at that job."

I glared at him.

Joc's eyes narrowed and he regarded me for a long moment. "You know what your problem is? You live in dreams. You live your entire life in the world of could-be instead of the world that is. That sounds pretty for some fucking poster but it makes piss-poor living in real life."

"Somebody's got to live that way, Joc."

"Sure. And maybe it's you. But I for one do not want to spend the rest of my days with a hopeless bunch of crazy people. Maybe you do. Maybe you want to wallow away your entire life like that, but I don't." He went to the coat closet and grabbed up his coat. He yanked it on. "I just hope your dreams are enough to keep you warm because nothing else is going to, the way you live. Your muse is going to be all the company you'll get."

And then he was gone.

Standing in the middle of the living room floor, I simply stared at the closed door. I felt nothing other than my beating heart. We had had arguments before, plenty of them. But this one was different.

This one, I knew, was the last.

21

Lori was not in school the next day. I think I had known she would not be. Still some little place inside me had held hope that all of this had been no more than a bad dream. But 12:40 arrived and Lori didn't.

The children were subdued. Boo was totally perplexed by Lori's absence. He kept rising from his chair and going to the door to look out. When he could see nothing in the corridor, he would walk around the room searching, his small, dark face wrinkled in confusion.

"Now what letter is this? What letter is this?" he would call over and over as he wandered. For the first time it occurred to me that phrase may have been a code for Lori. Such irony. Even Boo had Lori confused with reading.

Tomaso was frightened. "Where is she? What happened to her? Why isn't she here?" he asked constantly. Nothing I said satisfied him. Nor would he leave me alone in other ways. He wanted to be physically close, sitting on my side of the table, standing next to me at recess, remaining within a few feet of me all afternoon.

Only Claudia seemed to maintain any sort of normalcy. Indeed, she became my support. Without my request she managed Boo when Tomaso demanded too much time. She collected work folders, passed them out, picked them up, checked Tomaso's math.

After recess, after we had completed a modicum of routine work, I suggested we all go sit in the reading corner and I would read aloud for a while. We had been deep into *The Wind in the Willows* over the past week anyhow, and I thought a few extra chapters might take our minds off things.

As we sat down, Tomaso took the pillow Lori normally used and pushed it over to the side. Boo suddenly sprang to his feet. "Ah! Ah! Ah!" he shrieked at Tomaso. Then snatching the pillow up he ran to the door. "Ah-ah-ah!" he cried and pounded on the glass. "What letter is this? What letter is this? Ah! Ah! Aaaaaaaaah!" He turned back to us. There were tears on his cheeks, the first I ever recalled seeing. "Hello, little boy," he said in a high falsetto. "Hello, little boy. You're a nice boy, Boo. You're a nice boy anyway."

"Are you worried about Lori, Boo?" I asked. I tried to reassure him that she was okay, but he took no notice of my words.

Next Boo ran across the room to his cubby. Out flew a basket of counting beads. Down fell the box of disposable diapers. He scattered bits and pieces of various learning materials as he dug through the contents. Then up it came, in one hand held high over his head, the little booklet of pictures Lori had made him for Valentine's Day. Boo ran back to the table with it.

He was very much alert, no longer floating in inner space as usual, leaving us with just the shell of a little boy. Tears still flowed down his face, although there was no other

207

indication he was crying. Flattening the booklet out on the tabletop with slow, precise motions, he turned the pages.

"Doggie," he said determinedly. He looked up at us. Leaving the table he came over to me in the reading corner and grabbed my arm. Yanking me after him, he returned to the book. He held my arm by the wrist and thunked it against the picture. "Doggie. Doggie. What letter is this?" he asked in the lilting, stylized manner that always characterized that phrase.

The page turned. "Kitty. What letter is this? Kitty." He looked up at me. Then back at the booklet. Every page he went through in the same fashion.

All of this for Lori? I did not know. Perhaps it was. Perhaps the stress had provided enough pressure to trigger some synapse in his brain. There was no way of telling. Even after six months I did not understand Boo well enough to know.

Claudia and Tomaso sat spellbound. Neither said a thing. When he failed to communicate with me, Boo went over to Claudia. I thought he was going to drag her over too, but as he reached for her arm, he stopped midway. He looked at her, stared, as if it were the first time he was really seeing her. Straightening up, he put his hands out and touched her hair on either side of her face, lightly, as a hairdresser might do. His forehead was furrowed as he studied her. Again he touched her face, her hair. "What letter is this?" he asked.

Then he turned and came back to me at the table. Taking up the booklet he paged through it, dropped it, leaned forward on the tabletop, both hands flat, and gazed from one to the other of us. A real little boy was in there behind those eyes; he was seeing us. Desperately, I wished I knew what he wanted.

Boo looked around the room. Slowly, as if the decision had taken much thought, he walked over to the rocking chair. Reaching out, he set it in motion. Then before I knew what he was doing, he removed all his clothes. I was

208

startled. Months had passed since he had done that. Still, there was a difference this time. No silly laughter, no running. He just stood and slipped the clothes off. When he was totally undressed, he climbed in the chair and began to rock.

"What's he doing?" Claudia whispered.

"I don't know."

"B-I-N-G-O," he sang in a clear, light voice. "B-I-N-G-O, and Bingo was his name-o."

"Ooh, this is eerie," Claudia said. She took hold of my arm. "This is like 'The Twilight Zone.'"

Boo looked over at us. When he saw me he smiled. A very soft, angelic smile, as if he had come a long distance and was genuinely glad to see me. He lifted one hand and waved slightly. "B-I-N-G-O, B-I-N-G-O, and Bingo was his name-o."

I honestly did not know what to do.

Then Boo solved the matter for me. Although he was singing still, he raised one hand up and fluttered it at the overhead light. The song died away on his lips; he became absorbed in the motion of his hand. I had waited too long. Boo was no longer with us.

Lori did not come the next day either. I had tried to call her father the previous night but there was no answer. Dan Marshall had also tried. None of us on the staff spoke of Lori. Edna and I would run into one another in the hall or the office or the lounge and up would come a façade of pleasure at seeing the other. Talk would go on about seasons and Easter and all manner of nonsense. No talk of Lori. Dan was not much better. He and I spoke of her every time we met, but it was passed between us lightly as one does the weather, idle conversation. I do not know what we were all waiting for. Answers, I guess.

I recognized her. At least I thought I did. Seeing her brought up a nagging recognition, like one has during waking hours when one comes across something remembered from a dream. Her hair was dark and short in a Dutch bob, the way children in my mother's childhood wore their hair. Thin-rimmed, round glasses gave her an owlish look and all about her was the aura of another time.

Coming clear across the room to my desk without speaking, she halted at the corner of it and gave me a thorough looking over. "My name's Libby. I'm Lori's sister."

They were identical twins. Or so the charts said. I am not certain I would have placed her as Lori's sister, much less her identical twin. This child, so solemn behind her thick, round glasses, had none of the effervescence that meant Lori to me. She looked as if she shouldered the entire world.

"What can I do for you, Libby."

"I come to get my sister's homework."

"Oh." We regarded one another. "How is your sister?"

"She ain't coming back."

"Tomorrow?"

"Ever."

"Oh?" I said.

Libby nodded.

"Whose decision is that?"

"Hers."

"I see."

"But my dad told me to pick up her homework anyway." She tilted her head and the bangs and dark, straight hair fell sideways. "You're not so pretty," she said. "My sister said you were."

On Thursday, after Lori had been absent three days, Mr. Sjokheim came to school. "I don't know what I'm going to do with her," he told me as we waited for Edna and Dan. "I honestly don't. She won't even look at the work Libby brings home for her. She makes herself sick with worry about coming back. I know it isn't right to let her stay home, but what am I going to do?"

The meeting was grim. Early into it Dan suggested that Lori might need serious psychiatric intervention, most likely an inpatient evaluation. Heavy-duty stuff. There were no facilities of that kind in our community. The nearest were at the university where Lori had been taken for her neurological workup. After this suggestion Mr. Sjokheim kept trying to come up with alternatives. "Couldn't we do this instead? Couldn't we try that?" A dozen suggestions, many of them ludicrous, the ideas of a man who had no way to turn.

When we came to talk of Lori's behavior in school before the breakdown, Edna seemed obsessed with pointing out all Lori's little quirks: Her inability to do the work, her disruptiveness, her hyperactivity, her million other failures. Edna made Lori sound far worse than I had ever perceived her as being. It all painted a very bleak picture.

I did not know what to say. The things Edna spoke of were not altogether untrue. Lori did not get along well in the classroom. Undeniably her behavior in many ways was that of a disturbed child. It had been on other occasions; it certainly was now. She needed help. But that wasn't the real issue. Who the hell did we think we were fooling here? Had we really convinced ourselves that what had happened to Lori was her fault? Were we that blind?

It was not Lori. It was us. Dan, me, Edna, the entire stupid school system. We were responsible, not Lori. Was it maladjustment to give up? When you are physically incapable of doing something and have tried for three years to do it anyhow, are you crazy because you cannot take the pressure anymore? If Lori had been blind or deaf or without arms we would be brutes for bludgeoning her into a breakdown, but because she had a disability no one could see, we were able to put the blame on her. And we could sit here guiltlessly and do what professionals are so good at doing: playing God.

I felt physically ill. Perhaps the ethics of the matter would not have bothered me so much if the child had been someone besides Lori—Lori, my carer, who had already achieved the authentic goal of any form of learning: humaneness.

I am not an especially courageous person in many ways. I wish that I were. I was in a business sorely needing courage. I wish I could have said right then and there what I was thinking. At least I wish I had had the courage to get up and leave and no longer be a party to the proceedings. But my mouth would not open; my feet would not move. There would have to be another time for me to act. Thus, in the meeting while Dan and Edna talked, I sat mute and died a coward's death.

Mr. Sjokheim was also silent while they spoke. His eyes were clear and gentle, a soft hazel color. After each one of Edna's recitations he would nod. Never once did he offer any defense, any comment at all. Then Edna said she thought Lori was too deeply disturbed a child for the regular classroom. She needed some other kind of placement.

Mr. Sjokheim dropped his head and brought a hand to his face. I knew immediately that he was going to cry, and I was overcome by that horrid discomfort that always comes with seeing an adult cry. I rose to grab the tissue box from the window ledge.

"I'm sorry, I'm sorry," he kept apologizing for his tears. "It's just that I don't know what to do."

"That's all right," Dan said. "I know this must be hard to discuss."

We sat in silence and felt Mr. Sjokheim's humiliation.

Desperately, I tried to unglue my recreant tongue. It would not loosen. Finally, as Mr. Sjokheim regained control and sat with a shredded tissue in his hands, Dan wound up the meeting, saying that regardless of the alternatives we decided on for Lori, it was imperative that she get back into school immediately. Otherwise we courted adding school phobia to her other problems.

I asked Mr. Sjokheim to stay when the others had gone. All I had in the cupboard was instant hot chocolate. So I warmed water with an immersion coil in an empty mayonnaise jar, and we sat together drinking lumpy cocoa from Styrofoam cups.

We did not talk much. I had wanted to ask him how Lori was; I had wanted to know if he had found out from her what really had gone on in Edna's room that morning; I wanted to reassure him that I did not believe Lori was as unsalvageable as we had made her sound. However, the words could not be found. So we just passed small things back and forth between us. He was still on the verge of tears; I could hear them in his voice. The desire to touch him was almost overwhelming. I did not always realize how much I depended on touch to communicate. But social propriety kept me from it. And since I could not start to communicate with him in that manner, I never managed to start at all.

"Listen," I said at last, "it's all going to work out. We'll get things straightened around."

"Will we?"

"I think so."

He shrugged and stared into the empty white cup.

"But Dan was right about one thing. We *have* to get her back in school. No one can help her when she isn't here. And every day she stays home will only make it harder to come back."

213

"I don't know if I can do it," he said.
"We have to."
He nodded. "Okay. I'll try."

But of course Friday came and Lori was not in school.

22

Libby arrived as usual on Monday afternoon to pick up Lori's homework. It did not matter that I had told her the first night that Lori did not have any from this room. She came every night anyway.

A week had passed since the incident had taken place. My afternoon class was nearly back to normal despite Lori's absence. Routine was taking over.

Opening the door, Libby marched across the classroom to where I worked at the table. She was later than usual. It was almost quarter of four. I had assumed she had finally gotten the message and was not coming. Apparently, however, she had just gone home to change clothes because now she wore overalls and a shirt and I had only seen her in dresses before.

"I come to pick up my sister's homework."

I smiled. "Still don't have any for her."

Libby gazed at me intently. She had her short hair parted on the side and a red bow tied in it. More than ever she

215

looked like an escapee from the Depression era. Giving a swipe at her bangs and pushing up her glasses, she watched me.

"How is Lori?" I asked.

"Okay."

"We miss her. Is she coming back to school tomorrow?"

"Nope."

"No?"

"Told you once. She ain't never coming back."

We regarded one another. "Never? That's a long time to wait for her."

Libby did not reply. She was the strangest child. I felt unnatural in her presence. She continued to inspect me the way she always did. Her ability to maintain eye contact was uncanny.

She made no effort to leave, so finally I pushed out a chair with my foot for her to sit down. She did.

"Tell me, Libby, what kinds of things do you like to do?" I asked, desperate to break the silence.

"Play."

"Oh? Play what sorts of things?"

"Dolls."

"Mmm. Sounds fun. Do you have a special doll?"

"Yes."

"What's your doll's name?"

"No name."

"Just call her 'baby,' I suppose? I used to do that."

"I don't call it anything. It's just a doll."

"Oh."

Great conversation. If I had not heard her before, I would not have guessed she had a multisyllable vocabulary. I raised my eyes from my work to see her studying me. As always. The damn kid was driving me mad. So silent, so self-possessed, so very different from Lori.

Libby watched me as I worked on my children's charts. She seemed content just to sit there staring, not the least ill

216

at ease. After that futile period of small talk, I decided to go ahead and work without talking. I sort of hoped she would leave.

She did not.

I looked up. Again the exchange of long, appraising stares. Shutting the logbook, I sat back. "Libby," I said, "I need to know something. Maybe you can help me."

That steady gaze.

"Do you know what happened to Lori in Mrs. Thorsen's room last week?"

"She ain't coming back to school."

"Yes, I know. But do you know why?"

"Yes."

A little silence. She shifted in her chair and the large red bow bounced.

"Will you tell me?"

No reply.

"I really need to know, Libby. I can't help Lori without knowing what happened to her, and she just hasn't told anyone."

"Lori never tells people secret stuff. Me, I don't either."

"But she told you."

"That's different. We're twins. We tell each other everything that happens to us."

"Lib, Lori needs more help than just you can give her. She needs some grown-ups in on this too."

"Me and Lori, we're the only real family we got. Even our dad, he's adopted."

I smiled. "Yes, I know. I know a lot of things already. But I need to know more."

For the first time Libby hesitated and looked away. She studied the bulletin board. "You know what I done once?" she said softly.

"What's that?"

"I spit at her."

"At whom? Lori?"

217

"At that old lady. I spit at her. Then at recess I told her I was going to the bathroom and then I went in her room instead and spit on her desk."

"What old lady is that?"

"Mrs. Thorsen."

"Mmm."

A long pause.

Libby leaned forward intently, folding her arms on the table. "I'll tell you what she done to Lori." Her small face was close to mine and for the first time I could see the resemblance to her sister in her eyes.

"She was making her read. She told Lori to stand up in front of the whole reading group. You know, all the Ravens. Even Robby Johnson was watching and he can read better than practically anybody in the whole first grade. Even me. And she told Lori to read. She gave her big books with the hard backs on them like I got and I'm in the very best reading group. Well, Lori can't read them. And everybody laughed. They didn't never used to laugh at Lori but now they do. So that old lady kept giving her babier and babier books and kept telling her what was the matter that she couldn't read them. And even when she got right down to the book Lori sort of can read, Lori was too scared to do it right. Everybody just laughed at her and she was crying. But Mrs. Thorsen wouldn't let her sit down. She said she was gonna teach Lori good. So Lori threw up. She made Lori throw up in front of the whole class and she didn't even say she was sorry."

"Is that what really happened?" I asked.

"Cross my heart and hope to die! You can ask anybody. Ask Nancy Shannon or Mary Ann Marks or anybody. Ask Robby Johnson even. He's a Cub Scout and he never lies to anybody. You just ask him and he'll tell you!"

Libby's eyes were ablaze. Her small mouth was set. "I hate her. And someday I'm going to spit right in her face. I mean it, I will."

Ah, here was a good hater, if I had ever seen one. The disgust was vivid in her dark eyes.

"Lori isn't stupid," she said. "She's just as smart as anybody. She just can't read 'cause she got hurt once."

I nodded. "I know."

Libby sat back and the intensity of the conversation relaxed a little. "Lori isn't ever coming back. I don't think she should have to."

"Well, I differ from you there. I think she has to. But we need to change things for her."

"Yeah. I think somebody ought to run over Mrs. Thorsen with a car."

I regarded this child. What things hate does. And at such an early age.

We talked a little longer but the conversation was less vigorous. Eventually Libby fell back into monosyllables. The hands of the clock had moved around to almost 4:30, and I wanted to go home. The lesson plans were still unfinished so I opened the plan book and bent over them. Libby watched.

"I need to finish these," I explained. "I haven't a lot more time to talk."

"That's okay." She made no effort to move.

"Won't your father be worried when you're gone so long?"

"No. My dad ain't home yet. And I told the baby-sitter I was going to my ballet lesson."

"Oh?"

"Yeah, I got my leotard on under this, see?" She unbuckled her overalls to show me.

"Well, I don't mean to make you feel unwelcome, but it's getting kind of late for me and I need to get my work done before I can go home."

She smiled. "That's okay. I don't mind."

I went ahead with what I was doing. Libby sat quietly and watched me.

At 4:45 I closed the plan book and carried it over to my desk. I hesitated before turning. "It's time to go home, Libby."

Still she sat. Her back was to me; she had a hand up twisting her hair. No effort to get up.

"Libby?"

She turned.

"It's time to go, honey."

She continued to sit there. Continued to stare, to twist her hair. Her brow was slightly creased as if I had spoken to her in a foreign language and she did not quite understand what I had said. She tilted her head, a characteristic I was coming to know in her, and the dark hair fell sideways. I went to the closet to get my jacket.

"Teacher?"

"Yes?"

"Is she always going to be like this?"

"What do you mean, Libby?" Carrying my jacket, I came back to the table. For the first time I was aware of how young she looked.

"Is Lori always going to be this way?"

She was such a storybook child. The dark, straight Dutch-bobbed hair, the big ribbon on one side, blue denim overalls over a plaid shirt (and leotards). In the beginning the eerie long-ago quality had put me off. Now as I looked at her I was afraid I would never be able to look at her fully enough to remember her. She was too transient. Like a dream. Or a memory.

"I mean," Libby started and then stopped. I think I heard tears behind her voice, although I could tell this was a girl mostly without tears. She cleared her throat. "I mean, Lori really is bad. Badder than I think sometimes people know. She just can't do anything. Even baby books with just letters in them, like I could read two whole years ago. Lori can't even do that. And she can't really write her own

220

name. She can't even tie her shoes. She really, really is bad."

My heart ached for her, the abruptness of it making my breath catch. This is too much to worry about, I thought, when you aren't even eight.

Putting my jacket on the table, I again sat down with her. Libby dropped her head. She examined her hands. In the stark classroom light I could see her trembling slightly. Then she looked at me. *"Is* Lori retarded, Teacher?"

What a hard question that must have been to ask after risking so much to defend Lori. Yet apparently even Libby was suspicious that that might be the truth.

I was momentarily without words. When I did not answer immediately, Libby rose from her seat. Her face was anxious. Perhaps she took my silence for an affirmation of her own fears. I was afraid she was going to run.

"Libby, don't go. Sit down with me, love." I reached a hand out to her.

Libby stayed in her spot half a step beyond my fingers. "But *is* she, Teacher?"

I shook my head. "No, she isn't." I rose to get hold of her as she stood trembling and to bring her back. With an arm around her shoulder, I sat down again in the small chair. "I think you know her problems. Probably better than all the rest of us because the two of you have been together all along. She has brain damage. That isn't retardation. That's a kind of sore on her brain that makes it hard for her to learn the way you and I do. But from what I've read, the doctors say that maybe someday she will read. Maybe not ever so well as you do, but as she gets older and her brain learns new ways of doing things, maybe she will, some."

Libby's shoulders sagged. She leaned very slightly against me so that I could feel the merest shadow of her weight. Bringing a hand up, she rubbed her nose. She acknowledged nothing that I said.

"But Lori isn't retarded, Lib. You're the very rightest person to defend her on that account. Because there's nothing wrong with Lori's mind. Look how good she is at other things. Like math. When she doesn't need to write it down, she's a whiz. And more important, a lot more important, look how good Lori is with people. We have a little boy in here who can't even talk at all and Lori's very special with him. She understands people better than almost anyone I've ever met. She reads hearts like you and I read books, and Libby, that's far better than anything they teach in school."

A long and heavy silence. Libby was taking in deep, slow breaths. With my arm around her, I had her as close as I dared.

"How come it happened to her? How come there's nothing wrong with me?"

"No one knows those things, love. All we do is guess."

"My dad said her head was broke. He said it showed in the pictures they took."

I nodded. "I heard that too."

Libby's head was still down, her eyes narrowed as if she were studying something on the floor. Light as a breath, her hand came up to my shoulder. Even as it rested there, I could hardly feel it. "I know how it happened." Her voice was soft and flat. "My father, my real father, he used to hit Lori a lot. My mother hit us too. But my father, he had this stick thing. He did it when we were bad." A pause. "And I guess we were bad a lot. He hit Lori more than me though. Sometimes he hit her so much she'd just lay there and wouldn't even cry anymore. No matter how much I'd shake her."

Libby took down her hand. She ran her fingers along the skin of her other arm. "Once my father broke my arm. My mother wrapped it up with a pillowcase but it hurt so much I cried. And I couldn't stop. So she had to take me to the doctor. My father told me I better never tell how it got broke. I better tell them I fell down the stairs. And we didn't even have any stairs at our house. But he told me that. So I did it. And once he tied me to my bed too." She sighed wearily and shook her head. I was so scared then."

Libby looked at me. "You know what? I still sometimes dream about my old home and wake up scared. Sometimes I'm even crying. I'm always afraid maybe they might find where I live and come and take me back." She chewed her lower lip. "Sometimes in the daytime I sort of miss them. You know, I sort of draw these little pictures about them. But not at night. When I get out of those dreams I can't ever go back to sleep the whole rest of the night. It gives me a bad headache and makes me sick to my stomach. Daddy has to come in and sit with me." She paused. "I don't know if Lori remember that. She never tells me."

"You know, don't you, that that would never happen," I said. "Your daddy would never let anybody take you away from him. He loves you. You're his little girls now and he wouldn't let you go. No matter what you did or anything else. That would never happen. And you tell Lori that."

She nodded. "I know that. Sometimes I know it. . . . But sometimes, well, you sort of forget."

Her eyes were on my face then, her beautiful long-ago eyes. "I bet my father did it," she said. "I bet it was him that wrecked Lori so she can't read or anything."

"We don't know those things. We'll never know."

"I do," she said with no emotion. "And when I'm big, I'm going to find him. I'm going to get a big knife and I'm going to find him and I'm going to stab him right in the belly. I'm going to kill him. I will. You just see. I'm going to kill him for what he done to Lori. And me. And there won't be anybody who's going to stop me either."

Nothing I could say to that. Seven years old and the cycle of destruction and abuse had already been passed on to her. And the hate.

We sat in silence. Then Libby looked up at the clock. "I

223

gotta go. My ballet lesson got over at five o'clock. I'm going to get in trouble for being gone so long."

"May I give you a ride home?"

She shook her head and moved away. "I like to walk."

"All right." I pulled on my jacket. Libby headed for the door. "Lib?"

She paused and turned.

"Bye."

She gave an odd jerk of her shoulders, almost a shrug, and a tightness across her lips I could hardly call a smile. "Good-bye."

23

The house was dark and cold when I got home. Every night some small spirit in me kindled that Joc would be there waiting when I arrived. Every night the house was empty.

A week now for him too. He had left and there had been no more. No phone calls, no notes, no nothing. He had not even come back to get his records. I knew the night it happened that was going to be the way it was. I think I always knew it would end that way. Yet something within me kept hope. I did not take down the pictures. I did not package up the records to send. I did not pull the bolt lock to prevent entry with a key. Just in case.

I congratulated myself on handling his leaving well. No crying. No depression. No desperate, humiliating calls. He had walked out. It was over. Just as I knew all along it would be. I complimented myself on remaining rational and dignified, on understanding and accepting it.

But I knew I hadn't. I could not lock out the emptiness

he had left in his wake. I did not know what to do with myself. The deal at school had so absorbed me that I was eating, sleeping and dreaming Lori Sjokheim. With no way at home to diffuse my thoughts, I walked around haunted. Nothing could reduce the nagging restlessness.

Also, I discovered, Joc had completely taken care of my social life. I had not realized that until now, as I sat night after night alone. Certainly I had never been a social butterfly. My world had always been confined to a small circle of friends and my colleagues at work. But since I started dating Joc, even those few close friends had either drifted away or were his. I was left stranded.

Billie rescued me over the weekend when she invited me to dinner Saturday night. For survival lessons, she told me. "Oh, just like me when I was divorced," she said with a flap of one hand. Her voice still carried the low burr of South Carolina. "Never knew they were all his friends until then. Never want just a woman on her own."

"Well, it's not that exactly. It's . . . well, I don't know. I guess we just never had any friends collectively. Just acquaintances and places Joc liked to go to have a good time."

Another flap of her hand as she threw meat into the pot for stew. "Don't worry about it, honey. Men! Who needs 'em?"

Well, for one person, me.

It was a very hard time, I had to admit that, even without the outward trappings of distress. I needed someone in my life on a daily basis. Joc had been right about one thing: My muse was not warm enough in itself. I needed people too much. This, of course, raised the age-old question my family always kept fresh for me: Why not marry? Why not indeed. I picked up a pillow off the couch and threw it with all my might at the wall. And why didn't the rest of life have easy answers?

* * *

What were we going to do with Lori? Libby's account of what had happened in Edna's room was not far from what I had guessed. I knew Edna well enough. And I knew Lori.

Edna would not admit defeat. She saw nothing amiss in her behavior, and unfortunately there was little anyone could do about it. She was an old, tenured battle horse. The bureaucracy of the school system would be on her side all down the line, if for no other reason than that she was in her last year of teaching, and by the time the officials got geared up, she'd be through. Thus, to challenge her on the inhumanity of her treatment of Lori and undoubtedly of other children in the class would be quixotic.

I did discuss the matter once or twice with her as diplomatically as I could, but they were futile discussions. I always ended up feeling worse afterward than when I started them.

Behind the intellectual reasons for not pursuing the issue was my own lack of courage. Edna intimidated me. I was never sure exactly why; the issue was complex. There were superficial reasons. I disliked arguments. I did not like people to be angry with me and sometimes I placated them just to keep peace. I was vulnerable to emotional con games that emphasized my youth or my past mistakes. And there were deeper reasons; the ones I did not fully understand. Edna and I were universes apart in our thinking. She was completely ignorant of what I was saying and what I was trying to do. My beliefs had no meaning within her teaching career. Yet I knew that I had as little comprehension of her side as she did of mine. My age, my lack of experience sat as vultures on my shoulder. How *did* I know I was right? If I had learned anything along the way it was how much I did not know. And how often I had been wrong. I had a hard time facing her. She seemed so sure that she was right; I had so many doubts. So our confrontations always ended up the same way—with me feeling like a little girl.

I had a million reasons why I did not stand up to an apathetic, insensitive old woman. I didn't have much trouble rationalizing them to Billie or other people. Yet in the deep hours of the night I would find myself awake and unable to go back to sleep. At those times it was just the darkness, the truth and me. I was not very proud of it.

Because I could not face Edna, I tried to work things out with Dan.

"We're the ones who fouled up here, Dan. I don't want to see her stigmatized the rest of her life when what happened was our fault."

Dan was at his desk. He put a hand behind his neck and began to rotate his head as one does when one has tense muscles.

"I keep asking myself what our true goals in education are. What are they? To teach reading and writing and math? Or is it to provide the tools to create the kind of human beings who will someday help us out of the wretched mess this world is in?"

Dan shook his head. "Don't be romantic."

"Is that romantic? Is wanting something more out of people than what we have romantic?"

We gazed at one another.

Again he shook his head. "Our job here is to teach, Torey. Reading, writing, math and whatever else is in the curriculum. That *is* the way to make more out of people. There are no shortcuts."

I did not reply, not knowing how to.

"Listen, Tor, what Edna did with Lori certainly was not as kind as I would have liked. But that's life. She wasn't expecting anything that unusual from Lori. If Lori breaks under the pressure of first grade, she'll never make it the rest of the way through the system without psychological help."

"Then maybe we need to change the system."

"For one child? I really do know how you feel on this. Believe me, I do. But this is a school. We're here solely to teach. If a child can't make it, I'm sorry, but that's the way it is."

"Dan, no system should be that important. When you start sacrificing people to keep the system going, then something is wrong."

He nodded wearily. "Yeah. Who knows. Maybe something is."

The decision of what to do with Lori when she did return was no easily resolved matter. We all knew we had to remove her from Edna's class. But where to put her? The only full-time special education room was Betsy Kerry's group of profoundly retarded children. Lori, whatever her problems, was no candidate for that class. There was the possibility of putting her into the other first-grade class in the building, the same class Libby was in. However, the teacher of that room was a young, first-year teacher who was having considerable difficulty managing the children she already had without adding someone with problems like Lori's.

In the end I volunteered to take Lori in my room all day. Although she would remain on Edna's roster as a first-grade student, she would be with me for everything except music, physical education, art and social studies. I would fit her in around my other resource students in the mornings, and afternoons would continue as they were. Hardly a foolproof solution, but we hoped it might relieve some of the pressure on Lori and allow for more intensive teaching.

Tuesday. Still no Lori. At lunchtime I went down to the office and called Mr. Sjokheim at work. He was apologetic but he could not bring himself to force her to come. A cold sensation tightened my stomach. The time had come for offensive action; we had been passive as long as we could afford to be. I said to him that we could not allow Lori to go on much longer or she would need outside help to get back. Mr. Sjokheim explained that he had made an appointment with a local psychologist for Lori, and she was to see him the following week. No, I said, that was not enough. Lori had to come back to school. Now. That was no news to Mr. Sjokheim. The psychologist had told him the same thing. Could I come over? I asked. He agreed. We settled on 7:30 that evening.

My time had come. As I drove through residential streets, shadowy in spring darkness, on my way to the Sjokheims, I did a great deal of thinking. Here was the place to commit myself. Now was the time. And if I promised her, then I knew I would not back down when I had to face the others.

Mr. Sjokheim welcomed me at the door and let me in. Libby was in the living room when I entered. She had just had her hair washed and was rubbing the dampness out with a towel. Without her glasses on, the resemblance between her and Lori was obvious. When she saw me, she stopped drying her hair and stared. I meant to say hello but an unexpected shyness overtook me and I only managed to smile. Libby did not smile back. As I came to think about it, I did not remember seeing her smile very often.

Mr. Sjokheim led me down the hall to where Lori was waiting in her bedroom. Butterflies flittered in my chest. The door was open. The shyness stayed with me and I did not want to go in. What was I going to say? A moment's hesitation in the hallway. I could feel my heart. Around the corner Libby was leaning against the wall, watching us. With a smile of false confidence to Mr. Sjokheim, I entered.

Lori sat on her bed in yellow, footed, terry-cloth sleepers, with her long, dark hair loose and uncombed about her. She

230

stared at me. No smile. Not even the slightest flicker of friendliness crossed her face. In the dim light of the bedside lamp, her eyes were black, black and deep as a night with no stars. A vast desert stretched between us.

"Hi," I said.

No answer. I saw her taking deep breaths. She was sitting with one foot up on the bed, her hand resting on her knee.

"Lori, hello."

"Hi, Torey."

I relinquished the safety of the doorway and came over. "I miss you, Lor. I had to come see you. We all miss you."

Again no answer. Only those dark, deep eyes on me. Cloaked around her and as tangible as she herself, was an aloofness of which I would never have thought her capable. She was giving me no benefit of familiarity.

"May I sit down with you?" I asked.

She nodded. I pushed back the rumpled bedclothes and sat next to her. She moved a little away so as not to touch me.

"Lor, we want you to come back."

She turned her head to look me squarely in the face. A tiny shiver quaked along my skin. I knew I was seeing Libby's eyes. And Libby's hate. I could have wept.

"I'm never coming back."

"I know you feel that way."

"I feel that way 'cause it's the truth, that's why. I'm never coming back."

"But I miss you, Lori. Boo misses you. And Tom. And Claudia. We need you, Lor. It isn't a good class without you."

"I don't care."

What have we done to you! I honestly thought I was going to cry. It forced me to look away.

A soft, muffled thunking noise permeated the stillness around us and I turned. Outside the window beyond Lori's bed were daffodils in a window box. Most were faded and

231

dying but one remained fresh, the golden cup knocking insistently against the glass. When I turned back, Lori's head was down; she traced around the pattern on the bed sheet.

"Lor?"

"Yeah," she answered without looking up.

"Lori, we were wrong."

Silence while I swallowed.

"We were wrong to treat you the way we did. And we were wrong to ever make you think reading was so important. It isn't."

"Sure it is," she retorted at the sheet, her voice half aloud, half a whisper, and angry, as if I had been ridiculing her.

"No. It isn't. And it's our fault for ever making you think that it was. That was wrong."

"Sure it's important," she said again and looked up at me. "She made the kids laugh at me. She made me throw up. In front of everybody. I am never going back to that place, no matter who says I have to go. I'll run away if you try to make me. Even you."

"Lor, listen to me. Please?"

"No! Just go away. I'm *not* going back. And I don't want you here. Just go away and leave me alone."

"Lori."

"Can't you hear me?" Tears came to her eyes. "What's the matter with you? Go away. I don't want to see you." With that she turned away and flung herself face down on her pillow. Her dark hair splayed out to cover her.

I sat watching her and feeling helpless beyond words. Thunk, thunk, thunk went the daffodil against the window, the only noise in the room. I wanted to pick Lori up and hold her and brush away all the awful things; she was so small. I wanted to reassure myself that there still were problems solvable with a hug and that, being an adult, I

232

could fix things, when in fact I knew it was not so. And so did she.

"Lor?" I touched her back.

"Get *out* of here!" she repeated.

My hand fell back into my lap. Turning my head, I saw Libby standing in the doorway. Clad only in her underpants, she held her pajamas to her chest. Her hair was still damp but combed now; she brushed her bangs back with one hand. We exchanged a long, wordless gaze, and I could not read her feelings. Then she turned and left.

Gently I reached over and rubbed Lori's back. She jerked to get away from my touch at first, but when I persisted, she relaxed. Her face remained in the pillow.

"Lori?" I said after a while, "will you sit with me? Please?"

With much effort she rose up from her position and moved over next to me. Rugged dignity kept her my equal and I did not dare touch her too intimately. Instead, I rested my arm in back of her, my hand on the sheet.

"Lor, Lor, Lor, what have we done to you?"

She studied her fingers.

"I'm sorry," I said.

She looked up at me.

"I *am* sorry."

"What for?"

"For letting you think such unimportant things were so important. We were wrong about a lot of things, Lori. Sometimes when people live in a small world, small things start looking awfully important. Even when they're not. We should never have made you feel that reading was more important to us than you are. That's a very untrue thing."

"But I can't read."

"I know you can't. And I know it's a handy thing to be able to do. Someday maybe you will be able to. Who knows. But even if you never did, it wouldn't really matter.

233

I wouldn't care. We'd get around it somehow. You don't need to know how to read to be happy."

Her eyes were dark and bottomless.

I smiled. "Besides, you already can do something that's so much better than reading."

"What's that?"

"You can look at people in a special way and know just how they're feeling. Like you did with Tomaso and his teddy bear. You know how to understand those feelings, what makes people happy and sad. And you care. All the time I've known you, Lor, you've cared. And that's much more important than reading is. No matter what happens, don't ever forget that. In this world we so badly need people who care. There's more than enough readers to get all the reading done. But we're terribly short on carers."

Lori continued to watch me without wavering. I could see myself in her eyes. Then she dropped her head and let out a deep breath. Pulling up a strand of hair between her fingers she rubbed the smoothness against her lips. "But I still want to read."

I felt tired. And old. "You know, if there were some way to do it, I'd make it so you'd read. If I had a million dollars and could buy it for you, I would."

She seemed nonplussed.

"Lor, I only want you to be happy. Believe me, if I knew of any way to get reading for you, I'd do it. We're not holding back any secrets from you, just like you aren't." I stopped. I was running out of words. "You know, if somehow God could take away my ability to read and give it to you, I think I'd let Him. I think I'd be glad to let you have it."

Lori looked up. Her forehead creased. "But . . ." She turned away, looked out the window at the daffodils, then down at her hands. "But if that happened, then you couldn't be my teacher anymore. Not if you couldn't read."

She looked at me again. "I wouldn't want you to do that."

I smiled. "It isn't that important, is it?"

Although the smile never touched her lips, even in the dimness I could see it slip into her eyes. She reached over and gently patted my hand.

24

Lori came back to school, though not without a certain amount of trauma. At lunchtime the next day I drove over with Billie to Lori's house to get her and had to carry her crying and screaming to the car. On the four-block trip back to school, she vomited in my litter bag, and then I had to carry her crying and screaming into our room. But Lori got back to school.

Once she was there and the other children had gotten settled, I did a daring thing. Out of her cubby I took all the workbooks Edna had brought me to use for Lori's future edification. I took out the beautifully colored reading book, the new Rebus cards and all the other miscellany I had collected to teach Lori reading. And I threw them in the trash basket. I took the books, each one of them, and tore out the pages individually and ripped them in half, letting the shreds flutter down into the garbage. Tomaso and Boo were fascinated. Claudia, our book lover, was horrified. Lori watched from a distance, her eyes wary.

"What are you doing?" Tomaso ventured.

"I'm getting rid of all this. Lori isn't doing any more reading."

"She isn't?" Great surprise in his voice. Then his face lit up. "Can I help you?"

"Nope."

Lori came a little closer.

"But this is school," Claudia said. "You have to have reading."

"Nope," I said. "No more reading for Lori. No more writing. No more spelling."

Tom's eyebrows rose. "But what's she going to do?"

"Plenty." I finished pulling out the last page and tearing it into quarters. "There."

Lori edged closer. The other children stared a moment longer and then went back to their work. Finally Lori came all the way over and peered into the garbage can. I smacked my hands together. Her eyes came to me. They were not happy.

"You worried?"

She seemed on the verge of saying something, or at least wanting to, but did not speak.

"I know how much you want to learn to read. And write. And all the other things kids learn to do in school. I know that. And I'm not giving up on you. I think you'll learn. Just not now. It isn't the right time."

Still the furrowed brow, still the well of unhappiness in her eyes.

I pulled the chair over and sat down. Grabbing her under the arms, I set her on my knee. "I need you to trust me."

Her head was down. With one finger she explored the corduroy of my pants.

"Let me give you a little example, okay?"

She looked at me.

"Remember back in December when we planted the hyacinths?"

237

A nod.

"Remember how we had to put them in the refrigerator all those weeks to make them grow?"

"Yeah."

"What happened to them while they were in the refrigerator?"

Lori thought a moment. "They made roots."

"Yup. But did you see them making any roots when you looked? Did it look like they had done anything in the fridge at all?"

She shook her head.

"But did they? And did they bloom afterward?"

"Yes."

I smiled. "So tell me, Lor, what would have happened if you had decided that you wanted them to bloom right when we got them in December? What if you had gone in with your fingers and peeled back the bulb and yanked up the little embryo flower? Could you have made it bloom?"

"Uh-uh. It'd die."

"That's right. It would die. No matter how loving you were, no matter how much you tried. The flower wasn't ready to bloom and you only would have killed it."

Her eyes searched my face.

"People are like hyacinth bulbs. All we can do is make a good place for people to grow, but each person is responsible for doing his own growing in his own time. If we get in there and mess, all we do is hurt. No matter how well meaning we are. And sometimes growing is a very silent thing, like the bulbs in the refrigerator. Sometimes we can't even tell it's happening, but that doesn't mean it isn't."

Still the solemnity as she watched me. She did not speak.

"So trust me, Lor. I want to give you a little more time to grow. You'll read, but in your own time. Do you understand that?"

She nodded earnestly. "You're putting me back in the 'frigerator to make more roots."

And so the Great March Reading Crisis was over. Lori, now with me most of the day, turned to doing other things. Math, science, whatever we could do with manipulatives. For those assignments that absolutely needed reading, when I could devise no way around it, I appointed Tomaso Lori's official reader. It became his responsibility to read to Lori anything she needed read. Likewise, if she needed anything written down, Tom did it. I explained to Tomaso that Lori was totally dependent on him for this skill, and, as with a blind person and a guide dog, it was his duty to make sure Lori never got into a bad spot without him. Tomaso took the job to heart.

Every day Lori and I worked together on the many little things she was still slow at doing, which, while not exactly in the same category as reading and writing, seemed either affected by the same part of her brain or crippled by her inability to recognize symbols. Tying her shoes was one example. Telling time was another. I even went so far as to obtain a braille clock to help her learn to tell time by the approximate position of the hands rather than by the numbers.

Any extra time was filled with nonacademics. Lori became our chore person. She helped Boo with his Montessori boards, she fed the animals and cleaned their cages and watered the plants; she distributed and collected papers. I color-coordinated the files of the morning resource children, and Lori became responsible for taking their assignments from my desk, putting them in the correct folders, sorting out the folders at the end of the day and filing them. We staked out a corner of the playground to make a garden, and Lori raked and spaded and chose seeds from a seed catalog. She helped Tomaso set up a weather station in the middle of the garden to measure rainfall, temperature, humidity and wind direction. None of the things she did were great things, not things that would probably destine her to be first woman president or make the maiden journey to Mars. They were instead things that I hoped would make her simply Lori, growing girl in Room 101. That, in my opinion, was worthy enough.

Yet while the reading crisis had ended for Lori, it had begun for me. I had made the commitment and taken the action. Now I skulked in the hallways, terrified that Dan or Edna would discover what I had done. Lori was still designated Edna's pupil, and I knew I stood in grave danger by not teaching her the curriculum that Edna had given me. Edna would be furious. And Dan would not be happy with the way I had gone about it. My days until a confrontation came were numbered.

Worse, I think, than my fear of Dan and Edna was my fear of myself. Would I be able to stand up for what I thought was best? Making the commitment to Lori had been relatively easy. And I had known it would be. Lori still had faith in my omnipotence, and when we were in our classroom with the door to the outer world closed, I knew there was nothing I was not willing to try. All things seemed possible there.

I had used that knowledge to secure the courage to carry out what I believed. Now I feared. I dreaded that when the moment of confrontation came, that courage would not be enough. Living according to one's convictions, I soon discovered, was not nearly as soul satisfying as the novels make it out to be.

Lori had so absorbed my thoughts over the previous weeks that I had not devoted as much headwork to the other children as I normally did. However, I did not forget them.

Of the three, Claudia visited my thoughts most frequently. She continued to remain around the edges of the class. Three months now and still I hardly knew her. She stayed with me frequently after school, but we seldom really talked. Just small talk. All the time. Our whole relationship reminded me of an occasion in college when I was on a zoology field trip. We were all out in a swamp one night in the moonlight watching the courtship dance of cranes. That was Claudia and me, two cranes dancing: up, down, back, forth, fascinated, frightened, always coming close, never touching. I thought sometimes that perhaps this was just the way it was with "normal" children. Perhaps a teacher never did get to know them with the brutal familiarity one achieved with disturbed children. Perhaps never touching was usual. I could not tell; my experience with normal children was too slim. Whatever the truth of the matter, I wanted more of a relationship than we had. She seemed so hungry for something I did not appear to be giving her. Or at least not enough. But I could not identify what it was or how to increase it.

Over the previous month Claudia had begun to gain tremendous amounts of weight. Although I did not know it at the time, this apparently is common with very young mothers. At home Claudia became the proverbial lunatic relative locked in the attic. She had no friends to come to see her. Her father forbade her to go out except in special circumstances. Claudia's world was bound by school, television, books and her four-year-old sister Rebecca.

My own knowledge of prenatal activity and care was limited. My only resources were books from the library and what I could pry out of a girl friend's husband, an MD doing his residency at the hospital—unfortunately in orthopedics. I never found a support group of any sort for Claudia and I finally realized that I probably never would in time. If there was going to be any support, it would have to come from us. That was a miserable position for me, without knowledge, without experience, without even an intimate relationship with Claudia. Of all the kids, she was the one I brought home most often in my head, I think, just because she left me feeling so helpless and because I knew she needed help.

"Tor?"

After school, mid-March. I was at the worktable as usual making out the next day's lesson plans. Claudia had stayed to make some learning materials for Boo and Lori. She had been over at her desk near the bookshelves. I looked up when she called my name.

"What's this?" She took a magazine from inside the desk. Opening the magazine up, she came and sat down across the table from me.

"What's what? What have you got there?"

"This." She handed it to me. It was a copy of *Cosmopolitan*. She had it open to a psychiatrist's question-and-answer column. The letter Claudia was pointing to told of a woman who could not now achieve orgasms.

I read the piece.

"What I want to know," she said, "is what's an orgasm? Exactly."

Wow. They never told me about questions like this in teachers' school.

"Well, it's kind of hard to explain. I guess you'd say it's a sensation, a physical feeling, that starts in your body when you get sexually stimulated. Usually when you're having intercourse."

"But what's it feel like? Does it hurt?"

"No. It's sort of an electric feeling. Rhythmic." I paused to think of what to say next. "A really, really pleasurable feeling. It's one of the main reasons people like to have sex together."

242

"It feels good?"

I nodded.

A confused and rather skeptical look came over her face and she took the magazine back from me and reread the column. "You mean, it's supposed to feel *good* to have sex with a guy?"

Again I nodded.

Claudia shook her head in disbelief. Still she stared at the open magazine as if it would suddenly clear up this odd bit of information. "Golly." Another shake of her head. "You're supposed to *want* to have sex? Wow. I sure never knew that." Back to me with her incredulity. "I thought it was just something you did because you had to, to get a guy to like you and not leave you for somebody else. I sure didn't know you were supposed to feel good doing it."

A soft, aching sadness came to me as I watched her cope with this heresy I had proposed. Claudia sagged down into the seat wearily. "Boy, I sure didn't like it. It was awful. It hurt."

"Things went a little wrong for you," I said. "You didn't understand. There's a lot more to sex than just anatomy and being old enough to do it. You were too young, Claudia. Your body was ready but your head wasn't. It might even have been the same for Randy. I hope when you're older it will be different."

Claudia's head was down. She bent the corners of the magazine. "You know, they make you think sex is such great stuff, all those shows on TV and stuff. They make you think it's easy and if you do it with a guy, everything will be all right. You'll be happy and junk. And you'll live happily ever after. Really, it's a lot different from that."

"Yes, it is."

The room was filled with the small ripping sound of her fingernail running along the edges of the magazine. "I get so lonely sometimes. I think maybe I've been lonely all my life. I think I was born that way. Sometimes I think of

243

myself as a little dot on a piece of paper—you know, just a little black speck of nothing and all that emptiness around me."

She sighed. "Randy was so nice. You know what? He'd buy me milk shakes and stuff at McDonald's just for the fun of it. I didn't even have to ask. Randy, he was good to me."

Selling her soul for the price of a McDonald's milk shake and here was a girl whom no one thought needed help.

A powerful, although not altogether uncomfortable silence grew up around us. I could not think what to say that would carry sufficient meaning, so when she stopped talking, there was only the silence. I turned briefly and looked out the window. Windy and gray. When I turned back, she was watching me.

"Tor?"

"Yeah?"

"Am I a bad person?"

I shook my head. "No. There's no such thing as a bad person."

She braced her head with one hand. The silence came again. This time, however, it was diseased. I did not want it there but I could not make it go away. Claudia was self-absorbed, looking somewhere within herself and not at me.

Finally she looked back at me. "You think I'm dirty, don't you? Because of what I've done."

"No."

That silence again. "I do," she said slowly. "Sometimes I take three showers a day and still I feel dirty."

25

The day following my discussion with Claudia, I renewed attempts to get her parents to find psychological help for her. It was not so much what Claudia had done but why she did it and how she felt about it that made me feel help was essential. I wanted her family to understand that the kind of help Claudia needed could not be provided for her in the schoolroom. I was a teacher and my jurisdiction was only over those things that happened during the time the child was with me. Claudia's problems were much more far-reaching, and they needed intervention if we were not to end up confronting more serious problems down the line. The mother was willing to agree to my face that Claudia needed help but she would not carry through with it. The father was much less tactful. And because Claudia was presenting no problems at all in my classroom, my hands were tied when it came to initiating any action myself.

I had decided to eat lunch in my room so I could catch up on some paperwork that Lori's troubles had caused me to put off. In addition, report cards were due soon and as always I was behind on that.

The door opened. Mrs. Franklin stood there hesitantly, her head in, the rest of her out. "Am I bothering you?"

"Come on in."

A joyful smile broke over her face. She pulled Boo in behind her and shut the door. "I came to show you . . . Boothie had . . ." She halted just in front of the table. "Well, Boothie . . . I think, I think maybe he's getting better."

She hoisted Boo up on the table and took off his shoes and socks. Boo dissolved into a fit of giggles over all this attention. Putting away the last of my lunch and brushing off the crumbs, I moved my chair over for a better view.

"Now look," she said. "Here, Boothie, here." She began to wiggle his bare toes. "One little piggy? What's this, honey? One little piggy went to market?"

Boo leaned forward to see his feet. Excitedly, he flapped his hands out to the sides. Again Mrs. Franklin wiggled his big toe with her fingers. Boo was definitely interested.

"Come on, Boothe Birney, show your teacher what you can do. Come on, be good for Mama. One little piggy . . ."

By this time I was curious too. We all bent over Boo's bare foot.

Then very slowly he stopped the fluttering. Reaching forward he grabbed a toe. "One little piggy go to market," he said. "One little piggy stay home. One little piggy oi-oi-oi-oi all the way home!" Boo let out a squeal of pleasure.

Mrs. Franklin's face was bright. "See? See? That's just the way he used to say it before—" she paused. "Well, before he got older. Just like when he was a baby. Do it again, Boothie, do it for Mama."

"One little piggy go to market. One little piggy stay

home. One little piggy oi-oi-oi-oi all the way home! Oi-oi-oi-oi all the way home!" He shrieked, lifted his toes high in the air and clasped them. "Oi-oi-oi-oi all the way home!"

You would have thought he had just discovered a cure for cancer from the response he got from us for that accomplishment.

Mrs. Franklin was at least as excited as Boo. Over and over she caressed him, hugged his curly head to her coat, demanded the rhyme be repeated. "It's just the way he used to say it," she kept telling me. "Boothe Birney was too little to say it right when Charles would dry his feet and do it with him. Boothie always said oi-oi-oi. This is just like before he changed. It's the first time he's talked to us."

Her words touched me. If love could have cured this boy, I had no doubt he would have been well. The hopes and fears of so many years rested in her words. Yet I think both of us knew love was not going to do it. We were like relatives of a terminally ill patient savoring this present moment of health, however illusory. We both knew that there would probably be no future, save dreams.

Boo capered off the table and out across the room, leaving a trail of jacket, gloves and hat. Mrs. Franklin looked at me. "He's getting better, isn't he?" The hope in her voice made it quiver. "He is getting better. This is a good sign, isn't it?"

"Every little thing matters," I replied.

"We might get him to say mama," she said softly. "Just once. Don't you think?"

I nodded.

And Tomaso was blooming. Of all the children, he was making the most noticeable progress. Most of his annoying little habits were entirely gone. Even the swearing had decreased to a more acceptable level. Most important, we

247

were at last getting a handle on his explosions. They still happened but were much shorter and more easily controlled. I no longer had to hold him. Telling him to go sit down until he had things under control was enough. With the single exception of his birthday party, he no longer exhibited violent, destructive behavior.

A major contributor to his improvement was his relationship with Lori. Appointing him her reader had been an unexpected bonus for both of them. Tomaso took the responsibility with the utmost seriousness, and whether the change was caused by the boost to his self-esteem or by being tangibly so important to someone, I did not know. Perhaps he was just too busy to get mad. But from that mid-March appointment on, he became much calmer and more even-tempered.

Tom, himself, recognized his new status in the room. "I have to watch myself," he told me one afternoon. "She depends on me to get things done. I can't get mad so much anymore because I always have to stick around to make sure she's all right." He had grinned at me. "I'm what you'd have to call a real good friend, huh?" I had to agree to that.

The only problem of Tomaso's that continued to trouble me was his reliance on his dead father. I think he did know his father was dead and had been dead more than half Tom's life. Yet every day there was a comment or two spoken as if the man were still alive and very active in Tomaso's existence. My own conclusion was that Tomaso was living a fantasy much of the time in which his father played a major part. I did not especially object to the fantasy itself. Undoubtedly it served a necessary purpose in Tomaso's unstable life. Still, I had a hard time when he persistently tried to coerce us in the outer world to be a part of it. And the realism of some comments unsettled me.

I did not know how to treat the problem. For a while I simply ignored the situation and hoped it would go away. It did not. And sometimes I worried that perhaps he really could not always tell the difference between what was true and what he wished were. Worse, the kids on the bus he rode had begun to tease him about "superdad." The time had come to confront the issue.

Tomaso provided the opportunity himself. One afternoon late in the month he came in carrying a large plaster statue of a bullfighter. I had seen similar statues in the windows of stores which cater to people who do crafts. By the looks of the thing, it was something he had colored himself. The paint job was bright to the point of being garish, put on with eleven-year-old expertise.

"Lookie here," he called, lugging the statue over to the worktable. Lori and Boo swarmed up to check the item out. Claudia had not yet arrived. "It's a bullfighter. Just like my father's grandpa used to be. Just like him."

"Wow," Lori said appreciatively. "It's big."

"Ain't it pretty?"

"Yeah!"

Tomaso puffed out his chest. "Guess what."

"What?"

"My father made this for me. My real father."

I gave him a suspicious look. "Oh?"

"Yup. He made it for me. Just for me. See, first he sculptured it and then he baked it in this real hot oven to make it hard. Then he painted it."

"Wow," Lori said again. "You mean he just took a lump of clay and made a bullfighter out of it? Wow."

"Yup, that's what he did."

"He sure is a good artist," Lori said. "I wish my dad could make something like that for me. You're lucky. My dad can't even color and stay in the lines."

"Well, my father's special. He can do lots of things. He can make you anything you ask him to. Why, if I see a toy at the store, I just ask my father to make it for me and he does. He's made me probably five hundred toys. And they always turn out better than anything in the store."

"Would he make me something?" Lori asked.

249

Claudia came in at that point. When she saw us all around the table, she walked over. "What's this?"

"It's a bullfighter," Lori said. "Tomaso's father sculptured it himself just for Tomaso."

Disbelief broke over Claudia's face and she leaned forward to examine it. "Oh come on, Tomaso, you lie. Your father didn't make this. This is one of those things from the ceramic shop. You pour it in a mold."

"He did so make it, Claudia. He just saw one of those things in the ceramic shop and made one that looks just like it."

"Oh hah, Tomaso. You probably did it yourself. Look at it. No grown-up would paint it like that. You lie and you know it."

Tomaso's face reddened. "What do you know? How come you think you're so smart anyway? My father did so make this."

"Okay, you two, enough," I interjected, intent on heading off a battle. "It's time you got started on school work anyway. Tom, put your statue up on the window ledge."

"She's calling me a liar. Why don't you do something to her?"

"Tom, calm down. Put your statue over there now. We'll deal with the issue when I don't hear upset voices."

"No! You're on her side. You always take her side."

"Tomaso." My no-nonsense voice.

"Shut up! Just shut up. What does everybody pick on me for? Just shut up. I don't want to talk to you."

"I know you feel I'm being unfair but getting angry won't help. Sit down."

The other children began moving out of range. They too knew Tom was reaching the boiling point. I signaled them to get busy. Lori grabbed hold of Boo. Claudia loitered a moment longer. She and Tomaso had a maddeningly siblinglike rivalry on occasion, and Claudia seemed to love seeing him get into trouble. "Shoo," I said to her with a flick of my hand. She took up her work folder and went to her desk.

Tomaso glared in my direction and continued to stand. I took the statue over to the windowsill. Then I pointed to a chair. His eyes narrowed. I pointed again. After a long, face-saving delay, he sat.

"Okay, let's talk," I said.

"I don't wanna. You always take her side. You take everybody's side but mine."

"Suppose you explain your side of it."

"You heard. Are you deaf or something? She called me a liar. She made fun of my statue and you didn't even say anything. Some teacher you are."

"She said your father didn't make it."

"He did! He made it for me. He knew I liked Spain stuff and he made it for me."

What to say next? His dark eyes blazed, no denial in them.

"Tom?" Not a question really, my voice quiet.

Silence from him.

"Sometimes life isn't exactly the way we wish, is it?"

He shook his head. His displeasure made the motion more of a jerk than a shake. He looked down at his hands in his lap.

"And sometimes we sort of need to tell ourselves small stories. They aren't always very true but they make us feel better. That's an okay thing, Tom, to an extent. It's all right to pretend things as long as we know they aren't the truth. But it isn't right when we start trying to make other people believe them. They're just stories for ourselves."

"It *isn't* a story," he muttered at his fingers.

"Tom."

"It *isn't!*" His head remained down.

I did not reply. The silence grew long and cold around us. And it was brittle.

At last he brought a hand up and braced his forehead. "I

251

wish he did make it for me." His voice was so small I almost could not hear.

"Yes, I can understand that."

Dark eyes met mine. There was such sorrow in them. "I miss him. Why did he have to go away for?" Tom folded his arms on the table and lay his head down. He was not crying; there was not even the trace of tears behind his voice. Only desolation. I reached my hand out and pushed my fingers through his hair.

Tomaso turned his head to look at me. His eyes fixed on some invisible point between us. "He's dead. You knew that, didn't you. My father is dead."

"I knew."

"I tried not to hear them. I kept my hands over my ears," he said. "But they were yelling too much. I tried not to hear them but you couldn't help it, they were so loud. And me and César, we were on the couch."

"César?"

"My brother. Him and me, we slept on the couch. But she had this gun. I don't know where she got it from; I never seen it before. But she had it. And when César saw it, he got off the couch. She told him not to, but he got off anyway. He was crying. And she says, 'You better get back on that couch or I'll beat you with the lamp cord but good.' And my father, he yells at her. He yells at her . . . he yells . . ."

Tomaso still stared, his eyes unfocused. His fingertips were turning white from pressure against the table.

"There was a lot of noise. I couldn't make it go away. They were yelling so loud. And César was crying. He got back on the couch and he was crying so loud, screaming. Right in my ear . . . I thought it was my blood. I thought I was bleeding. I got up off the couch and ran . . . it was so warm . . . right in my ear and I could still hear it. The blood made so much noise."

An eerie pause. Bewilderment flooded Tomaso's features.

252

He lifted his head abruptly and looked around the room. "I wonder where César has gone? Where is he?" Then just as suddenly Tomaso dropped his head back down on his folded arms again; it seemed too heavy to hold up.

I could hear my own breathing.

He whispered something almost inaudibly in Spanish. I did not know what it was. His eyes still stared into the emptiness between us.

So many sounds make up a silence. A small, susurrant wind slipped from the north corner of the building and suckled up against the cracks in the weather stripping of the window. In their cage across the room the finches were making little whirrs to one another. The female had just laid a clutch of eggs, and they had much to discuss in regard to housekeeping. Claudia, absorbed in her schoolwork, rustled pages. Boo's and Lori's voices were only an undulating murmur in the background. Yet all of it together created a silence.

Tomaso was watching me now. I smiled.

"Why do people die, Torey?"

"I'm not really very sure."

"I wish it wouldn't happen."

"Sometimes I feel that way too."

Without raising his head, Tomaso's gaze moved beyond me to the bullfighter on the windowsill. "My father didn't really make that for me. I made it myself at Boys' Club." His voice was soft, almost peaceful sounding. His attention never left the statue. "That was dumb of me to say. My father couldn't make it. He's away in Spain right now, looking for a home for me and him. Why, probably right now he's found one and pretty soon he'll come get me."

A single tear slipped out of the corner of his eye and ran in a wet path down onto his hands.

26

Edna appeared in the doorway before school on the first day of April, April Fools'. It was not a social visit. I could see that immediately.

"You show me Lori Sjokheim's reading books."

"I don't have them."

"Where are they? What are you teaching her out of? I want to see it."

I had been hanging my down vest in the closet when she came in. Now I closed the door and leaned on the knob. "I don't have her reading books."

The severity of Edna's features made her look cold. The same fear was running through me that I suppose had run through Lori on countless occasions. I felt myself shrinking, a misbehaving child called to task by her teacher. It took all my courage just to keep looking her in the eye.

"You are teaching her from the curriculum I provided, aren't you?" Edna said. The softness of her voice belied anger held on tight rein.

"No." I shook my head. "I'm not."

"And just who do you think you are? Lori Sjokheim is a student enrolled in my class. You have no right to interfere with the curriculum I chose for her."

"Lori isn't ready for reading yet, Edna."

"Says who? You?"

Arrgh. This was no fun at all. I had had almost three weeks to work up the guts to say what I believed. And here I was, the cold sweat under my arms a nasty dispiriter to my heroics. Two sentences and I had already run out of ammunition.

"Let me tell you something and you listen good," Edna said. "This is a school, not some baby-sitting service for your poor little morons while you bleed on them. Our job in this place is to teach. Nothing else."

I was taking in deep breaths to keep my composure. I was afraid I was going to do something humiliating. Like cry.

"I don't mind telling you right to your face, if these children can't make the grade, get them out of here. Put them someplace they belong. That's what's wrong with this country today. Socialism. Everybody taking care of everybody else's business. And do you know what it is?" she asked. Her shoulders were trembling as she spoke. Her face was red. "It's cruelty. It's cruelty letting these kinds of children think they can be like everybody else. And keeping them out to grow up and produce more of their kind. It's in nobody's better interest. In the name of equality, we're forced to settle for mediocrity. How many of your children know who wrote the "Gettysburg Address"? How many of them would recognize *Hamlet?* How many even know the pledge to the flag?"

Silence.

"Well, how many of them, Torey?"

"Probably none of them."

"That's right. None. And you're standing there daring to tell me that you will not teach Lori Sjokheim reading.

255

What *have* you taught them? How do you even dare call yourself a teacher?" She turned. "I've had it with your bleeding-heart liberalism. I better find out you are following that cirriculum or there's going to be one big stink."

The door slammed.

At 9:15 Dan Marshall appeared. He beckoned me into the hallway. After giving instructions to the resource students, I went out.

"Edna's been down in my office for the last hour, Tor, and she's fit to be tied. She's going on about some nonsense over the curriculum you have Lori in. She's trying to tell me you aren't teaching Lori reading at all."

My stomach was knotted around the Grape-Nuts I had had for breakfast.

"Now I hate to bear tales, but I do need to find out what you're doing in here with Lori. Edna is plaguing me about it."

I gazed at him as steadily as my wilting spirit would let me. "She's right, Dan. I'm not teaching Lori reading."

His whole body sagged. "Oh gosh, don't tell me that. Say anything, just not that."

An anguished pause.

"Dan?"

He looked at me.

"I can't. Lori isn't ready for reading. She isn't even capable of reading. Or writing. Whatever her problem is, she hasn't matured out of it yet. But I *am* teaching her and I think we're really doing super in those other areas. She's a bright child; she has a lot of potential. So just trust me on this, would you?"

Good old Dan, the policy man. He was one good guy. I loved working with him. He was good-natured, easy to talk to, sincere, helpful. I found him countless times better than other administrators I had had. But basically, he was weak. He tended to make decisions in favor of whomever

256

the most aggressive party was. I never knew what his own beliefs were on any serious issue—or if he even had any. And when things got really rough he fell back on policy. The district policy book was the bottom line on everything.

"Tor, it isn't a matter of trust. We have obligations to these kids as students. They deserve to be taught the curriculum. And the book says . . ."

"Lori *can't* do it. It's not a case of her not wanting to. Or of my refusing to teach it to her."

Dan shook his head. "Then what's she doing in regular education? If you don't think she's capable of learning, then let's just face the fact that she doesn't belong here. But for pete's sake, make up your mind, Torey. On one hand you're going on about how normal she is and then you turn around and say she can't learn the normal curriculum. Either she's a regular student and she does the regular program or she goes special ed. You can't have it both ways."

"A full-time special ed class? Where? Betsy Kerry's class? You want to put Lori in with a bunch of kids whose IQ's together won't equal hers? Come on and think, Dan. You're beginning to sound like Edna."

We struggled back and forth over the issue like two mongrels over a bone. Neither of us was angry and in truth I'm not even sure we were on different sides. But the issue had gotten so mucked up that we could not pull ourselves away.

I hated what I was doing. I hated standing there in the hall arguing when I should have been in my classroom with the children. I hated the way I sounded when I got upset. I hated the way it made me feel. Yet I did not know what to do. So I just kept arguing my side of it.

In the end, I think I was the one who blew it. Instead of calmly discussing the real and valid points I had for not teaching reading, and instead of showing him all the good

257

things Lori had been learning, I became increasingly frustrated with the argument. This turned me to sarcasm when
I should have remained earnest and loudness when I should
have stayed soft. Dan, in response, became authoritarian.

"We're going to have to settle this," he said. "If that
means calling Birk Jones in, I'll do it, Torey."

"Fine with me."

"Okay, then." There was a long pause while we regarded
one another, both of us, I'm sure, wishing desperately that
the other would soften. Then he turned and went back
down the hall.

I was left leaning against the wall and watching him.
Grape-Nuts continued to grind mercilessly against my
diaphragm. The kids in the room were whooping and
hollering like savages. Things had been blown completely
out of proportion. Even in my elevated emotional state, I
could tell that. And it had become serious.

What a horrible day. I could not remember any that
equaled it. All the terrible things that had ever happened to
me with the kids had never carried this impact.

I think what heightened the offensiveness of this entire
program was my own uncertainty about the mainstreaming law, which lay at the root of our difficulties. Since it
had been enacted, I had lived in an uneasy alliance with it.
I found it a pathetically idealistic law. It was a stepchild of
that bitterly misunderstood Constitutional phrase about
all men being created equal. No one is equal. We are born
human beings and with that should go the innate right to
be accorded all the dignities of being human, regardless of
race, religion, sex or circumstances. But none of us is equal.
Unfortunately, Congress still believes that with sufficient
bureaucracy, money and laws, equality is achievable.

For many children the mainstreaming law had been a
godsend, particularly, those children with physical hand-
icaps. They were "normal" children. Their disability

touched only their physical selves. In the same way that some people cannot run as fast as others or jump as high, they could not see or hear or walk. To educate them away from their seeing or hearing or walking peers was to no one's advantage in many instances. Other groups of children, however, especially the retarded and the emotionally disturbed, received more pain than benefit from the law. To try one's hardest, to constantly be putting out one's best effort and always be the stupidest kid in the class, as in the case of the slow-learning child, was emotionally devastating. And for kids like mine who had skewed perceptions of the world or who needed intense, provocative interactions in the classroom, there was no way this could be given them with thirty other children and a harried teacher. For them the law could be slow death.

So Lori's case was hard for me. I objected to our placing more emphasis on reading than on the child. I objected to blaming Lori for her actions and reactions when we had induced them. But in regard to how she should be handled, I don't think I was as far apart from Edna and Dan as I seemed. The truth was, if there had been appropriate facilities available in the district, I too would have chosen for Lori full-time special education placement. She had suffered too much because we did not know how to teach her. I would have liked to have seen her out of the regular classroom for the academic subjects until we could develop a decent curriculum for her needs, but we had no place for her to go. When I had volunteered to take her all day long, I had thought I could simulate a special education placement. The problem rested in the fact that the mainstreaming law had taken away my legality. To me, Lori was a full-time special student and needed a special ed curriculum, which I thought I was giving her. To Edna I was reneging on my duty as a resource teacher who carries out supplementary classroom work. To Dan neither of us was right. In his policy books there was nothing governing rooms like

259

mine—special classes which, because of the law, did not exist.

I was so upset by the incident I became physically sick. All day long the children were a trial; my temper was short, my voice harsh. I had no patience at all. I even yelled at Lori until she cried. Perhaps I yelled at Lori most of all.

As I sat in the teacher's lounge after school and drank 7-Up to calm my stomach, Billie came banging in under a huge pile of books. With a gasp she dropped them on the couch beside me.

"Whooooo-ee, am I glad to unload those," she said. "And Lordyma, what a day! You know what Lambert Nye did to me? You know what a little twit he is anyway. We were making sound charts for the letter R and Lambert gives me this jar of glue, you know, one of those mucilage jars, to stick the pictures on with. I go put the whole damn chart full of it. Then I pick the chart up and the stupid pictures ooze right down the front and into my lap. You know what that little twit gave me?"

I shook my head.

"Honey. Honey instead of mucilage. And he says, 'Apwil Foolth, Mith Wobbinth.' I could have smacked him. I really could."

I smiled.

Billie gave me a hard look. "Somebody been April Fooling you a little too much today? You look lower than a run-over possum."

I told her.

Tenderly Billie reached out and touched my hand. She said nothing. And it made me cry.

"I just wish I could turn the clock back to this morning. I wish I could say to Edna that I'll do anything she wants me to and that this would all go away. I'm not cut out for this sort of thing, Billie. I'm just not."

Billie patted my hand. "Isn't a person in the world cut

260

out for it, honey. It takes hard work to stand up for yourself."

"Maybe if it made you feel better, more people would try. Mostly, it just makes me feel sick."

A loud, infectious laugh. "Hah! Well, I have a cure for that. Right over on Wallenda Street under the sign of the Golden Arches. Big Macs on me, how 'bout it?"

"Billie, I'd love to, really, but . . ."

"Come on." She nudged me. "And take that run-over possum look off your face. My daddy always had a saying for times like these. Said, you got a hard problem, well, you're either gonna live through it or you aren't. Live through it and you're happy. You die, you're either gonna go to Heaven or Hell. Go to Heaven, you're happy. Otherwise, least you got lots of company."

I had no answer to that.

The kids made sure, however, that I never had too much time to brood. And whatever I thought the magnitude of my own problems was, they unknowingly helped me keep things in perspective.

The next evening Claudia had stayed after school to help me clean up a science experiment. We were working together at the sink washing test tubes and glassware.

"Remember that other time we were talking?" she asked. "When you were telling me about sex and stuff?"

"Yes."

"Well, I've been doing some thinking. Do you have to be in love to like having sex with a guy?"

"I think it helps."

"I don't guess I was in love with Randy. Not really, really. I guess. I don't know. What is love?"

I pushed hair out of my face with a wet hand and looked over. "Boy that's a hard question, kid. And it has so many

261

answers I'm not sure which one to give you. Or if I even know."

She shook her head. "It's funny, sex and love. I don't understand it. And nobody ever seems to know how to explain it." She rolled her eyes. "All my mother ever tells me is about angels and cherubs and bells ringing. She makes it sound like going to church."

I grinned and plunged my hands into the soapy water.

"Tor?"

"Yeah?"

She had walked over to the cupboard to put the things away and paused, leaning on the door. "How old were you when you first had sex with a guy?"

I hesitated, weighing the intimacy of the question. "I was nineteen."

"Did you like it?"

I nodded.

"Were you in love?"

The question made me smile. Back into my thoughts came memories of a time that seemed almost like another lifetime. My student-protest days. College. The war. It was a long time ago. "Yes, I was in love."

"How did you meet him? Did you go to school together?"

"Once." I was still smiling with the sheer innocence of the memory. "I thought he was the greatest guy in the whole world. I was very much in love."

Claudia's eyes grew dreamy. She wandered back to me and the sink. "Where is he now?"

"There was a war on then. In Vietnam. He was a helicopter pilot." I took a breath. "He didn't come back."

"Ohh." And the soft, sad silence that always follows words of a long-ago death, particularly when one is talking with a child. She watched me closely, her eyes filled with a romantic intensity. It made her inordinately pretty.

"What was his name, Torey?"

"Tag. Taggart really, but we called him Tag."

"Tell me. Tell me what it was like."

And I did.

We were still leaning against the counter by the sink, the glassware long washed and put away. Still talking. Claudia paused. She placed her hands on her abdomen. "He's moving. I can feel him move. Here, put your hands here. Feel him?"

I reached down, laying my hand over her smock. Beneath was the slow, fluid motion of the baby.

Claudia was studying my face. "Do you think I'll ever be like you are?"

"What do you mean?"

"Do you think I'll ever be happy?"

27

In the end Birk Jones was called in to settle the matter of Lori's curriculum. Edna and I could not agree and Dan simply refused to discuss the issue any further. He called Birk and set the meeting for the following Tuesday.

The six days between were a special torture for me. Aside from the sheer mechanics of avoiding Edna, and even Dan, my waking hours were filled with soul searching.

The matter had grown so complex. The greatest issue on my mind was my own perception of the problem. Was I being hopelessly idealistic? The line between tilting at windmills and standing up for one's ethical beliefs was so fine. At the same time I dreaded the descent into cynicism so many of my colleagues termed simply professionalism.

I was growing tired too. This made the urge to give up or give in much stronger than it had been. I kept thinking of such things as having Lori transferred. Maybe some other teacher at some other school could teach her the things

Edna and I had failed to. When I thought about it, I knew it was untrue but I was becoming too tired to care.

The meanest thought to go through my head during those days was whether or not Lori was worth this. I was not proud of having such thoughts but they were not unusual. Some days I would sit in class and watch her. She remained her crazy, lovable self throughout the six-day period, chattering to me and the other kids about all the small details only Lori seemed to know. I would catch myself wondering if she would mind how all this came out, if it would matter to her one way or the other. The corollary of that question, of course, was did she matter that much to me? After all, she was just one kid, one of so many I had worked with over the years. I had lost a lot of them in that time. Would one more matter? No one would blame me. After all, officially, she wasn't even my kid.

I hated myself for thinking those thoughts. I hated knowing I even had them. But they were there and the only way I could dispel them was to envision the future. Not Lori's future, because regardless of how things came out, I could not see into that. Rather, I would envision my own. And I did not want to be the person I saw there.

So the six days passed.

My evenings were my own. Joc had been gone for a month now. I had finally packed his things and sent them to him. I put a new lock on the door. To me it seemed ironic that he, too, had left me over this one small girl. How I wished I had scales to weigh the problem, to see if the price I was paying was too high. But lacking them, I went about my life the best I could. I joined the YWCA and started swimming a mile a night. Billie lured me into taking a cake-decorating class. A local priest helped me refurbish my Latin and I began to read the original text of Geoffrey of Monmouth's *Rex Brittanicum*. Yet busy as I was, there was still too much time to think.

The meeting was scheduled for 1:30 on Tuesday afternoon. One of the office aides came down to take over my class while I was gone. We met in Dan's office, the four of us. It was, as Birk liked to say, a "family gathering." By his tone I could tell he planned to settle the entire issue right then and there.

The meeting was quiet. Birk questioned each of us. Edna first. What was her side of it? Where were she and I not in agreement? What in her opinion were Lori's major problems? How had she treated them? What objections did she have to my approach?

I watched Edna as she talked. She spoke quietly and I wondered where the slavering idiot I had perceived her to be had gone. I noticed instead the deep lines around her eyes and across her forehead. What had put them there? What had her life been like? She looked like somebody's grandmother, big, bosomy, gray haired. She talked like somebody's grandmother, too, using all the little expressions that intimated a survivor of the Depression and the War to End All Wars. Like my grandma used. Beneath my anger at her I was only unhappy. We would never know one another for the people we were.

Birk then turned to me and asked me all the same questions he had asked Edna. He sat slouched down in an office chair, his sports coat pushed up in back to touch his hair. One hand braced his head at the temple. An unlit pipe dangled from his lips.

Then he moved to Dan. How had Dan managed thus far? How was policy in these cases normally handled? How could it all be interpreted in regard to the mainstreaming law? Who was in charge of what?

At last he asked for Lori's file. Dan handed it to him and then minutes passed as Birk read it carefully, piece by

266

piece. Dead silence. Edna shifted position and I could hear the soft slurk of sweaty skin being pulled up from the plastic seat of the chair. Dan checked his watch and made a comment about recess. I stared out the window and did not think.

With a snap Birk shut the file. He looked around to each of us in turn. When he came to me, he made a little click with his tongue. "Can you and I have a moment alone?"

Terror! *Oh Jesus!*

Dan and Edna rose in unison to leave us. Desperately I did not want them to go. My heart was beating in my ears. Click. The door shut. There we were, Birk and I.

He smiled at me. A disarming, paternal smile. "So what's this all about?" Still the smile.

My hands came up in a gesture of bewilderment. "It's just like we said, Birk. That's all."

"But why did it come to this? To me? How come you and Edna couldn't get it settled between you?"

"I'm not sure."

"Dan gives me the impression that you really don't want it settled."

"Me? I want it settled." A pause. I was unnerved. My composure was wavering. If he was going to read me the riot act, at least he could be mercifully quick.

"Then what's the problem?"

All the fight drained right out of me and it was all I could do just to keep from tears. "I can't do it."

"Can't do what?"

"This!" I brought my hands up in a wide gesture.

Birk nodded and I had to put a hand up to my forehead and pinch the bridge of my nose to keep from crying. Beyond I could hear him tapping his pipe on the edge of Dan's desk.

"So," he said. "What do you want to do?"

"I want Lori, that's all. I want to keep her in a modified curriculum. I want to keep trying." When he did not answer after I spoke, I felt pressed to fill the vacancy. "Birk, we're killing this kid—as surely as if we put her on a rack. And you all are asking me to be the executioner. I can't do it. At this point in the game, I'm too tired to care about anything else, but I won't kill this kid. Nothing's that important to me."

"Mmmmmm." Tap, tap, tap with the pipe.

Taking my hand down, I sat up straighter. "Just give me a little time, Birk. You know me. I'm not out jumping on some bandwagon. This isn't some gimmick or some experiment. I *do* want her in the regular classroom. I do want to teach her to read. Just not right this moment. Maybe later. Maybe next month. Or next fall. Just not now. She can't do it and I can't make her."

No answer from Birk. His attention was on the pipe. Thoughtfully he extracted tobacco, tamper and matches from inside his suit coat. His lack of response frightened me.

"Please?" I asked.

"Tell me something. As one professional to another, what do you think this girl's chances are of ever learning to read?"

I tensed. Trick question?

Birk looked at me over the bowl of his pipe.

"Not too good, I think," I replied.

"No, I don't think they're good either. Not with this kind of injury. Not without some sign by now that she's maturing out of it." Birk was still watching me. He sucked in on his pipe and tried to light it. "So what's all this fuss about? What you're doing with her seems reasonable to me."

I stared at him in disbelief.

Another smile and Birk wrinkled his nose like a rabbit.

Relief washed over me with such suddenness that the tears really did come to my eyes. I leaned forward weakly. These last six days had been too hard to end so anticlimactically.

"You don't have much confidence in the system, do you?" he asked.

"No, I don't."

A congenial shake of his head. "You think you're the only person in the business who cares? There's plenty of us out here. If you know where to look. What you need, Torey, is a little faith."

"I use it all up on my kids."

"I know you do."

I needed a few moments to put myself back together. I thanked him and apologized for having been the source of so much trouble. I had not meant to be, that was the truth! Birk kept working his pipe, trying to get it lit. The room was filled with his inhaling.

"Listen to me now," he said, pausing from the pipe. "What went on here was just between you and me. I'll explain it all to Edna. You don't stir up muddy waters. Just go back and do your job."

I nodded. "What about Dan?"

Birk leveled most of his attention back at the pipe. "If we were making flashlights or automobiles or garbage disposals here, I'd be mighty upset with you for all the trouble you've caused Dan and me, for pushing us out on a limb and then trying to saw it off on us. But the way I see it, we're working with human beings. And once in a while things just have to bend."

The kids were at work when I came back into the classroom. Claudia was reading. Tomaso labored over math problems at the table. Boo and Lori were on the floor near the animal cages. Lori had a huge sheet of blank newsprint in front of her and she and Boo were drawing on it, only Boo was more absorbed in coloring the fingers of one hand rather than the paper.

I came over to them. Taking a pillow from the reading corner, I propped it against Benny's driftwood and lay back.

"You want to help us?" Lori asked.

"What are you doing?"

"Me and Boo, we're drawing ourselves a flower garden, aren't we, Boo?" She held up a handful of felt-tipped markers. "Here. You can help us if you want to."

"I think I'll just watch, if you don't mind."

"Okay." Lori again bent over the newsprint. Boo grabbed a red marker and started scribbling in his corner of the paper. Lori paused momentarily to watch him.

Sun streamed down through the window and illuminated hundreds of dancing dust motes. As I was watching Boo and Lori work, I thought of the blue bird picture she had made for me back in January. Even now it made me smile.

"Where were you gone at?" Lori asked.

I shrugged. "Just out."

"Tomaso said you weren't coming back."

"I'll always be back, Lori."

She smiled at me and went back to drawing. "I know you will."

"Lor?"

"Yeah?"

"How's Libby?"

"Okay."

"She used to come visit me every night when you were absent."

"Yeah, I know. She told me. She even told me when she skipped ballet. Daddy found out. Libby got a spanking for it." Lori gave me a private grin. "But she didn't mind too much. I think she wishes *she* got to be in this here class."

"I like Libby."

Lori nodded. "But Libby's not like me. She's smart. She can do anything."

"Oh? And you can't?"

Another grin. "Well, I can do *almost* anything."

"Yes, I thought so." I sat up and slid across the floor to

270

them. Sorting through the markers I found a blue one. "Are you going to make any birds in this garden?"

In an appraising inspection of the artwork, Lori even moved Boo's hand back to get the full effect. "I don't know. What do you think, Boo, should we oughta have birds?"

Boo gave her a wide, goofy smile.

"May I make some?" I asked.

"Sure. Go ahead. Over there. Above the flowers. You can make some birds."

I nodded. "Good. I feel like making blue birds."

28

April lay across us gently. Easter vacation came and went. The lilacs began to bloom. Buds on the dogwood promised May. As I was sitting at my desk at home one Saturday, I flipped forward and counted the weeks left to us this school year. Only six. My time was almost up.

Boo continued to make erratic, snail-paced progress. More and more frequently he would talk to us, really talk. I had discovered a few ways of orienting him to the reality and seducing him into communicating. Wiggling his toes to elicit the nursery rhyme was surefire. The kids and I were thrilled by even this modicum of progress, but having to take off his shoes and tickle his feet every time we wanted him to talk to us was not the most convenient method.

Boo advanced in other areas too. With Claudia's help, I had managed to indoctrinate him in the proper use of the toilet. Pretty much, anyhow. Although I think the training was probably more of us than him, he did stay dry about three-fourths of the time now. Another area of progress was Boo's increasing ability to attend to a task over a period of time. In the beginning he could never stay with things more than a minute or two. Now, depending on the task, he could remain involved up to a half an hour. Most of the credit went to Lori for that improvement. She had devoted hours, especially during the last month since she had been released from reading, to including Boo in numerous activities and making sure he knew how to do them. Together they colored, used the Montessori materials, cooked, cleaned the animal cages, put together puzzles, sorted books and generally kept the room in order. Now Boo could do several of these tasks alone without supervision or with minimal guidance, if we could keep him from self-stimulating.

Even better was the fact that this new behavior had carried over to home. Mrs. Franklin reported that Boo was now picking up things in his room when told, and he could occasionally participate in family activities. Although Boo still did not call her Mama, Mrs. Franklin was tearfully excited while telling us that Boo had actually hunted for Easter eggs with his cousins and had helped prepare salad for the Easter dinner. Hardly a notable accomplishment for most nearly eight-year-old boys, but for Boo it was the top of a small Everest.

Tomaso, too, continued to show improvement. No explosions at all for almost four weeks, a real record. No more foul language—well, almost no foul language. Gains in all his academic areas. Since he had arrived in November, Tomaso had gained nearly eighteen months in reading scores. That meant he had acquired more than three months' worth of reading skills for every month in the class. Although he was still behind his peers in that area, the gap had closed considerably.

Math was coming slower. While Tom had never been as far behind in math as he had in reading, he seemed to have a learning disability in that area. No matter how well he memorized the facts, he could not put them together meaningfully. Word problems were especially difficult. If a problem said that Janet had ten apples and wanted to give each of her five friends an equal number, Tomaso had no way of determining how many each would get. He could not discern whether he needed to subtract five from ten or multiply it or whether the five went first or the ten did or the other way around or if both numbers were even important. On the other hand, if I simply asked him what was ten divided by five, he knew immediately that the answer was two.

Despite these difficulties, Tomaso was an energetic learner, fascinated by science. Hardly a day went by that he did not come in with something he had found outside or some tale about volcanos or dinosaurs or air balloons. His greatest love was a set of outdated *National Geographic* magazines I had in the back of the room. He knew more about the tombs in China, foxes on Gull Island and trekking the Northwest Passage than I ever would.

Tomaso's father still lived with us, perhaps not so obviously as before, but he was still there. At one point I suggested to Tom's social worker that Tomaso might profit from some therapy at Mental Health. It was never followed up. Unfortunately, in Tomaso's case I had been a little too effective. To the social worker he had improved so much since entering the class that additional psychotherapy would, in her opinion, be redundant. I hesitated to point out that I was a teacher, not a practicing psychologist, and I had no business messing with the head of a kid who daily fantasized about the father murdered in front of him six years earlier. Yet someone, I thought, ought to be paying attention to that. My suggestions came to naught. Since it could not be clearly shown that these fantasies made Tomaso dangerous or about to go off the deep end, getting psychological help for someone of his status in the system was remote. So Tomaso and I continued to stumble along together the best we could.

Claudia was an excellent student: orderly, mannerly, task-oriented. She had progressed through her studies with ease, and we had long since finished the required work to pass her out of sixth grade. Now I designed enrichment activities, broadened her knowledge in weak areas and often let her choose research fields in which she was personally interested. But it was not Claudia's intellectual state that gave me worry. There had been no progress in getting her any sort of support, either with her pregnancy or her other problems. I continued to watch her cope, day after day, and I knew we had a time bomb. Helplessness became second nature to me in relating to Claudia. I hated it. I hated every minute of it.

And Lori. There was Lori with me all day now. She was learning too, in many ways. I tried to validate all the trouble she had caused me by reviewing how much she had gained in areas other than reading and writing. The truth was she was progressing, but the lesion on her brain continued to cast a shadow on many tasks. In math she excelled, even among her peers in the regular classroom. Of course, it all had to be done orally or with manipulatives because once reading or writing got tangled in, there was no way to tell what she did or did not know. However, without the bondage of symbols, Lori could rattle off answers as fast as I could ask her questions.

Lori also shared Tomaso's fascination for science. In the last weeks, since the moratorium on reading, she had turned more and more to science projects. I had a book of simple experiments meant for older children with reading problems. The steps were illustrated clearly with line drawings and relied minimally on words. If someone explained the point of the experiment to her, she could usually conduct the process on her own. And recently she had decided that what she wanted to be when she grew up

275

was a scientist who worked in a laboratory with animals and chemicals. I did not disillusion her. Free time invariably found her and Tomaso with a *National Geographic* spread out between them and the soft murmur of Tom's voice as he read the text and the picture captions. In time Lori, too, knew all there was to know about tombs, foxes and ice.

In the areas that Lori and I were currently working on since dropping reading, she was not progressing as fast as I had hoped. She could tell time to the quarter of the hour now but we could not refine it any more than that. It was just too confusing. She still could not tie her shoes, a frustrating fact for both of us. I could not tell if the problem was in poor fine motor control or an inability to follow the pattern of a bow. We tried and tried and tried, with shoes, with Montessori boards, with things I made. When finally she managed to make a loose bow in a large strip of cloth I had brought to school one morning, she wore it around her waist all day long.

We spent a lot of time in what I was coming to think of as "pre-reading" activities, things I hoped would help her get around old reading troubles by using environmental clues. I taught her how to recognize all the other children's names, not by reading them but by counting how many letters there were in each one, how many high ones, how many low ones. We went out in the neighborhood and matched road signs and billboards with pictures, their locations and what good sense should tell us they would say. Lori worked doggedly at it. I decided that if she could never become a scientist, she might make one hell of a good detective.

Now the year was about to close. As I sat at my desk and fingered the calendar, I wished that I had more time. Another year, another quarter, another month. If only I could stem the tide of time, hold off their growing up a moment longer, then maybe . . . It was a perennial wish.

Claudia was absent for five days. Attendance in our room was always good, a thing I had noted with other special education classes. Thus, when she did not show up, I was concerned.

On the second day of her absence I called her house. No answer. Over the next days the secretary in the office continued to call, but apparently the family was out of town. I thought it was strange that they had not notified us, but maybe it was an emergency trip. After enough days passed, I ceased to think about it.

On Monday of the next week Claudia was back in school. She looked dreadful, with white, almost translucent skin, and dark circles under her eyes.

"We missed you," I said when she arrived.

She came over to where I was standing near the animal cages. The female finch had laid another clutch of eggs that had failed to hatch and I was trying to extricate them before they rotted. Claudia watched me for a short time and then held out her hands to take the eggs.

"Guess what?"

"What's that?"

"I'm going to a psychiatrist."

I turned. Was there something in the tone of her voice. Pleasure? Hope? Relief? I could not tell. So I just nodded with a smile.

"His name is Dr. Friedman. He's really nice."

"That's good."

An expectant pause followed. It was full of that same hungry eagerness to communicate that she had brought

277

with her when she first entered the class. Although not quite smiling, her lips were turned up at the corners. "I'm glad about it," she said. "I'm real glad."

The afternoon passed, and Claudia fell back into her routine without difficulty. I was troubled by her appearance; she did not look at all well. And she seemed tired. I caught her once, nodding against her geography book.

Not until nearly the end of the day, when the others were occupied with their own activities, did I have a chance to sit down with her. "Do you feel okay, Claud?"

"Yeah, I'm all right."

"Sometimes when a person wants to get back to school, he or she might come back before really feeling good. I would hate that to happen. I mean, with the baby and all."

Claudia was sorting out some Ditto copies for me. She rustled one pile noisily. "I'm not sick. I never was." There was a small interlude in the conversation before she looked over at me. "I was in the hospital over in Falls City. Because I tried to kill myself last Saturday night."

"Oh." Outside it was raining, a dark, misty rain that brought an almost primal longing in me that I could not identify. Turning away from Claudia, I rose to watch out the window. And wonder how all the big things in life can slip themselves into such small conversations.

"I just couldn't stand it anymore," Claudia said, her voice flat and unemotional.

The rain fell. Hard. Spring-cold.

"So I got put in the hospital. And now I go to see Dr. Friedman. He was the doctor who took care of me. He's nice. He looks like Richard Dreyfuss and I like him. But he gave me some pills that make me feel tired all the time. Just until I get used to them, he said, but all I want to do is go to sleep."

I kept my back to her and watched the rain. I did not

want to turn around. I did not want to look at a twelve-year-old mother-to-be on antidepressants. Sometimes the job seemed just a little too heavy.

"It's not so bad, really. Now I get to go to Falls City every week. And my mom's taking me. She bought me a Kiss album last time we were there. Maybe she might even see Dr. Friedman; she said she might. And she said we could eat dinner out together on those nights. So, it's not so bad."

"No, I know it isn't. I'm glad for you, Claudia."

Stillness. Unexpectedly complete. I turned to check the other children, things were so quiet. All three of them were drawing together on one sheet of paper. They were unaware of us. Back to the window. I ran my finger along the caulking at the base and felt its rough edge.

"You know what I did?" Claudia asked.

I shook my head.

"I put a plastic bag over my head and tied a rope around it. Then I went and tied it in my closet to the bar. I closed the door and locked it so no one would find me." She sighed. "But it didn't work. Someone did."

29

I reckon I must have done something pretty awful in God's book. To the Egyptians when they fouled up, He sent plagues. To me, He sent Ariadne Boom.

Ariadne Boom was not your ordinary person. We all knew about her. A short, wide, gray-haired grandmother with an undisclosed age and a Ph.D., Ariadne Boom had been in the employ of the state Office of Public Instruction for the last decade. She had made herself famous as the most bandwagon-jumpingest jumper the OPI had ever found. I have no doubt that somewhere there is a *Guinness Book of World Records* trophy for spending the most tax dollars with the least recoup and Ariadne Boom's name is on it.

Some of her ideas would have been funny if they had not been so expensive. For instance, several years earlier she had become enamored of teaching machines, and one was purchased for every elementary classroom in the state. Not a single teacher I knew had ever used his or hers, partly because by the time they arrived, Ariadne Boom was believing in something else and none of us was ever instructed on how to use the things.

Her name was a company joke. Yet at the same time I think we all held her in awe because she had gotten so far and stayed so long in a position of power. Although I had never seen her, I suppose I should have known my days were numbered. Her new fancy was special education and child abuse, and she was making an informal tour of the state's classes.

The first of May a little note slid across my desk. Ariadne Boom was coming to visit. No date. She liked to pop in unannounced and catch teachers acting "natural." But Birk said she was headed my way. I was not sure why he chose to send her to my room when officially I did not even have a class. I suspected, however, that it was tongue-in-cheek disciplinary action for all the trouble I caused in March and April with Lori. It had to be. Nobody would willingly wish Ariadne Boom onto his friends.

What a lady. She was short; indeed, if she topped five feet I think that would have surprised me. Almost as wide as she was tall, she wore a bright maroon and red striped polyester top, black pants and, around her neck, half of Fort Knox pounded into jewelry. The odor of Emeraude preceded her. And followed her. Swinging open the door to the classroom one afternoon midweek in May, she rolled in with her entourage of two women and a man. About her was such an air of complete confidence that the room suddenly seemed like hers, not mine, and I felt to be the trespasser.

"What instructional model do you use here?" she asked me. The kids and I had just started opening exercises and we were all gathered in the reading corner on the floor. Boo stared wide eyed, his mouth hanging open. "I see your charts there. Are you a behaviorist?"

"Uh . . . uh," I was saying intelligently. I honestly had expected Birk to at least tell me she was in town. As it was, she caught me a whole lot more natural than I would have wanted. Boo was in just training pants because he had had an accident right after arriving and I had his corduroys hanging over a chair to dry. We had begun to make a huge papier mâché dinosaur over by the worktable the week before but had not had time to get back to it. Thus, huge buckets of moldy, soaking newspapers were all over the room. And I was wearing dumb clothes. I had on a shirt with pink hippopotamuses on it that I had found at a secondhand clothing store. The kids loved it but it was hardly adult fare. Worse, I had worn suspenders instead of a belt. Superman suspenders, no less, a bright, almost fluorescent blue with small Superman emblems all over them, a gift from Tomaso at Christmas. When I saw Dr. Boom come in, I scrunched down and hoped my clothes would escape notice. I felt like a clown.

She marched over to us in the corner to question about my methods of teaching. I pointed to the logbook on my desk. She could look at that while I finished with the children, then I would talk to her.

Lori leaned against me when Dr. Boom had gone over to the teacher's desk. "Boy, she sure smells, doesn't she?"

I gave Lori a black stare. She opened her mouth to defend her position and I clamped my hand over it and shook my head. Tomaso giggled.

The afternoon was long, endlessly long. Dr. Boom and her attendants leaned over my desk and read the logbook for a while. Out of the side of my mouth I whispered wicked threats to the children about behaving. Then the visitors wandered back. They were as unobtrusive as a cyclone on a summer's afternoon. I knew their interest in the class was genuine. Dr. Boom asked many valid, intelligent questions. But they were out of place. She took no notice of the children and spoke to me as if we were alone in the room. I could not tell if she was simply insensitive or if she believed that because these were special education children they did not hear.

What amazed me was her self-assurance. It oozed from her pores. Part of me was envious that anyone, regardless of how shmucky, could have that kind of confidence. The rest of me was intimidated by it.

The kids were nervous. Visitors were not that unusual in the room. Occasionally students from the community college or from the university in Falls City would come out for the afternoon. Nursing students, particularly those in psychiatric nursing, or medical students would often be with us two or three days at a time. The children never seemed to mind. But this day they did, I think because I was insecure. We were all feeling like bugs under a microscope.

Boo in particular was affected. Usually he completely ignored human beings. This time he did not. He seemed uncommonly alert to the environment, a condition I normally would have cherished. At the same time, he engaged in more bizarre behavior than usual. For instance, at one point he crawled the entire length of one wall underneath the rug to avoid having to pass the visitors. At another point he closed himself in my coat closet and I could not get him out. All the time in there he kept yelling, "And herrrre's Johnny! And herrrrre's Johnny!"

I took him aside and explained to him and to the others that these were merely people who had come to see how we did things and nothing to worry about. Did he remember how we had talked about having visitors at different times? No, he had forgotten. I patted him on the back and told him to go help Lori with her puzzle. Boo refused. Instead, he retreated to a spot near Benny's driftwood and sat with Claudia's sweater draped over his head. As I watched him, I thought I could exude a whole lot more confidence about the situation if he would help me a little.

283

Time raced by at the speed of a fly swimming in molasses. All I wanted was for recess to come, for dismissal to arrive and the whole thing to end. My own insecurity was beginning to diffuse into a kind of nervous nastiness.

At one point Ariadne Boom took a small chair to the far side of the room and sat down. Then she rose and strolled over to the animal cages not far away. The finches chirped merrily to her and she smiled. Benny was not in his cage but wrapped instead around the uppermost branches of the driftwood nearest the heat lamp. Being the friendly snake that he was, when Dr. Boom approached, he dropped his head and probably three feet of his body off the branch to be scratched. A silly snake smile of anticipation made him wiggle, swinging slightly back and forth on the branch.

When she went over to the animal corner, I think Dr. Boom must not have been aware that Benny was there, or at least that he was quite the size that he was. And foolish me, I didn't tell her. When she saw him flopping off his perch, she gave a strangled little squawk that caused all of us to turn. A deathly pallor on her face, she quickly returned to her chair, picked it up and moved it to the opposite side of the room from Benny's driftwood. Filled with very mean glee, I smiled at Tomaso and we went back to work.

Boo came completely unglued. After a spell of sitting under Claudia's sweater, he skittered across to me and plastered himself to my side in an atypical display of physical contact. Finding no belt to hang onto, he chose to grip the waistband of my jeans. Cautiously he would peer around me to look at the visitors. What did he think they would do to him? For a while he was content to hang on and move when I did. Then he pressed himself close and gripped my pants with both hands. This made walking difficult and I almost tripped.

"Boo, for crying out loud, cut that out. I can't move when you hang onto me like that." My voice sounded harsher than I had meant and I was instantly sorry. I fondled his head a moment.

Ariadne Boom watched the two of us intently. I could hear her whispering about the kids to her colleagues and I wished she would talk more quietly. I could also hear her whispering about me.

Moving to the table, I dragged Boo along. An irritated discomfort was growing inside me at not being able to present what I perceived she was looking for: the perfect class. I was acutely aware of all sorts of things—Lori's overtalkativeness, Tomaso's constant requests for teacher attention, Claudia's failure to look anyone in the eye. And Boo's incontinence. Still in only training pants, he released another stream of urine, all down the leg of my jeans.

"Oh, Boo!" I shrieked.

He clamped his hands around my leg and I nearly fell over. Shaking my leg, I tried to break loose. Lori and Tomaso looked up. Boo continued to cling, his hands clamped together in back of my leg where I could not reach them. When I tried to pull him off, he began to scream. Claudia came over and began the arduous task of unclenching his fingers. Prying him off, she held him long enough for me to reach down and lift him in my arms. As I carried him screaming to a less conspicuous corner of the room, I threw an apologetic glance to Dr. Boom. Already I could hear whispers about this severely disturbed youngster. Psst-psst-psst and the knowing shake of heads.

Boo continued to holler. When I set him down, he screeched and struck out at me although without hitting. Then a flurry of flapping and crying followed. I came down on my knees and took him in my arms. Boo clung so tightly that pain sprinted up my back where his fingers dug in.

When he quieted, he cautiously pulled himself up to look over my shoulder and check out the visitors. I could feel the tension in his small body, tension not meant for

285

me but instead for whatever mysterious thing it was about these people that upset him. His small fingers still gripped my shirt; his breathing still rasped. I felt frustrated not understanding what frightened him and not being able to comfort him.

Recess at last. An aide came to take the children out, and I stayed in with Dr. Boom and her attendants. The only positive outcome of Boo's upset was that it had involved me so much that I had forgotten my own nervousness. Now I met Dr. Boom on a more relaxed level than I would have if we had talked earlier.

And I had misjudged her.

She was not out for blood. Nor was she the caricature that she had seemed upon first entering the room. Beneath all the jewelry and Emeraude was an earnest lady. She saw through my foibles well enough to praise the class and the kids. I felt guilty for my misjudgment, but relieved.

Still, she wanted to know what I had avoided answering earlier: where I had come up with my teaching methods; what underlying theoretical model I ascribed to.

I had hoped I had eluded that question. The truth was, I did not know. My classroom methods were pretty eclectic. I used whatever seemed to me like it might work. But no matter how much I wanted to find the perfect method or the all-encompassing theory, I never had. God knows, I looked for it. Ever since I had walked into my first special education classroom almost eight years before, I had been searching for that secret way for me to open up every imprisoned child. So far I had never found it. Or anything else. Whose model and methods did I function under? Torey Hayden's, I suppose. But not because I was any genius at what I did, and certainly not because I had any magic keys. Instead, only for the ignominious reason that I was the only person whose thoughts I routinely understood. And some days I wasn't even sure about that.

Ariadne Boom fingered her chin and walked away from me. My silence had been long enough that she became distracted and I escaped that question once more.

One of the women, a young woman perhaps not much older than I, spoke. "We were over at that special class for the profoundly retarded this morning."

"Oh, you mean Betsy Kerry's class?" I asked.

Dr. Boom nodded. "Quite a group of children she has. And Birk tells me she comes straight from the regular classroom to teach those children."

I had to smile to myself. Betsy was one of our special people. Younger than I, no experience in special education at all, she was the only teacher in the district who was game enough to volunteer for that class after repeated advertisements had failed to turn up any interested applicants and the class was in danger of closing. She had eight kids all under ten, none of them toilet trained, few of them speaking, some of them not even able to walk. She and her two aides lived in a sort of controlled chaos six hours a day. Yet it was one of the best classrooms I had ever observed. Betsy loved those kids and they loved her. What she lacked in training and experience, she made up in sheer guts. And I knew that Betsy, like I, would never go back to the regular classroom if she had the choice.

I said this to Dr. Boom.

Dr. Boom shook her head. "I don't know though. I couldn't follow her methods too well. For the most part it seemed to me that she was just going around coping the best she could."

I mentioned that she must have noticed that that was pretty much what I had been doing all afternoon too.

"Ah no, Torey," she replied in a confidential tone. She then went on to explain that I, with my master's degree and doctoral training in special education, had been given the expertise Betsy did not have. I, she said, like she herself, functioned within the framework of our knowledge. "We have the training, the background. We are not merely coping. We know."

I stared at her. Maybe that was it. Maybe she *did* know. Maybe that was why she oozed such incredible confidence. But as for me in here with my children, I sure as hell didn't know. And what a price I would have paid for such knowledge. To straighten out the circuitry of Lori's brain, to open up the world of people and feelings and words to Boo, to give Claudia happiness or release Tomaso from his father's grave, I would gladly have gotten ten more degrees. But I was no better than Betsy and her idiots. My days, day in, day out, were one ceaseless string of copings. Coping and hoping and getting along the best we could. The university education, the experience, the training had answered few, if any, questions. Indeed, they only magnified for me how little I knew. And how little I probably ever would.

Dr. Boom had walked away from me, over to the bulletin board with Boo's, Lori's and my picture of the flower garden with blue birds. Thoughtfully she examined it. "You still haven't told me what model you operate under, Torey."

"That's because I don't know."

She raised an eyebrow skeptically. "Oh, come on now. You have to have some model for treating these children. Of deciding what to change and how to do it."

I shrugged. "I change what I surmise I have a chance at changing. The rest I accept, at least until I can figure out what to do about it. That's all. Nothing fancy."

"But what are your goals?"

"To make them humane. And strong enough to survive."

She smiled. A knowing smile. "You're young still. And still an idealist, aren't you?"

"I hope so."

The children returned and we resumed our activities. My outlook had changed entirely from the one I had had before recess. I was filled with a sadness I could not identify. I caught myself watching Ariadne Boom and wondering how it was she came to be the way she was. Was it a wearing down? Did all this pathos finally overpower a person? Had she been too long in too many classrooms? I knew she did not see any blue birds here in my garden. They did not sing to her as they did to me. I felt morbid fear. Could I too become like that, a woman immersed in things which did not fully kiss her?

The remainder of the day went quietly. Only Boo remained edgy. He sat on my lap as we worked. The others were shy but well behaved. After the bell rang and I had seen everybody out, I returned to Dr. Boom and her companions.

"I want to thank you for letting us come," she said. "Birk was right about you. This is a remarkable classroom."

I made muffled, embarrassed sounds.

"But I want to ask you something. And I want your honest feelings."

"Yes?"

"You are a gifted teacher, you know that. Why are you wasting yourself here?"

"I don't understand. What do you mean?"

"Here with these children who'll never amount to anything. I was sitting over there earlier and watching you with the autistic boy. And I was thinking, how *depressing*. There isn't one of them you're going to save. You ought to get yourself into university teaching or some other place where you can do some real good. You shouldn't waste yourself here."

I did not answer. Civilized behavior, I believe, is more often measured by what a person restrains himself from doing than by what he does.

30

May is the month for special programs. Mother's Day programs, May Day programs, end-of-the-year programs. The fifth grade was putting on a play. The entire school was sponsoring a talent show. The kindergarteners and first graders were presenting a special performance of songs and poems for mothers. Dozens of little heads adorned with paper flowers bobbed up and down outside our door for weeks.

We were doing nothing. In previous years when I had had a self-contained class, we had always arranged a special program for the parents. This year I could not manage it. With just four children, two of whom could not read, one who would not talk and one who was eight months pregnant, I could not think of anything for them to do. In the end I decided to do nothing because I did not have enough time or enough help or enough ideas.

This was fine with three of the children. Lori, of course, was outraged. If she had remained in Edna's class she would have gotten to be a woodland flower, wear paper tulips in her hair and sing "Now Merry Little Daisy Faces Say Hello to Spring." Libby had brought home her headgear and had taught Lori all the words to the songs. We were mercilessly plagued with Lori's rather inglorious singing voice as she serenaded us. Worse, she hauled in Libby's paper tulips. When she would not let up on the business, I finally became angry with her and told her if she wanted to go back to Edna's room and be a stupid flower, for pete's sake, go, but quit bothering us because we just could not manage a May program. That evoked tears and a lot of pouting, lower lip pushed out an inch. I felt very evil for having gotten impatient and tried to apologize, but Lori was in no mood to be placated.

The issue would not die. One Friday afternoon I had brought in my guitar. That in itself was not novel. We had no other way of making music. But this occasion sparked ideas.

"Hey, I know what we can do!" Lori cried. She had been at my feet on the floor but leaped up in a burst of excitement. "I know, I know! We can be in the talent show. Us four. And you can play the guitar."

My gut crinkled. I am no performer and the mere thought gave me stage fright.

"Oh, that's a dumb idea," Tomaso said. "What would we do?"

"Sing, stupid," Lori replied.

"I'm not stupid, you are. If you think we're going to get up and sing at some crappy talent show, you're crazy. We don't got no talent, for one thing."

A crestfallen expression. She looked sad so successfully that Tomaso weakened.

"Well, maybe it wasn't a *really* stupid idea. Just a little stupid."

Lori sat down and braced her cheeks with both fists. No words to any of us.

"Lor," I said, "I know you really want to do something. It

would be exciting to have a program. But right now we aren't in very good shape for it. Boo only knows one song and I don't think they'd like to hear "Bingo" at the talent show. Claudia's almost ready to have her baby. And that leaves just Tomaso, you and me."

"And *I* sure don't want to do it!" Tomaso said.

"And Tomaso doesn't want to do it, so that leaves just you and me, Lor. I don't think that's enough for an act. Besides, I don't even play the guitar very well. Just sort of good enough for us in here."

Her head was still down, lower lip out. No reasoning her out of this one. "We don't sing that bad," she muttered. "It's just nobody wants to do it." A resentful glare. "And we coulda put tulips in our hair and everything."

Tomaso made a face but I gave him the evil eye.

"If I'da been in the real first grade, I woulda got to *be* in a play. I woulda got my own flowers and everything. If I coulda stayed in real first grade." Abruptly there were tears over her cheeks. "But you made me come in this stupid kid's class and now I'm not ever gonna be in a play. And it's your fault." Trembling with her distress, she turned and stomped off across the room. On the far side by the closet, she hid her face in her hands against the wall and wept.

We all watched her in surprise. Nothing in the situation had caused me to believe she was so upset. Bewilderment kept us all immobilized an overlong moment.

It must have been hard. Hard being seven and relegated to the never-never land of a class like this. Hard wanting to be like everyone else and never quite understanding why you couldn't be. I had underestimated Lori. I had believed that if I could get her away from all the pressure of things she was incapable of, away from the abuse and humiliation, that was all she needed. I was wrong. This was not where she wanted to be. My room was safer, easier, but it was second choice. If she had had her way—if she could have managed it—Lori would have been a "real" first grader. Even Edna was worth bearing for that. And I guess that was the way it should have been, normalcy winning out over exceptionality. She could never grow, wanting anything less. Yet for me it was painful. The agony came from knowing that my real job was to put myself out of business. The sadness came from realizing that as the custodian of never-never land, I, like my room, would always have to be willingly left behind.

I started up on the guitar again, strumming a few chords. Tomaso asked if we could sing "He's Got the Whole World in His Hands." Tom liked that song because we had made up verses with each child's name in it.

"He's got the itty bitty baby in His hands," we sang.

"He's got you and me, brother, in His hands."

Lori came back wet cheeked and sat down next to my feet.

"He's got our little fellow, Boo, in His hands."

Tomaso, Claudia and Boo were holding hands and swaying back and forth to the music.

"He's got big, strong Tomaso in His hands."

"He's got our friend, Lori, in His hands."

Lori smiled weakly up to me. I smiled back.

"He's got Claudia and her baby in His hands."

"Torey?" Lori tugged at my pants leg.

I stopped playing the guitar.

"Can we sing 'He's got this little class in His hands'?"

I nodded, and we sang. It was a good verse; we all liked it and so we sang it again. All four of them had their arms linked now and were swaying in time to the music. Tomaso started us in again on the first verse.

As they sang I watched them. Boo, impossible, imprisoned Boo, his ethereal appearance making him all the more unreal in this everyday world. Lori, whose dark eyes reflected the other children's smiles even as the tears were still drying on her cheeks. Tomaso, whom I loved as much as I had ever loved any child, with his poignant, reckless

293

vulnerability. Claudia, shy, earnest, unhappy, bulging Claudia. They were so beautiful to me, so far beyond anything for which I could find words.

Unexpectedly, tears blurred my vision. They were so beautiful and I was so helpless. There was too much to do here. At least for one person. And perhaps there always would be. Perhaps if I had an army of aides, an eternity of time and a university of scholars, it would never be enough for Boo or Lori, or even Tom or Claudia. I think I knew that. But it did not matter. Whatever Ariadne Boom might think, it did not matter. They were the world to me. Yet, as I sat strumming the guitar and watching them, I was overcome. I worked only for the moments of the day, the aches and grinds and brutal beauty of being human. That was enough for me; it was all I ever wanted. I was never troubled by the future. But them—they deserved more. And I was filled with immense sorrow because I knew I could never give it to them.

Sometimes this happened. Not often and never at times I would expect it. But little moments still possessed the power to break my heart. I could not sing.

Lori rose up on her knees and touched my arm. "How come you're crying, Torey?"

"I'm not crying, love, my eyes just sting."

She shook her head. "No sir. You're crying. How come?"

I smiled. "I'm feeling sad because you can't be in the first-grade program. You ought to be. And I wish there were just some way I could make it so you were."

"Oh Torey, don't *cry* about it. I don't feel so awful bad, really. It doesn't matter that much. I don't really care."

"Yes, you do, Lor. And so do I. Some things in the world are sad and there's nothing wrong with crying over them a little. It gets the dirt out of your eyes."

Tomaso flapped a hand at us impatiently. "Oh, come on, you guys. Let's sing some more or I'm going to have the dirt out of my eyes too."

31

May rose up with great heat. Our room was on the west side of the building and it soon became uncomfortably warm in the afternoons. Since the weather outside was so nice, I took the children a couple of times to do our work in the shade of a hawthorn tree at the far end of the playground.

Claudia and Boo were doing Montessori materials. Lori was apart from us in the garden. Lettuce grew there now and spinach and peas and radishes. She was busy picking bugs out of the leaves of spinach. I lay stretched out on the grass while Tomaso read to me from his reading book. He was doing a skill lesson on distinguishing fact from opinion and was reading aloud all sorts of dreary things about January mean temperatures in St. Petersburg, Florida, and whether or not dogs made the best pets.

I had moved over to be in the warm May sunshine. The weariness of winter oozed out of my bones. Boo seemed like he needed to use the rest room so Claudia took him in.

The day was warm for so early in the season, in the seventies and nudging 80, and I had kicked my sandals off and closed my eyes.

"I've picked off twelve bugs," Lori announced.

"What kind are they?" I asked.

"I dunno. Spinach bugs, I guess."

"Lemme see," Tomaso said.

"Oh no, you don't. Finish your reading first." I kicked him with one toe.

"I just wanted to look at them. Sheesh."

"Not until I find out if it's a fact that red is the best color for a bike. Now read."

"I think it is," Lori said.

"Gotta be an opinion then," Tomaso said and flipped his book back open.

"I'll save the bugs for you, Tommy," Lori said. "Can I go get a jar to put them in, Torey?"

"Sure. And see what Boo and Claudia are up to. They've been gone a long time."

"Alrighty." Lori ran off to leave Tom and me alone on the grass with our facts and opinions.

I lay back and closed my eyes again. Tomaso's voice had that slightly petulant tone of one forced to do something he would sooner not do. He was tapping against the bottom of my bare foot with his shoe, like a telegrapher.

"Torey! Torey, come quick!" Lori ran across the playground toward us. "Help! Something's happened to Boo."

I bounded to my feet and took off. Tomaso was right behind. "What's the matter?" I asked as we all dashed for the doorway.

"I don't know!" Lori was crying.

Boo and Claudia were in the classroom. Workmen had begun installing insulation in the ceiling of the school during the last week; that had been another major influence for moving my class outside, because the banging and rattling were atrocious. Apparently when they had seen my empty classroom they must have thought it unused because a huge sheet of fiberglass insulation was leaning against the cupboard by the sink. On the side against the cupboard doors was the soft fiberglass itself. On the side facing us was the shiny Mylar covering. Overhead our fluorescent lights were on.

Boo stood before the Mylar, his hands flapping wildly as they did in the old days. His body trembled with an excited frenzy. Back and forth his head moved in a rhythmic, hypnotic manner like a charmed snake. Then I noticed that when not flapping he would grip his bare upper arms and rake his fingernails down them. Long tracks had been scraped in each arm.

Claudia's face was tight with fear. "I didn't know what to do. He just started to do that and he screams every time I try to pull him away. It's like he doesn't even know me."

"Boo!" I said sternly. "Boo!"

No response. He was so involved in self-stimulating that my voice alone could not break his concentration. The reality we stood in was gone for Boo. He lived only in his Mylar reflection. I saw him reach up and grab a handful of hair. With a deft yank he pulled it from his head.

I moved to catch hold of his shoulders. That was a mistake. Boo was further gone than I had realized. He shrieked hysterically when I touched him and then he tore off screaming. Tufts of black hair fell in his wake as he continued to rip it from his head. Intermittently, his hands would flap frantically and his head would flop back and forth as if there were no muscles in the neck.

"Boo!" I did not know if I should chase him or not. On one hand I was afraid that if I didn't he would hurt himself more seriously than just pulling hair. On the other hand I knew he would spook completely when being pursued. Turning, I pulled Lori and Tomaso inside the room from the doorway. For the first time in months I latched the hook and eye.

Boo rampaged, screaming maniacally. Then he started in on his clothes. Off came the shoes, the socks, the pants. But not with the old deft precision. Instead he tore them off. Rrrrrip went the shirt, buttons careening in all directions. He used the same brutal force he had used on his hair. Within seconds he was stripped. Only his training pants remained on; their material was too stretchy to tear. Boo ran in wide, reckless circles beyond our reach.

"Ohhhh," I heard Lori murmur sadly behind me. She captured my feelings exactly. Some little Pollyannaish dream that Boo was actually getting better sank and died agonizingly inside me. He ran now with more bizarre frenzy than he had ever shown when he first arrived.

Cautiously I walked out into the middle of the room to put myself more directly in his path. He veered to avoid me. The screaming never stopped. To the world beyond our door it must have sounded as if we had an injured wild animal in here.

Abruptly, as he was bolting past the Mylar, he stopped dead. The hands came up to ear level, the fingers fluttered. Once more he began to weave back and forth, enchanted by something none of us could perceive. His crying ceased.

Watching Boo was terrifying. Perhaps the fear came because the change after all these months of improvement was so unceremoniously sudden; the behavior was so alien to anything he had done before. He was a stranger.

I tried easing up on him from behind while he stood transfixed before the glimmering Mylar on the insulation. Boo was not that unaware of his environment. With a bloodcurdling scream, he ran from me in terror, as if I meant to kill him.

The other children stood in a fearful huddle against the door, their eyes wide and full of horror. I had had Tomaso turn off the overhead lights in case they were contributing to Boo's hysteria as they sometimes did, so now we were in a bright afternoon darkness that at any other time would have seemed natural. But now it only added to the eeriness.

Boo halted across the room near the window. Reaching up to cover his face with his hands, he shrieked, the cry changing pitch to a hoarse moan. Fingernails against his cheeks, he pulled them down into a long scraping motion. Reddened trails were left against his dark skin. Again and again he scratched at his face and cried out as if bees had descended upon him and he was trying to ward them off. Blood trickled through his fingers.

Lori screamed at the sight. I ran toward Boo, but as I got close, he tore off, his hands still over his face, now wildly gouging at his skin and pulling at his hair.

"Boo! Boo, come here. *Please*, come here."

But I could not win him away from himself.

Tomaso was the first to act. He broke from the others and came out at Boo with both of his arms spread wide like a goose girl herding her flock. Boo, blood running into his eyes and down onto the smooth skin of his chest, lurched away from Tomaso, but I was on the other side. Between Tom and me we were able to squeeze him into a smaller and smaller area. Finally I could reach out and grab Boo's arm, slippery with blood. I pulled him to me.

We fell into a little heap, Boo and I. I was still unable to squelch the demon in him, and he struggled savagely. One hand raked across my cheek, but I did not know if the blood that came trickling down my chin was his or mine. He bit my arm when I tried to check the bleeding. Finally I crushed him tight against me so that he could no longer move.

We sat. The other children watched us. Both Claudia and Lori were crying. Tomaso's face was pale and grim.

We sat. Still Boo struggled. Whatever he had been trying to tear out of himself was still unwilling to give up.

We sat.

Boo no longer fought against me, but I could still feel the foreignness in his body, rigid and tense. I did not let go.

The depression settling over me was unspeakable. All these months, all this time given him and he was as crazy as ever. In a moment of mental hopscotch I thought of Albert Einstein's famous comment about God not playing dice with the universe. I wondered what kind of game God did play. And why I never could quite grasp the rules.

When I finally let go of Boo, he was his normal goofy self. Grinning while I dressed him, he jabbered the sports report. A hundred scores and RBI's and errors were regurgitated. Then he giggled to himself and gave the weather. Partly cloudy.

We went about our activities the remainder of the afternoon with tremendous care lest too much noise or gaiety shatter the frail atmosphere. Tom and Lori pulled the insulation back into the hallway. We left the lights out. I took Boo down to the girls' rest room and tried to wash the dried blood from his face and hair. Both of us looked like warriors with the even tracks of his fingernails down our cheeks.

When his mother came to get him in his tattered clothes I tried to explain the best I could what had happened. She left with tears in her eyes.

It was Claudia who was the most upset of all. She wept intermittently throughout the afternoon. To her, what Boo had done was her fault. Over and over she kept telling me things she should have done to have prevented him from falling apart. No amount of reassurance from me helped. In talking to her I came to realize that Claudia in her quiet, earnest way had grown to love Boo deeply. She was more invested in him than I had ever known. That this had happened crushed her.

I allowed Claudia to stay after school to help me with miscellaneous tasks. She had not recovered from her feelings enough that I wanted to send her home. We sat together at the table and made cutouts for the bulletin board.

"Why did he do that?" she asked me. "He was okay when I brought him in. Really. We went in the bathroom and then stopped in here to get my sweater. That's all."

I nodded. "It wasn't anything you did. I don't know what it was. Maybe just the reflection on the Mylar."

"But why?"

"Because that's just the way he is."

"Is he ever going to be different?"

I shrugged with just one shoulder. "I don't know. Probably not a lot."

She gazed at me. The pause was intense. "How can you *stand* it here? I couldn't. I couldn't be here all the time and know I never mattered."

I looked over at her. "I *do* matter. That isn't the question. I matter to me. And day to day I matter to Boo. We all do. Day to day, is all there is, Claudia. And day to day is all I care about."

She shook her head. With her fingertips she felt along the smoothness of the tabletop. "Are all your kids like this? Like Boo?"

I was unsure of what she was asking.

"Is something wrong with all of them? Something inside where you can't see it? Even with Tom and Lori? Are all your kids like that?"

I rubbed my hand across my lips and considered the question.

"They're crazy, aren't they?" she said softly. Her tone was not derogatory. "My dad told me once that this was a room for crazy children. Where they put you before you grew up and they had to lock you away. That's really true, isn't it?"

"I guess. If that's what you want to call it. I guess you could."

"It's different than I thought it would be. I always

301

thought crazy people were bad. Like Jack the Ripper or Son of Sam. I was scared to even think about them. But that isn't the way it really is, is it? Boo isn't bad. Or Tom or Lori."

"No, they aren't bad."

"But they aren't good either, are they? Or else people wouldn't be afraid of them."

"No one is good or bad, Claudia. Those are only words."

She studied my face, really looked at me, her eyes locking mine. "No one's really any different, are they? We're all just pretty much the same."

We worked together in silence for a long while. Fifteen or twenty minutes passed and neither of us spoke.

"Claudia?"

She looked up.

"Remember a long time ago when I talked to you about your baby? About what you were going to do with it?"

"Yeah."

"I still worry about it."

"You don't have to."

"I know I don't. But I do. I don't want your baby to end up in here, in this room with me."

She wrinkled her forehead. "He won't."

"That's what all mothers think. What Boo's mom thought. Mothers love their children. But sometimes when life gets out of control for big people, the little people get hurt."

"That won't happen to me."

"That's what Lori's parents thought. And then one night . . . well, no one does think it'll happen to them. But remember kids like Lori. And Tommy with his dead father. And Boo this afternoon. I don't want to see your baby in here, Claudia, and sometimes when I think of all the things you have ahead of you, I worry."

"Well, don't."

"That's all I'm going to say on it. It's a closed subject and I won't bother you again."

Claudia rose from her chair and went behind me to the window. I turned. Beyond her I saw Tomaso's reading book and my sandals still on the lawn. A hawthorn flower had fallen from the tree and settled in the crack of the open book.

"Some days," she said, "I feel old. I feel like a grandmother. It makes me very tired."

32

Time had come to make decisions on placement of the children for the following year. I was being returned to full-time resource work, although I was remaining at the same school. Rumor had it that the district was considering reopening a few more all-day special education classes, but I had seen no job postings nor was I asked to be involved.

About Claudia there was no question. She would return to parochial school in the fall as a seventh grader. I only had to return her graded schoolwork to the home school and they would proceed as they saw fit. Basically, I felt that was good. If she had been my responsibility, I would have wanted her back in a regular program.

Tomaso, too, I hoped could go back to a normal class. He would be a fifth grader next year, and I thought he was ready for the daily ups and downs of ordinary kids. Even with his temper, Tom was a warm, sensitive, outgoing boy. His anger still lay with him in some areas but he could usually handle it more appropriately. What Tomaso needed most now was eleven-year-old male friends and that was something I could not give him. In discussing the placement with Birk, we decided to send him back to his home school where he would not need busing and could make friends within walking distance of home and school. The resource teacher at that school was competent, and we felt certain that with his help, Tomaso could successfully reenter the normal world.

I was much less certain of Boo. He could not go into a less restrictive environment than the afternoon class had provided. The outburst during the previous week underscored that. However, we could no longer continue to patch programs together for him as had been done this year. He needed a full-time class geared toward autistic-type children, one with a small teacher-pupil ratio and a strong program in language and survival skills. I knew he needed a summer program too. For boys like Boo there could be no vacations.

There was, unfortunately, no proper placement in the district for Boo. Before the wholesale clean-out at the passage of the mainstreaming law, we had had going a fairly adequate program for autistic children. However, the funding was cut and then mainstreaming came along and the program died. Two of the children in it went into regular settings with extensive help, two had been sent away to private schools, one was in Betsy Kerry's class and one had moved out of the district.

Boo's parents were as concerned about his placement as I was. Then mid-month Mrs. Franklin called to tell me that they had located a small private program in a nearby community. When I investigated, I found a good-looking place. We had a large population in the area of one of the lesser-known religious sects. With the changing policies toward special education programs in the public schools, they had decided to open a class in one of their parochial schools for that group of children who were falling between

305

the cracks. After a year of running a class for older disturbed children, they had decided to open a primary program expanded to include autistic-type children. The two teachers were young and eager. The room was bright and big and filled with ample, albeit worn, equipment. Aide positions were filled by the parents.

The Franklins, Birk and I discussed the program. I wanted them to be aware that Boo would receive religious training in a faith not his own and that because the family was not of that faith they were ineligible for tuition scholarships. The Franklins would have to pay the entire costs themselves. Yes, they knew. By cutting corners they felt they could afford the modest tuition. As far as the religious training went, they felt that if Boo learned anybody's religion that was a positive step.

Lori's placement had not yet come up. Because she remained on Edna's roster, I was not responsible for her placement. The matter seemed cut and dried to me so I did not worry much about it. I assumed the next year for Lori would be second grade and a good share of her day still with me. Both second-grade teachers were good, and one, an older woman who had been teaching for years, was superb. I was looking forward to planning out Lori's program with her.

After school, I was down in the lounge with Billie and Hal Langorhan, a sixth-grade teacher, when Dan came in. He pulled his mug off the shelf, filled it with coffee. Coming over, he pushed my logbook aside and sat down next to me on the couch. We made small talk for a while.

"Say Dan," I said during a pause in the conversation, "when are we going to meet on Lori Sjokheim's placement for next year? I've been thinking about it. I think Ella Martinson would be ideal, don't you? And the way my schedule looks right now, I could give Lori about three

306

hours of intensive resource help. Ella could handle her the rest of the time, couldn't she?"

Dan stared into his coffee mug intently, like a fortune-teller reading tea leaves. He did not respond.

"You don't think Ella is a good idea? Margery doesn't seem to have things quite as much together as Ella does, do you think? Her kids always seem in a dither. And I thought Lori might profit from someone as down-to-earth as Ella."

Dan's face was reddening.

"But if you don't want Ella . . . well, I certainly wouldn't mind working with Margery. She really is creative. I guess that might be good for Lori too. Real good, I'm sure. . . ."

Dan looked up "We're retaining Lori Sjokheim."

"What?"

Dan jerked his head. "Come on, let's get out of here."

We walked down the hall to my room. I was beyond words. Once inside, Dan shut my door firmly.

"Now what do you mean, you're retaining Lori? There hasn't ever been a meeting on her. Has there?"

Dan had sunk into a small kiddie chair. "I've been meaning to tell you. . . ."

"But—"

"We have had a meeting. Edna, Lori's father and I. And we've decided to retain her. There isn't much else we could do with her. She hasn't completed any first-grade skills yet. There's no way we could justify sending her on to second grade."

I was speechless.

Dan put a hand up. "Now before you go and get all upset, think about it. What else could we do?"

"Of all the sneaky tricks! You did this behind my back. You knew I wouldn't stand for it."

"Her father has already agreed, Torey. He thinks it's the right idea too."

"Dan, we cannot do this," I said. "We just can't."

307

He would not even look at me.

"She's seven years old, going to be eight in September. She's a great big girl already; she's grown like a weed this year. She'll be half a head over the first graders."

"But she has no reading skills, Tor. We can't lay a burden like that on Ella or Margery."

"And we can lay it on Lori? We've half killed this girl already with our stupid ideas. She's already failed one grade; how is it going to be failing another? The child has a physical disability. You could keep her in first grade until she is a gray-haired grandmother and she may never learn to read."

Dan's head was down. "Torey, don't make this so difficult on me."

"I'm not trying to make it difficult. I'm just trying to understand. You've got to know deep down in your heart, Dan, how wrong this is. Otherwise you wouldn't have sneaked around like a bunch of kids behind the barn. You're punishing the girl simply because she's different and we can't teach her. All the other excuses are crap."

"But she *is* different."

"Yes, you're right about that. But we're stuck with her, aren't we? So isn't it about time we start accommodating her handicap? Look at Ruthann Bye in the fifth grade. She can hardly see. Everything Carolyn gives her has to be magnified on that machine before Ruthann can see it. What's so different about Lori?"

"But Lori can't learn. Ruthann does."

"Lori can learn. The truth is that we haven't taught her. Why can't we start taping her reading material? We could quiz her orally. Lori isn't dumb. She simply has a disability. All the time in the world in first grade isn't going to change that, unless her teacher moonlights as a brain surgeon."

My words were so much hot air. The decision had been made. Lori's big mistake was being left with a handicap that did not deform her. We had not yet learned mercy for things we could not pity.

Dan clasped his hands together and gave a weary shake of his head. "I'm sorry. I'm sorry this upsets you but I will not argue it further. Edna, Mr. Sjokheim and I all talked it over and decided together that repeating first grade would be best for Lori. It was a consensus. Edna's and his. And mine."

I stared at him. I wanted to hate him. To hate him the way I had Edna in April. I felt nothing. I was just too tired of fighting.

"Edna sure got the last laugh on this one, didn't she? All the time you made me think I was doing the right thing not putting Lori through the first-grade curriculum. And all the time you knew Edna had the trump card. Just humoring me."

"Now come on, Tor. You know better than that."

"I hope the laugh was worth the price."

There came between us a great, solid silence. I think Dan thought I would protest further. He sat hunched up in his chair, steeled for the worst. I said no more. The fight had gone out of me. It had just been too hard and too long, and there was something in his eyes that told me I could not win this time. The decision had been made. So I said nothing. Not all of me was satisfied with my silence but that would be a matter I would have to come to terms with in myself.

Turning away I looked past the flower garden on the bulletin board, past the finches, past the art cabinet Lori had hidden under, to the window. My mind was vacant. Then I turned back.

"Does she know?"

Dan shrugged. "I'm not sure. I don't think so."

309

"I certainly hope you don't expect me to tell her. I won't. The dirt belongs to you."

I went home in a state of weary depression. After all the trouble earlier, I just could not rouse myself to fight one more time. It seemed too futile. I was not a born fighter and one needed to be for this job.

For the first time since he had left, I sorely missed Joc. The need to lean on someone, to be physically close was so great I was in tears. I was sick to death of being "strong." I had not cried about Joc's absence since the night he left. Now I folded my arms on the kitchen table, lay my head down and wept.

Later, I heated up a glass of milk and laced it with molasses, an old trick I had learned years before for insomnia. Then I sat staring at it, waiting for it to cool. My head hurt. I sat in the dimly lit kitchen and thought of other times. My childhood, growing up in the mountains of Montana. My college years. All the times of my life when I had not been teaching. The innocent times. I was tired of teaching.

The hardest time was the next day when I saw Lori. She did not know. As I watched her gaily going about her tasks, I tried to think of some way to salve the future for her.

By afternoon I had a plan.

"Lori, come here," I said. The other children were at work on their tasks. Lori had been with Tomaso but rose and came across to the worktable. She pulled a chair out and sat down. "We're going to do something different today, you and me."

"What's that?" She was wiggly. I could not tell if it was anticipation or normal Lori-squirminess.

I lay a book on the table. "We're going to read."

Her eyes grew wide and dark. Immediately tears formed and ran down her cheeks. "I don't want to."

"Lor, Lor, Lor, now don't," I said and reached across the table to catch her face in my hands.

"I can't do it."

"Hey, now stop crying. I won't make you do anything you can't do."

She snuffled noisily.

"There are two of us here, Lor, you and me. I'll set the limits. And because I set them, I'll never make you do what you can't do. When we come to things you can't do, we'll do them together. There won't ever be a time in here that I let you in for something that you and I can't handle together."

My hands remained on either side of her face. The tears still ran. I could feel her trembling beneath my fingers. "Don't cry, Lor."

"But I'm scared. I'll goof up. I know I will."

"No you won't. I've already told you I won't let you. Just like when you learn to ride a bike and someone holds on until you can pedal by yourself. I'll be holding on too, and just like I said, if we can't do it together, we won't do it."

"But, Torey, I *can't* read."

I smiled. "Well, I can."

The book was Dick and Jane. Good old dull Dick and Jane from 1956. Just the kind of book I needed. Few words and a story carried along in pictures. For all the faults of these old books, I liked them. In their extreme simplicity, they worked for me and my school-weary kids.

I put the book on the table. Just a little book, paperback, as all pre-primers seem to be. Lori looked at it askance.

I explained to her about the kids in the stories, Dick, Jane and Baby Sally. Lori was not ready to trust me. Her eyes were huge and dilated, still bright with unfallen tears.

She would chance brief peeks at the cover of the book but she would not touch it.

"You haven't ever read this book. It's called *We Look and See*." I picked it up and opened the cover. "Come over here on my side and we'll read it together."

Lori rose and came to me. I pushed the chair back and took her on my lap. Holding the book in front of us, I showed her the title page of the first story. On it was Sally taking off her white baby oxfords and pulling on her father's big black galoshes. Underneath the picture was printed the word "look." I pointed to it. "That says 'Look.'"

"Look," Lori whispered tentatively.

I turned the page. Sally and Dick outside. Dick has the hose on, Sally is stomping through the puddles in her father's galoshes. "Look, look," the text reads. Obviously it is what Sally is saying to her brother. "See, here is the very same word as on the other page. Do you remember what it was?"

"Look," Lori said.

"That's right. See, it says it two times. 'Look, look.' Sally wants her brother to see her walking in her daddy's overshoes."

"Look here," Lori exclaimed. "Look what happens. Her feet fell out of the boots. Ooooooh, she's gonna step in the water." A twist around to see me and Lori grinned. "Her daddy's gonna be mad at her for that, huh?"

"I'll bet," I agreed. "See, here's what Sally says. She's surprised and she says, 'Oh, oh, oh.' See, that word's 'oh.' Can you read it?"

"Oh, oh, oh."

"Good, there you go. Now let's see what happens when we turn the page." Last page of the story. Dick sees his little sister in this terrible dilemma and wheels his red wagon up behind her. Sally falls into it. The day is saved. Underneath, the text reads "Oh, oh. Oh, look." Not Nobel literature material, but Lori was delighted. She clapped her hands.

"All right, scout, now let's read it straight through from the beginning. You and me together." I turned back to the title page. "Look," we said in unison.

Turn page. "Look, look." Other side. "Oh, oh, oh."

Turn page. "Oh, oh. Oh, look." End of story.

"Now," I said, "I want you to try it on your own. See, look at the words carefully. The long one is 'look.' The short one is 'oh.' Ready?"

Lori nodded and held the book up close. Deep breath. Another deep breath. "Look," she said hoarsely.

"Super! Next page."

"Look, look." When she got to the next page she hesitated.

"Look at Sally, Lor. What happened to her? What does she say?"

"Oh?"

"You bet! And how many times?"

"Oh, oh, oh."

"Terrific!" I turned over to the last page for her.

"Oh, oh," Lori said immediately. "Oh . . ." Long pause. "What was that other word?"

"Look. Oh, oh. Oh, look."

I took hold of her chin and turned her face to look at me. "Do you know what you just did, Lori Sjokheim?"

Her eyes widened.

"You read that story, didn't you?"

A tremendous, face-splitting smile.

"You read that story all by yourself. You just picked that old book up and read it like anybody would. No fooling you."

"I read it," she whispered incredulously. She snapped around and snatched it up again. "I'm gonna do it again. Watch me, Tor. I'm gonna read it right through with no mistakes. Watch me."

313

She flipped back to the first page. A long wait while she took breaths in preparation. "Look," she announced and turned around to grin. Then flipped the page. "Look, look. Oh, oh, oh." Over to the next page. "Oh, oh. Oh, look." Back to me. "I *did* it! I DID IT!"

Before I could stop her she had bounded off my lap. "Hey, you guys. Hey Tomaso! Claudia! Listen! I can read! Listen to me. Come here and watch me. I can *read!*" Grabbing the book up she ran over to them. The story was read. And read and read and read.

From my chair I watched her. It was not really reading, I suppose. Not really. By this time she had memorized the story. Only two words, not much of a feat. And I had little doubt that if I took them out of the context of that Dick and Jane story she would not be able to recognize them any more than she recognized any other symbol. But that was not important. Not now. What was important was a scrawny seven-year-old kid waving a twenty-five-year-old pre-primer at me from across the room, squealing delightedly, reading out the text to Boo and Benny and the finches. Come what might in her future, I knew I had given her the best I had. Never again could anyone say she could not read. She now could prove that false. Lori Sjokheim was not anybody to be messed with. Lori Sjokheim *could* read.

33

What a crazy week we had! Lori was intoxicated by her success. She never put the book down. She had to take it home to read to her father and Libby. She had to read it to each and every one of the morning resource kids. She even had to read it to Edna. For Tomaso, Claudia, Boo and me, it soon got to be a bit much. Tom would come up behind me in the room some days when I was absorbed in doing something else and whisper in my ear, "Look, look. Oh, oh, oh." He could make it sound obscene. That never failed to provoke a lot of good-natured yelling on my part and some fierce threats about bamboo under the fingernails of students who drove their teacher batty.

In the back of my mind the entire time was the specter of Lori's retention. I refused to let it dampen our high spirits but nonetheless I anxiously searched her face each day to see if her father had told her. I only hoped that when he did, the glory of Dick and Jane would be enough to sustain her.

My birthday was on Friday of that week and I told the children I would bring a cake. We planned a sort of Happy Birthday/Reading-celebration party.

On Thursday, new excitement. Tomaso came galloping in, whooping at the top of his lungs.

"Guess what's going to happen to me!"

"What's that?" I asked.

"I'm gonna move!" Roaring across the room to me, he bounced up on the worktable where I was grading papers. He slid across the table on his seat and knocked papers into my lap.

"You are?"

"Yup, my uncle's coming to get me and take me back to Texas."

The others gathered around.

"Is this the same uncle you lived with before?" I asked skeptically, thinking of child slavery, abuse and abandonment.

"No siree! This here's my Uncle Iago. My mama's brother. He's gonna take me to live with him. I'm going to have me a real family! Yessiree! No more foster homes for me." Tom's excitement burst out of him and he whooped up onto his feet atop the table.

"Tom, that's really super."

"Are you happy for me?"

"You bet I am."

Lori socked his leg. "Well, I'm not."

"*Lori!*" I said in surprise. "This is a wonderful thing to have happen to Tom."

"But I don't want him to go." Her lower lip shoved out. "I want you to stay here, Tomaso."

Tomaso was too high to care what she wanted. Still standing on top of the table, he threw pencils into the air and tried to catch them. "Now we're going to have a Happy-Birthday-Reading-Celebration-Going-

Away-Party tomorrow, huh? And the going-away part's for meeeee!"

Streamers from the ceiling, balloons, hats for everyone made it a party with all the trappings. My cake was on the table. Mr. Sjokheim had sent a plate of brownies, which Lori proudly announced she had helped bake. Orange juice had come courtesy of Mrs. Franklin, who also sent a box of crocheted animal finger puppets to be used as party favors. Claudia turned the record player on; rock music blared out. We were having an all-afternoon party that I hoped would make up for never having had a school program and any other injustices visited on us because of our status as a class.

Not until about halfway through the cake and orange juice did I notice anything amiss. I looked around the room. Tomaso was not there.

"Where's Tom?" I asked Claudia. She was in a chair next to the record player. The music was so loud I had to shout.

"I don't know. He was here a minute ago."

"Hey, Lor." She and Boo were out in the middle of the floor dancing to the music. Or so they fancied. "Do you know where Tomaso is?"

"Yeah," she shouted over the music. "He's in the closet."

"Huh? What? In what closet? What are you talking about?"

She stopped dancing. "In the closet. Over there. But you better oughtn't bother him. He's crying."

I stared at her. Boo was pawing at her to make her dance again. "Why's he crying, Lor?"

"He's lonesome for us already."

I went over to the coat closet. What a class of kids I had this year for hiding. The closet was small, perhaps less than three feet deep, meant only for the teacher's coat and boots.

317

I cracked the door open cautiously. Tomaso sat huddled up on the floor, his face hidden against his knees. I bent down and put my face to the opening. "Tommy, what's the matter?"

"Nothing, leave me alone."

I watched him.

"Go away."

"All right." I stood up.

"Well sheesh," he muttered and looked up. "I didn't mean really go away."

"Oh. Okay." I knelt back down. The door was still only open a little way. Light illuminated part of his face, but most of the closet was black. "You sort of wish you didn't have to go?"

He nodded.

"It's scary, isn't it, having to go new places."

"I don't wanna go. I wanna stay right here."

"You feel that way now; that's natural."

"I never wanted to go. My social worker, she said I had to. She says he's kin and he's got a claim on me. But I don't want to go. I don't even know him. I never seen him since I was a baby. I want to stay with my foster mom and dad here and come to this class. I'm tired of moving."

"Well, changes are hard to get used to."

"I don't wanna go! I wanna stay right here. But us kids, we don't got no rights. We just got to go where they tell us, those stinking bastards. When I grow up, I'm going to shoot them all in the head."

I reached a hand in to him and he took it.

Tomaso began to cry again with loud blubbery noises. He had my hand pressed to his wet cheek. My knees were getting sore so I adjusted myself around to a sitting position with only my arm in the closet. I watched the other kids as they played.

"I don't see why I should ever have bothered to do

318

anything," Tomaso muttered through the opening. "I don't see why I ever bothered to be good, if they're going to make me go away. It doesn't matter now, everything I did."

I turned to look at him. "Of course it matters, Tomaso. It matters to me. To all of us. We all care that you tried to be good in here. We'll always care."

"I don't see why people bother to care about anything. All it does is hurt you in the end. All you did was make me like you and now I wish I never did because I don't want to miss you. I spend my whole fucking life missing people. I'm never going to like anybody again."

"You're right there. It does hurt. Loving people always does hurt. It's part of the deal, I think."

"It hurts too much. It isn't worth it. I'm never going to like anybody again. Then I don't have to worry."

I watched him huddled on the floor of the closet. "Yes, Tom, you're right about that too. If you never love anybody, you'll never have a broken heart. But Tom, that's not what hearts were made for."

He dissolved into tears again. I was asking too much in wanting him to understand. Quietly I closed the closet door and rose to my feet to go join the other children.

We went ahead with the rest of the party, with recess and games. Tomaso remained in the closet. Later I noticed Lori over there. She was squatting before a small crack in the door and talking to him. A few minutes later she came to me.

"Tomaso wants you to tell everybody he hasn't been crying," she said.

"What?"

She wrinkled her nose at my denseness. "Come here." She pulled me down to her height to whisper in my ear. "I think he's *embarrassed*. He wants you to tell everyone he hasn't really been crying."

And so I did.

Tomaso emerged from the closet red eyed and snuffly. "Did you guys save me any cake? I wanted some cake. You guys didn't eat it all, did you?"

"No, we didn't. There's some on the back counter."

He headed off, then paused and turned around and looked at me. "Torey?"

"Yes?"

"Happy Birthday."

The day ended in a round of handshakes and back pats for Tomaso as he cleaned things out of his cubby. All of us were suddenly too shy to put our arms around him, even Lori. The unusual reserve lasted until after the others had gone home and I walked Tomaso out to his bus.

"My father's coming to get me," he said.

I looked at him.

"He's back from Spain. And he's coming to get me tonight. He's gonna take me off to live with him."

I nodded. Together we stood on the corner near the front of the school and waited for the bus. A spring storm was stirring up in the west. Anvil-shaped clouds soared high into the sky. The smell of rain was borne in on the wind.

"We're going to live in Spain together, him and me. He's got a house and everything. And I'll have my own room. And he's gonna teach me to be a bullfighter. This is probably the last school I'll ever go to. It's what I always wanted, to live with my father. Now I'll get to."

He gazed at me. His dark eyes were soft and wistful. "I'm really happy." There was no happiness anywhere.

"I know you are, Tommy," I said and ruffled his hair with my fingers.

"I'm going to live with my father."

I watched the clouds pile higher above us and wondered if we would get wet before the bus arrived. In my chest I could feel my heart thudding as if I had run a long distance.

"Torey?" He tugged at my arm. "I'm going to live with my father."

I turned and looked at him. A long, loaded pause.

"No, I'm not," he whispered. "I know that. I'm going to live with Uncle Iago. I'll never live with my father." His belongings clattered to the cement and he grabbed me around the waist.

The rain did come before the bus. But as it was, we never noticed.

34

It was a time of endings. Only a week and a half left to us. Tomaso's absence created a tremendous gap. I think we all were thankful to be leaving soon and not to have to continue for long without him.

In the middle of the next week Claudia told me that the night before she had had a false alarm with the baby. "I got pains right here. My mom timed them and they were twenty minutes apart. So my dad took me to the hospital." Then she rolled her eyes. "But it didn't happen. Still four more weeks."

Claudia looked at me. She wrinkled her nose. "Tell you the truth, I wish it was last week. My back hurts, my front hurts, my feet hurt, everything hurts. I'm sick of this."

I smiled.

"You know, I got names picked out. If it's a boy I want to call him Matthew. And if it's a girl, I'm going to name her Jenny. Don't you think those are good names? What do you want it to be?"

"Healthy."
She grinned.

I never saw Claudia again. The first time was a false alarm. The second was not. Early the following morning Claudia delivered a 4-pound 4-ounce girl prematurely. When Claudia's mother called, she said both mother and daughter were doing well, although the infant had jaundice and was in the intensive-care nursery. They named her Jenny.

"This is just like the old times, isn't it?" Lori said to me wistfully the next afternoon when I told her. "Just Boo and me."

I nodded. "Just Boo and you."

"And you too."

"And me."

She opened her reading book and stared momentarily at it before looking back at me. "You know, Tor, I don't think I like it so good without the others here."

"You know, Lor, I don't think I do either."

We went on with our normal routine. In our daily practice with Dick and Jane, Lori was beginning to show some of the old difficulties she had always had with reading, because the number of words was increasing and she could not rely so heavily on sheer memory of the story. Four stories into the book now, she was expected to have a reading vocabulary of seven words. I never gave her any other support materials such as workbooks or flash cards because I knew failure lay there. This venture with Dick and Jane was not for the purpose of teaching Lori how to read. I did not delude myself into thinking I could so easily do that. It was simply an effort to give her confidence enough to believe she was capable of learning. She had summer school coming up and then the next year. Time enough for reality. I needed to give her dreams.

Boo continued on, his usual wacky self. I remembered back to the days when I first had Boo and Lori together and how lost I had felt. How would I ever manage two such different students together at the same time? Now with Tomaso and Claudia gone, I had so much time on my hands that it seemed scandalous to have only two students. I could not imagine how I had ever felt overwhelmed.

I had made my own plans for the summer. I was going home to Montana for a while; then I planned to take some summer courses to keep my teacher certification up to date. Nothing spiffy. And I was moving. My current place had grown too small to accommodate all my books and teaching materials and the million and one other things I had acquired without realizing it. Besides, it was too far from school. I always had to drive. So I located a closer, larger apartment. I wanted to go home to Montana as soon as school ended and I wanted to get moved and settled first, so my evenings were filled with packing.

One night shortly into June, Billie came over to dinner to lend a hand in the boxing up. We had the place in shambles from one end to the other such that when the telephone rang I actually could not find it at first. Billie was laughing hysterically.

"Hello?"

Noises on the other end. I could not tell what they were.

"Hello? Hello?"

Someone was crying. Snuffling into the phone. I motioned Billie to be quiet.

"Who is this?"

"Torey?"

"Yes. Who's this?"

"It's me. Claudia."

"Claudia! Claudia, what's the matter?"

Sob. Snuffle. "I've been thinking . . ." More whimpering. "I've thought about things . . . about Jenny. She's so little,

Torey. She just got out of the incubator. She's so tiny."
Claudia dissolved into sobs.

"Claudia? Are you all right? What's wrong?"

"I'm gonna give her up, Torey. I signed the papers this morning. I did, and my mom did. I'm gonna give her up."

"Oh Claudia—"

"The lady at the agency, she said they had a good home for her. Her mommy and daddy've been waiting a long . . ." Sob. "A long time for her." Loud weeping.

"You did a good thing, Claudia. I'm proud of you."

"I didn't want her like Boo. I didn't want to hurt her."

And then it was the end. The last day. Nobody was working. There were parties all over school. Lori asked to spend the day in the first-grade classroom because they were having a celebration. She told me she would come by to clean out her things and say good-bye at the end of the day. Then she skipped down the hall.

Boo and I stripped the room of its final reminders of the year. The open bookshelves had to be covered with butcher paper and taped down. The sink and the counters had to be scoured. All the cupboards had to be inventoried and taped shut. We worked together silently, Boo willingly joining me. When we had finished, we took a walk to the park not far away.

So different this, from my other years as a classroom teacher. Last days had always been filled with that poignant sadness endings bring but yet with the promise of a long vacation and the raucousness of a final day. But now, here I was with my one vacant student, probably the least busy teacher in the school. To Boo it was just another day.

We walked around the duck pond and fed the greedy ducks and geese the last of the finches' food. Afterward we strolled through the small zoo. I took Boo's shoes off so

325

that he could run through the grass. In the end I took mine off too. We waded in the stream and tried to catch water skippers. On the way back to school I bought ice cream cones for us from a sidewalk vendor.

Mrs. Franklin was waiting for us when we returned. She took Boo's hand from me.

"Good-bye, Boo," I said.

He stared off into space. Mrs. Franklin reoriented his face so that he had to look at me. Even then he averted his eyes.

"Boo? Good-bye, Boo," I said and bent close to him.

"Tornado watch! Tornado watch!" he cried and let out the long, piercing warning signal that always came over the television to alert viewers to an impending storm. He raised his fingers between our faces and began to twiddle them.

Mrs. Franklin smiled apologetically. Then a few words, a smile, a hesitant pat on my arm and it was over. Standing alone with my sandals in my hand, I watched Mrs. Franklin and my fairy child walk away down the sidewalk. His beauty lay upon him with the shining stillness of a dream. I had not sullied him.

Back in the room I stood in the middle of the floor. The papered and taped shelves gave it a cold, foreign appearance. The animals were gone, the rug rolled up, the chairs upended on top of the worktable. Yet even so, the walls spoke to me. So much had happened here. Like every year, I wished it were not over.

The door opened.

Lori.

She did not look at me. Instead she went across the room and started yanking stuff out of her cubby and dropping it on the floor. She was on her knees, pulling the things out when suddenly she stopped. She let what was in her hands crash to the linoleum. Then she bent forward and covered her face with her hands.

"Lor? What's the matter?"

"I didn't pass." Grabbing her report card, she flung it out across the floor at me. Then she began to cry. Folding her arms across her knees she hid her face in them and wept the heavy, inconsolable tears of one who had really tried, of one who believed that evil old adage about trying hard enough. In the face of all the odds, Lori had never lost her dreams.

From my place in the middle of the empty room, I came and sat down beside her on the floor. We had no tissues left and had to make do with paper towels. Lori mopped furiously at her tears, pushing them back, swallowing them. "It's just that I don't like to think of myself as stupid."

"You're not stupid, Lor."

"I flunked kindergarten. Now I flunked first grade. I'll probably be a million years old by the time I get out of school."

"You're not stupid, Lor."

"It's just the same thing as being stupid, if I'm not."

Not knowing what else to say, I remained quiet.

"It hurts me to flunk. Didn't they know how much it hurts?" Then she looked at me. The resentment was obvious. "Didn't you?"

"It wasn't my decision."

"But didn't you know?"

A long pause. "Yes."

"Then how come you didn't stop it?" She was angry with me. Her eyes were full of accusation.

"I couldn't, Lori."

"Yes, you could have. If you'd really wanted to, you could've done it."

I shook my head. "No, Lori. It wasn't my decision. Other people thought it would be better for you to be in the first grade another year and I couldn't do anything about it."

She regarded me a long, long moment before turning

away. "You knew how bad I wanted to be in second grade. You knew. How come you didn't make it so I could be?"

"Lori! I *couldn't!*"

"But why not?"

I caught hold of her chin with my fingers and turned her face to me. "Listen to me. I could *not* do anything about it. There are some things in this world that I cannot do, no matter how much I wish I could. This was one of them."

She began to weep in earnest then, the tears bubbling up and over her cheeks and down onto my fingers. "You couldn't?"

I shook my head.

My fall from Heaven hurt—both of us.

We were without words for many minutes. Lori sobbed, bent over with her head against her knees again. I sat quietly and did not touch her, not knowing if my comfort would be wanted.

Finally she snuffled and swallowed and brought up the front of her dress to dry her face.

"What am I going to tell Libby?" she asked. "Now we're not going to be twins anymore. And Libby really wants us to be. She's going to be awfully upset."

"Sure you'll be twins. You'll always be twins, Lori. Nothing can change that."

"Uh-uh. We won't be the same age anymore. She'll be older."

"No, she won't. She'll just be in a different grade, that's all. Like this year she was in a different room. But you'll still be twins. Nothing can change a really important thing like that. Certainly not anything as silly as school."

"I wanted to be in second grade too. I wanted it *bad.*"

"I know."

Again we sat in silence. Lori had stopped crying, but I still did not dare to touch her, so we sat side by side on the floor. The building around us was absolutely soundless. Only faraway calls of children free from bondage could be heard. The emptiness of the room weighed in on me.

Lori picked up a paper from the floor in front of her, one of the things she had thrown out of her cubby earlier. It was a drawing she and Boo had done together.

"Is Boo gone?" she asked.

"Yes."

"I didn't even get to say good-bye to him."

"Remember, you said good-bye earlier. I told you he'd be gone."

She nodded. "He's not coming back next year, is he?"

"No."

"And Claudia, she's not coming back either?"

"No."

"And Tommy's not coming back," she said softly. "Just me. Just me coming back. Just me."

"And me," I added.

Lori looked over at me. Then she nodded. "Yup. Just you and me." She held out the picture and studied it. I pushed a piece of dirt around on the floor with my finger.

"Hey, Lor?"

"Yes?"

"Let's go celebrate."

"*Celebrate?*" Her face puckered with irritation. "What's there to celebrate?"

I shrugged. "I don't know especially. I just feel like it."

No response.

"Well, maybe we could celebrate its being the very last day of school," I suggested. "We have the whole summer ahead of us. How about that?"

"No. I have to go to summer school."

"Hmmm, well, I saw that Southby's have opened up the swimming pool for the summer."

"I don't care about that. I can't swim."

"It isn't raining anymore. It's a nice day out. We could celebrate that."

"It's too hot. I'm sweaty."

"You're making it hard on me, Lor. I'm trying and you're not helping."

"I don't care."

"Ho, ho. What a little Scrooge we've become. Well, listen, Boo and I discovered an ice cream man down on the corner of Seventh and Maple. What do you say we go get an ice cream cone? And guess what? He has butter brickle."

"I *hate* butter brickle!"

"Lori! For crying out loud."

There was a long, long pause and then suddenly she giggled. The tension shattered around us and both of us broke out laughing. "I'm being hard to get along with, aren't I?" she said.

"You definitely are!"

"Well, I sure don't want any butter brickle ice cream. That's almost worse than flunking."

We smiled at each other. Then she sucked her lower lip between her teeth and looked at me expectantly. "So, what we gonna celebrate?"

"You tell me. I'm out of ideas."

She shrugged. "I dunno. Just us, I guess. You and me. Let's just celebrate us."

"And what do you want to do?" I asked.

"I dunno. What do you want to do? You choose?"

I pushed myself up from the floor. "Let me see how much money I have."

"No, Tor, wait." Lori jumped up. "Let's get Libby too."

I hesitated. I thought about the humiliation awaiting her when she faced Libby, and I didn't want to spoil things again. "I was thinking maybe you would prefer just us, I mean . . ."

"Yeah, but Libby always feels so bad when school gets out. She likes it a whole lot better than we do."

"I see."

"And I got an idea." Lori dug into a pocket. "I got seven cents here. I could buy us all bubble gum. We could go to the park and roll down the Indian mound. And on the way we could stop at the Safeway store and I could buy us bubble gum." Her smile broadened. "See here, how much I got?"

"Yes, but I was thinking . . . I mean, I know how bad you feel about . . . I mean, I'm sorry I couldn't fix things and I thought maybe . . ." The words died inadvertently. We gazed at each other. Lori jingled the seven cents in her hand.

Finally she gave a little shrug. She opened her palm to look at the change, looked back at me and smiled. It was a quiet smile. "Don't worry so much, Tor. You always worry. It isn't that important. Now come on."

I came.

Epilogue

I stayed at the school and saw Lori through another year of first grade. Her family has since moved back East, and she attends a private school for the learning disabled. She never has learned how to read. Fortunately, for all of us, it has not been that important.

Boo remains in his parochial program for autistic children. We in this world have not yet succeeded in bringing him out of his. However, he has made small gains. He does speak now in a moderately coherent manner. And he does say mama.

Claudia returned to her former school. She went on to graduate valedictorian of her class. None of us, of course, knows where Jenny is. However, as the years passed I continued to search the faces of my students. Not one of the little girls has looked like Claudia.

Not long ago I read a story in the newspaper about a young boy who managed to lead four children to safety from a burning building, then ran back to get an infant. Along with the article was an AP photo showing the mayor presenting the boy with a hero's award for his valor and what the mayor deemed "his selfless love for others." The boy was Tomaso.